Christian Petzold

Contemporary Film Directors

Edited by Justus Nieland and Jennifer Fay

The Contemporary Film Directors series provides concise, well-written introductions to directors from around the world and from every level of the film industry. Its chief aims are to broaden our awareness of important artists, to give serious critical attention to their work, and to illustrate the variety and vitality of contemporary cinema. Contributors to the series include an array of internationally respected critics and academics. Each volume contains an incisive critical commentary, an informative interview with the director, and a detailed filmography.

A list of books in the series appears at the end of this book.

Christian Petzold |

Jaimey Fisher

**UNIVERSITY
OF
ILLINOIS
PRESS**
URBANA,
CHICAGO,
AND
SPRINGFIELD

© 2013 by the Board of Trustees
of the University of Illinois
All rights reserved
Manufactured in the United States of America
1 2 3 4 5 C P 5 4 3 2 1
∞ This book is printed on acid-free paper.

Frontispiece: Christian Petzold directs *Ghosts* (*Gespenster*, 2005).
From left to right: Benno Fürmann, Sabine Timoteo, Julia Hummer,
Christian Petzold. Photo by Christian Schulz.

Library of Congress Cataloging-in-Publication Data
Fisher, Jaimey.
Christian Petzold / by Jaimey Fisher.
pages   cm. — (Contemporary film directors)
Includes bibliographical references and index.
ISBN 978-0-252-03798-6 (hardcover : alk. paper) —
ISBN 978-0-252-07950-4 (pbk. : alk. paper) —
ISBN 978-0-252-09523-8 (e-book)
1. Petzold, Christian, 1960- —Criticism and interpretation.
2. Petzold, Christian, 1960- —Interviews. I. Title.
PN1998.3.P467F57   2013
791.4302'33092—dc23   2013010217

For Jacqueline

Contents

Acknowledgments | xi

A GHOSTLY ARCHEOLOGY:
THE ART-HOUSE GENRE CINEMA
OF CHRISTIAN PETZOLD | 1

Contexts 1: Biographical-Historical   6

Contexts 2: 1990s and Post-2000 German Cinema   9

Petzold's Ghostly Archeology of Genre   11

Pilots (Pilotinnen)   20

Cuba Libre   28

The Sex Thief (Die Beischlafdiebin)   32

The State I Am In (Die innere Sicherheit)   38

Something to Remind Me (Toter Mann)   60

Wolfsburg   67

Ghosts (Gespenster)   78

Yella   97

Jerichow   118

Dreileben: Beats Being Dead
(Dreileben: Etwas Besseres als den Tod)   131

Barbara   138

AN INTERVIEW WITH CHRISTIAN PETZOLD | 147

Filmography 169

Bibliography 177

Index 189

Acknowledgments |

For his initial interest and support, I would like to thank James Naremore, and then Jennifer Fay and Justus Nieland for their continued encouragement and edifying feedback. I am likewise grateful to Danny Nasset and other staff at the University of Illinois Press for their guidance and help. I am particularly indebted to Christian Petzold for being so generous with his time and thoughts as well as to Florian Koerner von Gustorf and Michael Weber at Schramm Film for their assistance on many fronts. Jeff Lipsky at Adapt Films was kind enough to allow me to view *Barbara* in advance of its U.S. release, and I thank Sophoan Sorn at the San Francisco Goethe Institut's Berlin and Beyond Festival for involving me in its prerelease screening. The staffs at the Deutsche Kinemathek and the DFFB library offered indispensable help all along the way.

My conversations with Brad Prager, Michael Richardson, and Marco Abel have made my thinking about Petzold's cinema and the Berlin School in general finer. I owe special thanks to Nora Alter for encouraging me to submit the original proposal as well as for her continuing guidance. Mark Breimhorst, Jeff Fort, Gerd Gemünden, Tina Gerhardt, Eric Gimon, and Daniel Stolzenberg read earlier versions and offered many perspicacious comments. Lutz Koepnick gave the manuscript a careful and illuminating reading. Eric Rentschler was encouraging at key moments, while Tom Clyde kindly invited me to present to the Think Visual group and offered advice along the way. Eric Smoodin was, as ever, supportive and incisive in his comments. Kriss Ravetto-Biagioli and the DHI Faculty Seminar she convened offered invaluable thoughts and encouragement. Thanks as well to Sascha Gerhards for helping me prepare the filmography and to Bastian Heinsohn for assisting with the interview. Tom Galarga and Nelson Martinez-Berrios gave the manuscript late and very helpful readings. Lutz Artmann and Jens Kempf offered typically astute counsel. Julie Nowka-Murphy helped with the transcription of the interview, while Joan Murphy and Uli Nowka offered their support and wisdom throughout. Joel Fisher contributed his considerable expertise on the images and many other topics. Randy Fisher and Jackie Garbo Yang Fisher offered unwavering support as always. Noah and Alexandra retained their good humor and boundless charm on too many trips to Berlin, and Jacqueline Berman, to whom this book is dedicated, offered immeasurable interest, discussion, and insight, beginning to (open) end.

Christian Petzold

A Ghostly Archeology |

The Art-House Genre Cinema of Christian Petzold

I will never make a film that tries to lead to some conclusion—instead [my films] try to narrate an abeyance [Schwebezustand]. Films that do not give answers, rather pose questions.

—Christian Petzold, interviewed by Caroline Buck

It's not really about how people are hiding something; rather, it concerns how they become economic.

—Christian Petzold, interviewed by Christof Siemes and Katja Nicodemus

Over the past twenty years and across eleven feature-length works, Christian Petzold has established himself as the most critically acclaimed director in Germany. Five of his last eight films have won Best Film from the Association of German Film Critics (2001, 2005, 2007, 2008, and 2012). It is not only the critics, however, who admire Petzold's work: his breakthrough *The State I Am In* (*Die innere Sicherheit*; 2000) won the Federal Film Prize in Gold, the equivalent of a best-film prize for its year, an unusual recognition for an art-house film. His more recent films have only affirmed his status as an auteur transcending art-house cinema: Petzold's participation, with two other directors, in the 2011 three-part *Dreileben* project has been called the most interesting development in German television in decades (Suchsland); and his *Barbara* (2012) not only won the Silver Bear for best director at the Berlin Film Festival but was also named Germany's submission for the 2013 Oscar for best foreign-language film. He is usually regarded as the most prominent and important of the group of filmmakers known as the Berlin School, which some French critics have declared a "German New Wave" (Lim). The themes Petzold unfolds in his films are global in scope and engage with the present moment in general, particularly with the spread of the economics, practices, and beliefs of neoliberalism. Although Petzold regularly invokes neoliberalism and its operations—for example, in the interview in this volume—his work approaches it in unusually intriguing ways.[1]

Midway through *Jerichow* (2008), for example, Petzold offers a brief, seemingly tangential conversation that is nonetheless revealing for his unusual approach. Two of the film's three main characters, Ali and Thomas, sit in the front seats of a parked work van, the vehicle with which they deliver supplies for Ali's snack bars sprinkled throughout the former East German Prignitz region. The camera rests, as it does in many shots of automobiles across Petzold's films, in the backseat. It shoots over the shoulder of the figures, a position that allows the bodies of the actors, as Petzold repeatedly emphasizes, to adapt to the relevant physical activity of driving (figures 1 and 2; Nord and Petzold, "Das Auto").

Such images of characters in a "movement space" (a space remade by the systems of mobility in modern society [Urry, *Mobilities* 45–46]) recur throughout Petzold's cinema. For John Urry, movement and mobility in general have been key developments in modernity, transforming spaces and individuals alike (6–7). These movement spaces, as I shall discuss in the sections on *Pilots* (*Pilotinnen*; 1995) and on *Wolfsburg* (2003), become for Petzold a crucial point of contact between individuals and the socioeconomic world changing around them. In fact, shallow-focus shots of individuals in such movement spaces, with natural surroundings (landscapes, forests, lakes, and so on) in the blurred background, rank among the most important images in Petzold's cinema. Here, in *Jerichow*, as they sit watching the traffic in the provinces, Ali quizzes Thomas on where he would suggest locating a new snack bar. Parked before an intersection—another key movement space in Petzold's cinema—they debate where the most

Figures 1–2. Thomas (Benno Fürmann) and Ali (Hilmi Sözer) discuss optimizing Ali's business at an intersection in *Jerichow* (2008).

customers would flock, what time of day they would most likely stop by, what impact a traffic light would have on customers' ebbs and flows. The casually cold calculus of the business-minded, car-based conversation seems all the more surprising because Thomas has just slept with Laura, Ali's wife, and will soon plot to kill him.

Thomas starts the film unemployed and broke, and Petzold offers this conversation to demonstrate how, as he says, Thomas is becoming economic—how love and economy intersect at this literal street-crossing. As someone unemployed and socially marginal, Thomas has become a "ghost," as Petzold terms such characters, in the modern economy. Petzold's films are devised to register and track developments in German economy and society, especially since unification in 1989–90—these rapid and accelerating changes generate ghosts out of older modes of individual existence, ghosts and/or near-ghosts that recur throughout his cinema (from Karin in his first feature to Ana and Barbara in his two most recent works). Such ghosts, and Petzold's interest in them, recall the "social dead" that Orlando Patterson and, more recently, João Biehl have sketched (Patterson 38–39; Biehl 41 and 68). But here, viewers sense that Ali's employing Thomas as a chauffeur and now asking him to think through his business options give this ghost an opportunity to return to "normal" life. Such economic spectrality is not a question of simple financial disadvantage or oppressions but rather one in which Petzold's characters are active agents in their own desperation and alienation, often through, as in *Jerichow,* banal acts of theft, betrayal, and even murder.

The scene notably revisits and restages one from *The Postman Always Rings Twice,* an American hard-boiled novel and then series of films noirs that Petzold cites, as he does with many other films, as a generic model. In *Postman,* the male friends, the entrepreneur Nick and the drifter Frank, discuss the details of how to advertise Nick's restaurant most effectively with a sign similarly at the roadside. *Postman* also seems symptomatic of what Urry terms (and what Petzold consistently explores as) a "mobility turn" in the contemporary world that has fundamentally remade natural and artificial spaces, bodies, and the psychologies that inhabit them (Urry, *Mobilities* 6–7). Petzold's recasting of *Postman* shows how he consistently restages a genre predecessor in contemporary Germany, offering mutually illuminating readings of both the classic film and his own contemporary context. This may be the most unusual achievement of his films, the level of socioeconomic and political engagement they attain while nonetheless deploying deception, crime, and love—very much the conventional purview of popular genre films.

It is no accident that Thomas falls in love with his employer's wife Laura, whom he imagines saving as he labors alongside her for Ali's business. Petzold's films explore individuals' tendency, consciously or not, to remake themselves for the socioeconomic context, not only by adjusting their overtly economic activities but also by adapting their desires, dreams, and fantasies. A key aspect of this remaking, what I call an economic "refunctioning," of people centers on how their desires change through work and the mobility it now brings.[2] The recent refunctioning of people, for Petzold, results above all from the fundamental economic and social changes wrought by neoliberalism in a country where political and socioeconomic developments usually lag behind those of the Anglo-American countries. If neoliberalism has privatized formerly public institutions, deregulated markets, and valorized entrepreneurial initiative, it has also shifted the risks generated by those markets and formerly insured against by those public institutions—like unemployment—to individuals (Peck and Tickell; Bourdieu and Wacquant 4). Such shifts are facilitated by, and have facilitated, the "flexibility" of labor, the fading of collectivized political solidarities, and the widespread financialization of the economy, with its ancillary explosion of debt (all of these, especially debt, figure repeatedly in Petzold's films). These developments in the dismantling of public institutions, the transformation of labor, and financialization of life have, as Petzold's cinema repeatedly underscores, changed how individuals experience work, relationships, and themselves (see Bauman).

Petzold's films consistently explore these new and transformational modes of individualities, especially the compromised, even tainted, character of desire in the wake of such economic adaptability, accommodation, and mobility. This kind of adaptability, productive desire, and subsequent movement are emphatically historicized in Petzold's cinema, in which history regularly intrudes upon individuals' dreams, fantasies, and desires as well as the spaces they inhabit. Such relentless "progress" of history is what has rendered people like Thomas ghostlike, spectral presences on history's inexorable march forward (see Gordon 8). As noted above, Petzold's ghosts, like Biehl's social dead, are invariably remnants from an earlier moment generated by socioeconomic change; in fact, as I shall detail below, this spectrality compels the viewer to confront history's transformations, dissonances, and losses. Individuals, families, even whole communities are knocked out of time and rendered undead before they realize it. Petzold's films consistently explore the coldness, paranoia, and fear bred of such economic adaptability, tainted desire, and sudden spectrality.

Contexts 1: Biographical-Historical

The wide-ranging constellation of themes that inhabit Petzold's films arises in part from the environment in which he grew up and now works. Petzold is the most distinguished contemporary auteur in Germany, but it bears underscoring that his training and career are well woven into recent historical events of tectonic importance: the fall of the Berlin Wall, the "reunification" of the two Germanys, the disappearance of the Soviet Union and the Warsaw Pact, and the accelerated integration of the European Union. Although our relative proximity to these events may obscure their significance, they have fundamentally recast the city, the country, and the continent in and on which Petzold operates. Indeed, during all of these events, Petzold was resident in Berlin, his adopted city, chosen in the early 1980s for cultural and political reasons. The Berlin Wall had not only divided Germany; it had kept the two Germanys, East and West, rutted in an ossified monument to the cold war and its Manichean logic. This charged, chosen place of residence interweaves Petzold's personal story with the history of Germany and the European continent. It located him at the most important front of the cold war that crumbled around him with unexpected speed and unforeseen consequences, an important subtext to many of his films.

Petzold was born in Hilden and grew up largely in Haan, in the western part of West Germany near the Ruhr region (*Ruhrgebiet*), more or less midway between the wealthy state-capital city Düsseldorf and industrial Wuppertal. The Ruhr region is Germany's industrial core, the engine of the country's spectacular economic rise from a fragmented mosaic of small states to, by the end of the nineteenth century, a world industrial power. For these obvious strategic reasons, the region proved a recurring target during Germany's twentieth-century wars. In World War II, the Ruhr region was heavily bombed to degrade the country's industrial capacity, but was then rapidly rebuilt in the 1950s and 1960s. The result was an industrial and often postindustrial landscape that seems to have left its mark on Petzold's vivid cinematic imagination (as reflected in *Pilots* or *The Sex Thief*). The area has a large number of small cities that tend, with the exception of notably wealthier Düsseldorf, to have more of a working-class character than Germany's better-known metropolises like Munich, Hamburg, or Frankfurt (Berlin constitutes an important exception on which I shall elaborate below).

Petzold recounts how his parents arrived in this region as political refugees from Soviet-dominated East Germany, where they had grown up. His father was originally from Saxony and his mother from what is now the Czech Republic. Their origins in a terrain of shifting borders and migrating masses is typical of the constant and fundamental remaking that has marked Central Europe in the twentieth and twenty-first centuries. In the interview contained in this book, Petzold discusses the impact of his parents' growing up as "refugee children" on his own childhood. He inhabited a series of "transit spaces," referring to bungalows and other inexpensive, semidisposable domiciles, and even called the site of much of his upbringing the German equivalent of "trailer parks" (said to me in English). Related to the movement spaces of modern mobility—they are by-products or second-order effects of such mobility—these transit spaces (like gas stations and roadside rest areas, but also hotels, motels, and other disposable buildings) play a central role in Petzold's cinema. His background recalls and underscores how Germany and its neighbors witnessed one of the largest (if self-inflicted) movements of people ever. An estimated fourteen to sixteen million people, including Petzold's parents, migrated in Central and Eastern Europe during the latter stages of World War II and in its aftermath. Later in the early postwar period, the 1949 creation and then 1950s political trajectory of East Germany created further westward-migratory waves. It was an era of often forgotten but utterly breathtaking movement and resettlement, whose magnitude and depths are only recently being tended and tallied by historians (Moeller).

Having left behind first eastern territories lost in the war and then East Germany itself, Petzold's parents became avowed anti-Communists, something against which a young Petzold reacted. The anti-Communist posture of West Germany not only positioned it against its immediate neighbors of East Germany and the other Warsaw Pact countries, it also helped integrate it into the western alliance of NATO and inclined it fatefully toward the United States. The Ruhr region was reconstructed with the help of the United States not least to bolster Western Europe economically and militarily as a bulwark against the feared westward expansion of the Soviet bloc. This postwar political inclination has created an abidingly complex relationship for many postwar Germans with the United States (memorably manifest, for example, in Wim Wenders's famous declaration that "the Yanks have colonized our subconscious" in his *Kings of the Road* [*Im Laufe der Zeit*; 1976]). This ambivalence toward the United States runs throughout Petzold's work, both in its love-hate relationship with Hollywood genre films and with the impact of what many Germans regard as the accelerating "Americanization" of their country. For one of many examples, in responding to a question about the spread of American economic and cultural practices in the former East Germany, Petzold said that he did not have to introduce such phenomena, as the American is already there, in fast-food restaurants, sport-utility vehicles, and exercise gyms (Uehling and Petzold).

Somewhat contrary to this anti-Communist background, Petzold chose to forego mandatory military service in favor of (likewise mandatory) civil service and then to study (modern) German literature in Berlin. In his civil-service position, he had his first professional experience with film, running a film program for young people at a kind of German YMCA, with whom he watched hundreds of films. The program was divided into popular and art-house cinema, a false distinction with which Petzold has never agreed and one I argue has been formative in his open-minded approach to genre films. After completing this civil service, he relocated to Berlin in 1981 and enrolled at the Freie Universität (Free University), the origins of which also rest in the cold-war history of the city and the country. The main campus of the university, including its literature departments where Petzold studied, is in the southwestern section of Berlin, in what was the U.S. sector of the city. During the 1960s and 1970s student movements, the Freie Universität became one of West Germany's most leftist academic institutions, hosting political actions, protests, and student strikes on a sometimes daily basis. This owed as well to the political demographics of West Berliners, often self-selected transplants from West Germany seeking to escape mandatory military or civil service, as West Berlin residence alone was seen as contributing sufficiently to the defense of the country. In the interview herein, Petzold stresses that his move to Berlin was driven by politics and by a cultural affinity for the (then once and future) capital.

This political atmosphere also informed the founding and trajectory of the German Film and Television Academy of Berlin (known by its German abbreviation DFFB), where Petzold enrolled after finishing his master's degree in German literature at the Freie Universität. Petzold wrote his master's thesis on the literary provocateur Rolf Dieter Brinkmann but, even during his time at the Freie Universität, was auditing classes at the DFFB and was always oriented, as he puts it, "in the direction of cinema." Founded in 1966, the DFFB was part of the wave of state-subsidized film schools after the Oberhausen Manifesto, which initiated the changes that would lead to the New German Cinema of directors like Rainer Werner Fassbinder, Werner Herzog, Wim Wenders, as well as Helma Sanders-Brahms and Helke Sander, among many others. German cinema luminaries of the 1970s and 1980s like Harun Farocki, Hartmut Bitomsky, and Helke Sander were associated with the DFFB from the beginning. Petzold recounts how, given his auditing of classes and familiarity with the faculty, he was surprised not to be admitted on his first try (he says that their reminding him that Fassbinder was never accepted there was cold comfort). He was admitted on his second attempt and entered in 1989, such that he was at the film school in Berlin, learning from important figures of 1970s and 1980s German cinema, when the Berlin Wall fell and Germany reunified (see the section on *Ghosts*).

Contexts 2: 1990s and Post-2000 German Cinema

Petzold's filmmaking career began at a 1990s moment when German cinema, like much of German society and culture, seemed unsure of itself and uncertain about its future direction. This uncertainty arose in no small part from the series of world-historical events outlined above. Germany had, after all, produced seven fundamentally different forms of state over the course of the twentieth century. The 1990s cinematic consequences of these disorienting events were, perhaps unsurprisingly, a turn away from the auteurist, politically engaged orientation of New German Cinema and to lighter fare, largely geared to distract from the anxieties that would accompany (yet) another fundamental transformation of state, economy, and culture. Eric Rentschler has influentially argued that the 1990s were marked by a "cinema of consensus," films that appealed to a popular, if not the absolute lowest, common denominator. For example, 1990s German cinema tended to treat the watershed events of 1989 and 1990, the end of East Germany, as grist for comedies and parodies (with titles like *Go, Trabi, Go* [1991] and its sequel, *Go, Trabi, Go: That Was the Wild East* [1993]), which, along with similarly escapist historical drama, dominated the domestic box office (see Naughton).

Petzold is usually regarded as the foremost figure in a post-2000 abreaction to this 1990s cinema of consensus. The emergence and rise of Petzold's work coincides with what Brad Prager and I have described as a turn away from the affirmative cinema of the 1990s in favor of a more critically and aesthetically ambitious mode of German cinema around 2000 (Fisher and Prager). Petzold regards these 1990s popular films as inane, a return to the kinds of banal entertainments that dominated German cinema in the 1950s. The post-2000 turn in feature film serves as a revival, or perhaps an echo, of "the collapse of the conventional" declared by the 1962 Oberhausen Manifesto, which helped usher in some twenty years of German film whose cinematic achievements were the greatest since the Weimar era (Fisher and Prager 2–3). It has sought to restore to Germany what Werner Herzog called a "legitimate cinema," something more akin to the achievements of Fritz Lang, F. W. Murnau, and the Weimar-era G. W. Pabst.

Petzold's work, especially with the 2000–01 success of *The State I Am In,* has galvanized, more than that of any other single director, this second collapse of the conventional and been a harbinger of German cinema's return to more artistically ambitious filmmaking. Petzold is, in fact, generally regarded as the foremost director of the so-called Berlin School—a bit of a misnomer, since it is not particularly based in Berlin and is not any kind of school. The term Berlin School emerged in the wake of *The State I Am In,* around 2001 in reviews of films by Angela Schanelec and Thomas Arslan, with whom Petzold had worked during their time together at the DFFB (Baute et al.). The phrase has now come into widespread usage in German critical circles, most often to describe the films of such contemporary German directors as Petzold, Arslan, and Schanelec, as well as those by a "second generation" of Christoph Hochhäusler, Valeska Grisebach, and Ulrich Köhler, among others. Coined as it was by critics, the Berlin School style is notoriously hard to define, not least because the alleged members rejected issuing any kind of manifesto. Although the group is loosely affiliated with the film journal *Revolver*, the journal covers a wide range of topics and has involved only some members of the school. Although leery of defining the Berlin School solely by style, Marco Abel observes that many Berlin School films do offer long takes and long shots, a minimal use of nondiegetic or scored music, and "clinically precise framings" (Abel, *Counter-Cinema*). For Abel, this, much more than a sum of its merely style parts, amounts to an attempt to establish a counter-cinema to mainstream aesthetics and concerns. The filmmakers associated with the Berlin School deliberately avoid popular cinema's "dramaturgy of overbearance" (Thomas Arslan) and its "shepherding effect" (Christoph Hochhäusler), both of which refer to the fairly closed, even manipulative aesthetics of mainstream feature films (qtd. in Kopp 287–88). Even if the Berlin School has not formally defined itself as a school or wave, filmmaking in this mode has become one of the most important aesthetic/artistic developments in post–cold war European cinema and art-house cinema in general.

Petzold's Ghostly Archeology of Genre

Although Petzold is usually placed at the forefront of the Berlin School, his films engage with popular forms, especially genre, notably more than other Berlin School works. While Petzold's themes demonstrate the social and political critique characteristic of the Berlin School, his explorations of this constellation also uniquely exploit popular genres to achieve their impact. This approach distinguishes Petzold's work from that of other important European directors like Michael Haneke or the Dardenne brothers, whose films follow a more conventional art-house mode, foregrounding their distance from, even antagonism toward, popular genre. More than any other major art-house cinema director currently working, I would suggest, Petzold describes and credits the influence of often very popular films on his work. He has named assorted mainstream genre movies as the inspirations for many of his most critically acclaimed and prize-winning films: Alfred Hitchcock for *Pilots* (*The 39 Steps*) and *Something to Remind Me* (*Vertigo*), Edgar G. Ulmer for *Cuba Libre* (*Detour*), Kathryn Bigelow's *Near Dark* as an inspiration for *The State I Am In,* Herk Harvey's *Carnival of Souls* for *Yella,* and *The Postman Always Rings Twice* for *Jerichow* (including Visconti's,

Garnett's, and Rafelson's versions). Petzold's films consistently negotiate between genre and art-house cinema, between globally circulating images and national particularity, leaving them deliberately suspended in crisis and abeyance—central themes, as the first epigraph to this essay suggests, within the films themselves.

It is precisely the abiding distinction between artistically ambitious and genre cinemas that Petzold discusses and problematizes in his "Mail Exchange" (*Mailwechsel*) with Christoph Hochhäusler and Dominik Graf. Hochhäusler, the cofounder of the journal *Revolver,* is among the best-known directors of the Berlin School; Graf is some ten years older than Petzold and counts as Germany's premier genre filmmaker, primarily of crime thrillers and *policiers* for television (see Wahl, Abel, and Jockenhövel). This "Mail Exchange" was carried out via email among the three directors in 2006, published in *Revolver,* and formed the basis for their three "episodes" of the four-and-a-half-hour *Dreileben* project in 2011. Despite being made for television, each of *Dreileben*'s three episodes is also a stand-alone, ninety-minute film. The "Mail Exchange" occurred when Graf was invited to participate in a panel on the Berlin School at the DFFB with Petzold and Hochhäusler, but could not attend. Their virtual panel quickly became a pointed debate on the advantages and disadvantages of the Berlin School style as well as the potential for popular genre in Germany. Petzold proposed making the "Mail Exchange" the basis for a shared film project and subsequently provided the story that serves as the foundation for all three episodes. The five years between the "Mail Exchange" and *Dreileben*—years in which Petzold made *Yella* and *Jerichow* and foregrounded their basis on popular genre—underscore how central these questions about art-house versus genre cinema have remained for Petzold's thinking and work.

In Dominik Graf's opening salvo, he admits that the Berlin School started promisingly but argues that the subsequent films failed to "expand [their] narrative possibilities," opting instead to "narrow . . . [their] gaze via style-proclamation."[3] He refers to the films as "Snow White films" (*Schneewittchenfilme*)—that is, films that put their increasingly lifeless subjects under a cold, museal glass. Although Graf professes to liking some of the Berlin School's works, he regards this tendency to lifeless formalism, appealing as it may be to film critics and scholars, as a problem for cinema as a whole. Quoting Fassbinder, who decried some of his New German Cinema contemporaries for "beginning to shoot their film reviews," Graf argues that this approach results in a thematic and stylistic standstill that is tantamount to "dying in one's own well-warmed socks." Questioning the consistently "arranged forlornness" of these characters, Graf recalls what François Truffaut wondered about Ingmar Bergman: does he think life is really as crappy as in his films?

In these criticisms of the Berlin School, Graf raises again and again what he regards as a fundamental problem in German cinema—a persisting, crippling polarization between art-house film and genre film. To this charge of widening the cinematic gap, Hochhäusler admits that his films aim to create a "GEGEN-Kino" (COUNTER-cinema), an effort very much in the mold of the 1960s and 1970s art-house approach cited above (and confirming Marco Abel's argument about the Berlin School). But I would emphasize that Petzold stakes out a position somewhat different from Hochhäusler's. Petzold demonstrates how much of his thinking dovetails with Graf's: he likewise laments the divide between popular and art-house cinema.[4] In an interview with Abel in *Cineaste*, Petzold reflects on the New German Cinema director Volker Schlöndorff's criticisms of German popular cinema, particularly his assertion that German directors need more film theory:

> I'm not sure about this. I don't think we will improve filmmaking in Germany by offering more film-theory seminars. We were in need of instructors who could think cinema rather than divide it into neat, teachable categories [. . .] and the German *Autorenkino* [auteur cinema] is at least partially to blame for this. They participated in this pigeonholing—art house over here, mainstream over there, nonstars versus stars, etc. Those who participated in divvying up cinema this way were the death of cinema. [. . .] By the end of the 1980s we had two kinds of cinema: the miserable cinema of literature and an escapist, lowbrow cinema, which wanted to be the opposite of this literary cinema. And before you knew it, someone like Dominik Graf, for whose attempt at making intelligent genre films I have the utmost respect, found himself in an incredibly lonesome position. (Abel and Petzold)

This conviction about the perils of separating mainstream from art-house cinema has persisted right through the 2012 *Barbara* (Lueken et al.). Although Petzold is well versed in social, literary, and cultural theory, he believes that an overacademicization and overtheorization in filmmaking has led to an aesthetic dead end. He thinks that one needs cinematic and, as we shall see, at least partially genre answers to aesthetic questions posed by the gap between art-house and popular cinema. For Graf, the solution to this pernicious polarization rests in the lonely task of (re)establishing the German genre film. Petzold is "fascinated" by this "Sisyphus work" of Graf's, but he then draws a suggestive distinction between Graf's undertaking and his own work, as he puts it, to "make films in the cemetery of genre cinema, with the remainders that are still there for the taking" (Abel and Petzold). At that point, Petzold did not elaborate, but in the interview herein, I ask him about his approach to genre and how it relates to 1970s directors like Fassbinder, Wenders, and Godard. Petzold explained:

> I think the difference is that we are twenty years on. [These directors] took genre as a grammar, and they used that grammar to destroy genre and to unleash a new kind of energy—they quoted, destroyed, deconstructed genre, no? But as we began to make films, there was not any cinema anymore, no genre cinema at all. . . . [I]t is all on television now, in the afternoons. . . . So we had to approach it differently. It was more the case that I wanted to rediscover genre; I did not want to destroy it, therefore not *de*construct it, rather *re*construct it. I guess that's the way one can put it. . . . It is a kind of archaeology.

The passage first and foremost confirms his productive engagement with genre, but the distinction he draws between the earlier generation and his own is revealing. For Fassbinder, Wenders, and Godard—all directors Petzold greatly admires—genres were still an extant medium, so they could undertake the productive dismantling of genres for an audience well versed in their grammars. For German filmmakers of Petzold's generation, however, these kinds of genres no longer exist in cinema—at best they exist in stultifying forms on television—so the task is one of recovery, rebuilding, and reinscribing genre for a contemporary moment haunted by history, failed by neoliberalism, and rife with loss.

How then to square Petzold's clear art-house and auteurist tendencies, including his challenging political and economic themes, with his stated attempt to reconstitute genre as the core of a better German cinema? His cinema reconciles these seeming contradictions, I would argue, with a particular, peculiar mode of generic (re)assemblage, not a mimetic reproduction of genre works nor an outright negation of them. It is indeed a peculiar sort of archaeology of genre, one that excavates piecemeal, recombines, and reexhibits in the service of his own aesthetic and political vision. This archaeology is neither sentimental nor nostalgic—as he makes clear with his unusual reading of Peter Bogdanovich's *The Last Picture Show* in the interview herein. Petzold's multiple references to *The Last Picture Show* are suggestive, I think, because the film self-consciously manipulates genre (as do many other classic films that he cites as inspirations, like *Detour, Near Dark,* and the various versions of *The Postman Always Rings Twice*). As its title suggests, *The Last Picture Show* is a film very much aware of its place in time: it registers radical temporal transformation, the passing of a distinct moment, but does so from the emphatic perspective of the present. *The Last Picture Show* depicts the crisis of a present aware of the unremitting passing of time—and achieves this depiction through a self-conscious manipulation of a late genre. In the character of Sam the Lion, played by Ben Johnson, a regular from John Wayne's (older) Westerns, the film registers the last vestige of the old Western that its West Texas setting and milieu would imply. The film's narrative and stylistic choices explore the gap between that Western milieu and the younger, altogether different generation around him, a gap registering not only the generational passing of time but also the inexorable unfolding of history. With Sam the Lion's antiquated presence and then death, the young are cut adrift from a cultural tradition and mode of being that had helped ground them and their whole small town. With its registering of the passing of time, and the marking of its casualties, *The Last Picture Show* displays throughout remnants, remains, and ghosts of an era becoming bygone—perhaps the very core aspects of Petzold's cinema that, I am arguing, characterize his manipulation of genre as well.

Remnants, remains, and ghosts fascinate Petzold: beyond his metaphor of his films' digging in the graveyard of genre—and repeated images of people actually digging in his films—he speaks regularly of remains in terms of remnant energies, gestures, and bodies.[5] Remains both structure his directions to his actors and, even more importantly, frame his three major films to date, the so-called Ghost trilogy of *The State I Am In, Ghosts,* and *Yella. The Last Picture Show'*s displacing the old cowboy out of generic context and resetting him in the present moment is precisely, I think, how Petzold approaches genre. He tends to tear generic remnants out of their contexts, to recontextualize them, and to allow them to illuminate a certain present in that present's collision with a rapidly receding past. This sensibility and approach recalls one of Petzold's stated influences, Walter Benjamin, the literary critic, cultural historian, and philosopher, especially of history. Benjamin's (unfinished) magnum opus is the so-called Arcades Project in which he sought to create an archeological history of modernity by immersing himself in the past, tearing out quotes and images to "mortify" them, and then recontextualizing them in work that would illuminate the present (see also Benjamin, "Excavation and Memory").[6] Similarly emphasizing remnants and remains, Petzold works in this mode with older genre films by conjuring a non-nostalgic, critical history of the present.

Benjamin's work and thought are shot through, from his earliest to his last writings, with a fascination with the ghostly and spectral (Richter, Introduction). What is a remnant, a remain, and/or a ghost? Remnants, remains, and ghosts are things that, above all, recall the past—that underscore the so-called presence of the past. But beyond the simultaneity of the past in the present, they indicate the very processes by which the present becomes past. Especially ghosts compel us to ask in an uncanny, non-nostalgic mode: Why does this remain? What happened that it survives in this liminal form? In this way, not only do remnants, remains, and ghosts make the past present for us now, but they also beg the question of why we have come to this particular present—the remnant, remain, or ghost is a melancholic reminder that things could have been different; their very presence queries why we have ended up here and now. As Derrida makes clear in his *Specters of Marx*—conceived and written in the same post-1989 milieu that so influenced Petzold—ghosts suggest the noncontemporaneity, the nonidentity, of the present with itself. For Derrida, this engagement with the ghost—to "speak *of the* ghost, indeed *to the* ghost and *with* it," as he puts it—can and should be a political gesture, one directed at responsibility and justice (Derrida xviii). Playing upon the pronunciation of "haunt" in French, he suggests the parallels between this ghostly existence of "hauntology" and ontology in general. In Petzold's cinema, a central goal for the viewer is not simply to exorcise these historical ghosts—emphatically not to uncover the secret that will banish it forever—but, in that posture of abeyance, to interpret the purpose and meaning of its abiding presence.

These remains, remnants, and especially ghosts thereby inspire for Petzold not an empirical or documentary search for history and historical transformation but a haunted and uncanny one, one that points to Petzold's elusive, spectral style. His is a ghostly archeology, one that dovetails with a recurring interest in the dissonant and disorienting effects of the horror genre (see the sections on *State I Am In, Ghosts,* and *Yella* below). Ghosts are not given to easy observation or facile explanation—in terms of images, they would not offer themselves up to the camera straight on, as star actors of mainstream cinema normally would; rather, they prefer shadows and the conceptually ambiguous. Petzold's cinema foregrounds this elusive aspect of the ghostly, its ephemeral character that lends to an ontological ambiguity, but one rendered ironically starker in the brightness and razor-sharp clarity of Petzold's images (shot by his regular, longtime cinematographer and collaborator, Hans Fromm). Such precise images deployed in the service of the spectral only exacerbate the fundamental cognitive confusion with which ghosts confront viewers (Carroll 32–33), a confusion Petzold refunctions, for example in *Yella,* to query our present socioeconomic condition. At the level of the image and of performance in his films, that elusiveness and transitoriness recall the paintings of Gerhard Richter, one of Petzold's favorite artists, whose painting *Betty* (1988) adorns the wall of the house in *The Sex Thief.* This elusiveness of the ghost and reference to Richter dovetails with how Petzold instructs his actors to gesture and move in elliptical, allusive ways—to tend, as he says, to the turned-away (*das Abgewandte*). His films are full of characters turning and walking away from the camera and viewer, looking back for a second before they, ghostlike, disappear.

Such a ghostly archeology also helps explain why Petzold can be more open to engaging and deploying popular forms (see, for example, his interest in comics: Petzold, "Hawaiian Getaway" and "Lucky to Have Her," discussed in Mitchell). This is perhaps the most distinguishing aspect of Petzold's celebrated cinema: its open acknowledgment and engagement with a wide array of popular genre films that went before. Much as Benjamin self-consciously uncovers and cites previous sources,

Petzold can be more open about engaging and deploying popular forms because he is conjuring them as remnants, remains, and ghosts to illuminate the present. The reinscription of popular genre, not least to critique dominant historical, political, and economic discourses, distinguishes Petzold's films from the 1990s cinema of consensus and from the aesthetic austerity of many Berlin School directors. It is not so much that Petzold is against mainstream cinema but that he is working against the way it tends to be coordinated to dominant modes of facile understanding and reductive thinking (much as Benjamin's discontinuous histories were directed against mainstream, "progressive" history [Albig, Gurk, and Petzold]). While admiring of and even obsessed with the efficacy of genre effects, Petzold's work destabilizes and politicizes them.

Petzold foregrounds two other aspects of mainstream genre in particular that contribute to his unusual style. On the one hand, he foregrounds how a new physicality, a new type of body, emerges in certain moments of popular genre—something that he realized while in film school when he went to a midafternoon matinee of *Pretty Woman* (see the interview herein). He sat with a crowd of professional women screaming "What a man!" as the unabashedly rich Edward Lewis (Richard Gere) turned on the bath tap with his big toe. For Petzold, this was a new type of neoliberal body, an emergent physicality concomitant with new desires, delivered in a popular genre film. This is perhaps a counterintuitive assertion, since one might think that genres would merely repeat their bodily forms, yet, as his example highlights, such moments of physical intensity can shine through (and partially because of) the dim redundancy of narrative. Precisely in its repetitions and variations, genre cinema is able to "discover" (*entdecken*) the new bodies of the emergent economic constellations foregrounded above, images of which Petzold recognized as both "sexy and dangerous." This corporeal mode of becoming economic is an insight that one of Petzold's own published articles confirms. In a 2003 piece in the *FAZ* (*Frankfurter Allgemeine Zeitung*, Germany's most important daily newspaper), he foregrounds, in yet another engagement with popular genre, the meaning of Demi Moore's hyper-fit yet desexed body in *Charlie's Angels: Full Throttle* (2003). For him, the distance between the bodies of the (1970s) Angels and Moore's (post-2000) villainous, fallen Angel registers fundamental shifts in physicality and in the wider culture around them (Petzold,

"Luzifers Tochter"). Petzold repeatedly isolates and intensifies new kinds of physicality that galvanize the ghostliness of older forms of corporeality, leading viewers to contemplate historical and political change written on the body itself.

Certainly related to these multiple spectral temporalities and new physicalities, Petzold foregrounds moments of crisis and transitions in popular genre. Although genre films often do tend to hackneyed conflicts and resolutions, Petzold uncovers and isolates within them moments of crisis, transition, and transformation for individuals and collectives (and the intersection therein). In fact, it is precisely to comprehend these transitions and transformations, these "discoveries of something new," within genre that one has to tell "the old stories and tales," as he says in the interview herein. Petzold showed me, from the preparatory materials for *Barbara,* a still image from *My Darling Clementine* of Henry Fonda (as Wyatt Earp) in cowboy kit, tipped back, almost suspended, on a porch chair. For Petzold, this image stages a crucial moment of decision in the Western, a genre that in general tracks the (ongoing) crisis of civilization and nature, of democracy and anarchy. Fonda's Wyatt Earp is surveying a town to which he has committed to bring civilizing law and order, a historical development about which he himself feels ambivalent. This image of hesitant balance, on the inside/outside space of the porch, is exactly what Petzold seeks in this and many other films, and that with which he briefs the cinematographer Fromm and his actors, including his recurring lead actor Nina Hoss.

Such images constitute, Petzold emphasizes, precisely the moment of *Schwebezustand,* of simultaneously individual and collective abeyance, one that he consistently explores in his cinema. If Petzold's films are full of ghosts—the remnants of such collective crises and transitions—then these residual specters haunt, in abeyance, emergent socioeconomic formations. In these myriad ways, his films excavate, as I shall track throughout this volume, such remnants and remains from the rich soils of mainstream genre as well as the nonfiction films of his regular collabator, Harun Farocki (see Fisher, "Times of Transition and Transformation"). In his ghostly archaeology of genre's transitional histories, Petzold extracts fragments of a quickly receding past that can illuminate our present. This deliberate excavation and studied extraction bring to the clear light of day, in a uniquely art-genre cinema, how the world is constantly transforming individuals politically and economically, at the most intimate level of their desires, dreams, and fantasies.

Pilots (*Pilotinnen*): Working Women on the Vehicular Run

Pilots (1995), Petzold's graduation film from the DFFB in Berlin, developed in part out of a thirty-minute short film he considers a personal breakthrough, *The Warm Money* (*Das warme Geld*; 1992). *The Warm Money* suggests a recurring narrative approach for Petzold: women under economic pressure forced to navigate an inhospitable world both economically and romantically, such that the two become insidiously intertwined. The results in the feature-length *Pilots* were auspicious. Some called the work not only the year's best television film but probably the best German film of the year, a considerable accomplishment for a final project at film school (Ertl and Knepperges 75). While *Pilots* takes up some of the plot and themes from *The Warm Money*, it extends them by building on one of most accomplished genre works of the 1930s—Alfred Hitchcock's *The 39 Steps* (1935)—in a highly original direction. The relationship between the work world, interwoven economic-erotic desire, and the criminal world becomes paramount. Although he returns to some of these themes in later films, in this early phase of *The Warm Money, Pilots,* and *The Sex Thief,* they are explored through unusually close relationships between two women. In *Pilots,* this relationship unfolds between two women of different generations, a divide ultimately overshadowed by their itinerant work and the movement spaces (cars, airplanes) as well as the transit spaces (rest areas, hotels) in which it locates them.

Although it was Petzold's graduation film from film school, *Pilots* received funding from television and underscores how, as with many postwar German art and art-house directors, Petzold's career from the beginning has relied substantially on television financing. Television was essential to the success of Germany's first postwar wave of celebrated art-house films, those of the New German Cinema: one prominent critic has even declared German independent filmmaking "unthinkable without television" (Elsaesser, *New German Cinema* 202; see also Hake 161–62. Given the modest size of the German theatrical market and limited export potential for even its most popular films, artistically ambitious works invariably require subsidy support, and in Germany, even for theatrical releases, this has been funneled to a large degree through television. These conditions have led to a symbiotic relationship in Germany between television and film, in which the lines between the two are not very clearly drawn or even drawable (Hake 181). For example, the long-running series *Das kleine Fernsehspiel* (The little teleplay) of the German channel ZDF continues to be an important player in the German film industry, having fostered German directors like Tom Tykwer and Fatih Akın and even supported established non-German directors like Agnes Varda and Jim Jarmusch. Petzold similarly first established his reputation with *Das kleine Fernsehspiel*, with his first two works, *Pilotinnen* and *Cuba Libre,* financed and playing therein. Although many of Petzold's early films were initially made as television productions, even the later theatrical releases like *Yella, Jerichow,* and *Barbara* were financed in large part by television, but the above should indicate how fine this line is in Germany, and Petzold has emphasized that he made even earlier works contracted by television as if they were cinema films.[7]

Originally entitled "The Summer When Frank Sinatra Died," *Pilots* begins with Karin, who is at the end of her forties and in Paris, where she and a French lover, Michel, try to negotiate when and where they might next meet (Suchsland and Petzold, "Der Schneidetisch eines Films"). Both are traveling salespeople, she for a German cosmetics company (Sinatra-sounding "Blue Eyes") and he for a German sparkling-wine company. With a lingering close-up on their hands plotting out their travels on a map of northern Europe, she says, "I have to go," to which he replies, "Someday we'll have a place." As Karin travels to various merchants in the Ruhr region, the film establishes that she is under increasing pressure from a new, young, and efficiency-obsessed manager, "Junior," to move "four thousand units a week." Junior orders his girlfriend, the much younger Sophie, to accompany Karin, likely to keep her under surveillance while training Sophie to take her job (as Jamie Peck and Adam Tickell note, changes in labor have yielded ever-increasing surveillance at work, a recurring theme in Petzold's cinema [391–92]). The film follows the two in Karin's car, which becomes the film's (and Petzold's cinema's) key movement space: the two women are at first openly competitive and then grow closer together as they realize that Junior is exploiting them both. When Michel is arrested for embezzling and Junior sells the company while cutting Sophie out, the women decide to take matters into their own hands (to extend a manual theme of the film, one close to Petzold's mentor and collaborator Harun Farocki; see Blümlinger 174 and Elsaesser, "Harun Farocki" 16–17). They first rob the kind of drug stores to which they have been selling cosmetics and then move on to a shopping mall with much bigger revenues and risks.

In depicting the makeup industry and its discontents, Petzold engages one of the themes that will recur throughout his career: the remaking and repurposing of people for, and through, work. Petzold has said that he thematizes work because it and its consequences are substantively absent in mainstream German cinema (see the interview herein). In this case, the character of the work (cosmetics) is related to the literal refashioning and recasting of people: the theme of makeup and its relationship to people's economic and political transformation returns, in fact, some seventeen years later in *Barbara* (Nord and Petzold, "Ich wollte, dass die DDR Farben Hat"). Petzold lists three encounters with the makeup industry and its salespeople that inspired the cosmetics-centered plot of *Pilots.* First, at a time when his father was unemployed, Petzold's mother tried to become a local Avon representative, so they had assorted Avon saleswomen visit their home. These women, Petzold recounts, were childless and, "as in an Elke Sommer film from the 1960s, sat in sunglasses in their own cars, waiting for their big chance" (Ertl and Knepperges 73). Second, another former teacher at the DFFB, Hartmut Bitomsky, reported to Petzold that he had observed, in the former East German provinces, a sales representative from a western makeup firm, expensively turned out and on her cell phone, with "telepathic defensive powers" against the womenless "brood of men" hitting on her (an ability manifested by Karin as she stays in hotels throughout the film). Third, when Petzold was traveling for research on a Farocki project, he encountered in a hotel a Merz-Spezial saleswoman (a company whose motto is "I Am Spezial") who was learning French. Petzold underscores how fascinated he was by these kinds of characters who were not by any means invented but rather living on the edges of society, belonging to no one, "not even to me when I depict them in a film."

People from the margins, especially marginalized women, are a recurring presence in all of Petzold's films and embody the socioeconomic changes his cinema is tracking. It is remarkable how, in all three of these observations, he links the cosmetics theme to new forms of deindustrialized, service-based labor (Avon and other corporate sales reps) as well as to both movement spaces (the car) and transit spaces (hotels and contemporary shopping malls), all of which contribute to the film's iconography. As noted in the introduction, Petzold is fascinated by how genre, as a recurring story tending to myth, can track the emergence of transitional types of individuals. All three of the sales representatives he cites underscore how a particular kind of labor in contemporary capitalism produces new kinds of people. Contemporary capitalism refunctions not only these women's work but also their erotic and fantasy worlds, worlds increasingly unburdened of family and even love, thus attaining the lack of attachment and lightness of being valorized in neoliberal capitalism (Urry, *Mobilities* 33; Bauman 4).

Along these thematic lines, it is worth noting that all these models above, along with the protagonists in the film, are women. Although Petzold is (at least somewhat) sensitive to the fact that so many of his protagonists are women, his consistent use of them in his work seems similar to that in the films of Fassbinder and Kluge, filmmakers he admires and who saw social reasons for favoring female protagonists in key works.[8] As Petzold has recounted, he regards women as more adaptable (and often more ambitious) in responding to new conditions (Demmerle and Petzold). Besides wanting to avoid becoming overly autobiographical in his work, Petzold also chooses to foreground women because he regards them as more problematically disempowered—they have it harder, he says (Ertl and Knepperges 75)—in that they still have to rely on men, as Karin and Sophie do on Junior, as the perpetual owners of the means of production (Abel and Petzold). Whether or not one might regard this as feminist, many of his female characters are strong, active, and determined despite victimization, particularly as his late films *Yella* and *Barbara* demonstrate.

In *Pilots* the two female protagonists are, in fact, a notable revision to the genre model he cites for the film, Hitchcock's 1935 *The 39 Steps*. Petzold recounts how he regards the Hitchcock film as, above all, a rumination on the production of desire (Ertl and Knepperges 75). *The 39 Steps* follows a Canadian, Hannay, who is compelled to flee through England and Scotland when he, in familiar Hitchcock fashion, becomes the "wrong man" to whom guilt (for murder) is accidentally attributed.

On his flight from both police and the actually guilty criminals, he ends up handcuffed to a woman, Pamela, who is at first openly hostile to him. Escaping in thrilling manner, Hannay and Pamela pursue a spy ringleader and predictably fall in love en route to discovering that the secret plans that they are chasing do not exist in material form. In a typical Hitchcock MacGuffin, they have been memorized by the aptly monikered "Mr. Memory," a performer at the music hall where the film concludes (with Memory's murder).

Petzold's analysis of this film as a study of desire is actually quite close to Slavoj Zizek's: Zizek argues that *The 39 Steps* was an early masterpiece that marked Hitchcock's "epistemological break," consolidating and developing his classical style (Zizek 3–4). Like Petzold, Zizek regards the film as exploring how the couple's desire is produced not from within the individual(s) but from without. Hannay and Pamela are thrown together by the police on the train and then literally handcuffed together by the killer's men before they know each other, a material attachment before (psychological) desire begins. The characters absorb desire from their surroundings, from the context, one of the recurring themes of all of Petzold's studies of transformative individuals amidst changing contexts.

Why would such a reconfigured desire—one constituted by the outside and desiring, in MacGuffin mode, nothing—interest Petzold? Even at this early stage, in his graduation film, his intervention in Hitchcock's genre film demonstrates his preferred mixture of genre with his own auteurist interests and engagements. Karin and Sophie are, at first, like Hannay and Pamela, deliberately cold, distant, and even cruel to each other—recurring aspects of interpersonal relations throughout Petzold's work. In *Pilots,* however, it is an interpersonal coldness and cruelty not of the prevailing sexual mores (as in *The 39 Steps*; see Wood 275) but rather of capitalism itself. As Zygmunt Bauman notes, the new economic conditions attenuate traditional interpersonal bonds, rendering them more distant, cold, and often paranoid (Bauman 4). This competition and subsequent coldness pervade their interactions until a turning-point scene at almost precisely halfway through the film, when the women stumble upon a potential, though ultimately criminal, solidarity.

In this watershed scene, Sophie, stuck in the car with Karin and angry at her boyfriend-boss Junior, throws her Blue Eyes jacket against the dashboard, which suddenly releases tear gas within the car. Karin keeps tear gas close at hand, reminiscent of Petzold's recounting the paranoid posture of this new type of itinerant female salesperson. The trauma of the event, and the tears imposed from the outside, leads abruptly to the two competitors' first heartfelt conversation. Sitting on the car hood, they confess their dreams to each other and admit their defeats at the hands of Junior in particular and work more generally. Beyond these externally imposed tears, the scene is remarkable because it shoots them at an airport and underneath flying jets, more movement spaces central to the assiduous flows of contemporary capitalism. But the scene also deliberately locates them beyond the end of the runway, at capitalism's margins (figure 3).

They confess to each other that both had aspired to be flight attendants, but Karin could not due to her lack of foreign languages. Although Sophie did ascend to this coveted aerial movement space, she discovered that it was no longer so great anyway—everything is now a charter flight, and the men are up front with the pilots while the women

Figure 3. Karin (Eleonore Weisgerber) and Sophie (Nadeshda Brennicke) at capitalism's margins in *Pilots* (1995).

are in the back with the vomit bags. A second plane flies overhead and overwhelms the sound track in apparent response to Karin's question if she is to be dismissed from the company—she fears becoming the kind of socioeconomic ghost with which Petzold becomes preoccupied in his later work. Sophie responds revealingly with resignation that perhaps everyone is done anyway. The image (and, above all, sound) of aircraft flying overhead recurs later in Petzold's cinema, as in *Yella, Jerichow, Dreileben,* and *Barbara,* and reminds us of the very different socioeconomic scales at which movement spaces, and therefore contemporary individuals in them, operate (Smith; Marston). At this potentially spectral moment, in response to "everyone is done anyway" and the divergence of scales, their dream of becoming their own (figurative) pilots is born.

If *The 39 Steps* offers a typical Hitchcock plotting of the wrong man Hannay and the malleability of his desire, Petzold, as that watershed scene demonstrates, deliberately diverges from Hitchcock in the specificity of the context that produces desire. For Petzold, the crucial outside impinging on the individual's desire, dreams, and fantasy is very specifically the economic milieu of late West Germany and early "unified" Germany. For example, when he was asked whether the beginning of the film in Paris signified his own longing for the French New Wave or a wish on his part to travel abroad, Petzold averred that it had much more to do with the film's engagement with cosmetics and how they function in the consumerist imaginary—Paris is, of course, a city listed ubiquitously on perfume bottles and makeup packages (Abel and Petzold). Petzold cites how Paris is one of those cities, like Milan or New York, that is listed on fashion goods as a fantasy site of the production of beauty, a materialist MacGuffin offered to consumers to colonize the construction of their own bodies and to navigate their place within the global economy.

Such an imagined, even fantasized geography is a central aspect of this new mode of individuality that Petzold explores here and in many of his films, especially in its relationship to the movement spaces described in the introduction. In the wake of Karin's constant driving and the metaphysical itinerancy it implies—the mobility in the movement space of the car embodying changes in work and self—the film deploys what Petzold terms, in the interview in this book and elsewhere, "transit spaces" (*Transitorte*), by-products or second-order effects of modern mobility such as gas stations, rest areas, or hotels. For an example, in an early scene, an alarm awakens Karin (was the opening Paris sequence only a dream?), and the camera finds her at a freeway rest stop where she meanders over to the bathroom in her pajamas to brush her teeth. The rest area and gas station, important transit spaces since near the beginning of cinema, serve as recurring, key location settings for Petzold's films (for example, in *Cuba Libre*, *The State I Am In*, and *Dreileben*). Much later in the film, when a pregnant Sophie begs Karin for a place to rest, Karin matter-of-factly divulges that she does not even have an apartment, that she only has a mailbox in Germany. She resides full-time in the travel hotels that punctuate the film and that likewise recall Hannay's flight through Scotland (hotels are a key transit space for Petzold; see the section on *Yella* below). Karin's late revelation that she does not have a home reinscribes the film's early rest-area scene. Viewers realize that her sleeping and washing next to the autobahn was not just a stopover but, rather, that such transit spaces are her very mode of existence—despite earning quite well, she chooses to be homeless. This mobile ontology of our contemporary moment entails novel modes of transient domesticity even for the economically successful.

The women's relationship to the economic milieu that produces desire from the outside—one much more specific than in *The 39 Steps*—is underscored in a revealing story that Petzold recounts about an early screening of *Pilots*. When he screened it for his fellow students at the DFFB, they wondered why Karin and Sophie, instead of resorting to crude and clearly doomed robbery, did not just go to the unemployment office and seek other work. Petzold's answer is revealing. To him, these kinds of questions showed that he should have spent even more time depicting Karin's and Sophie's work lives—despite some criticisms that he had dedicated too much of the film to them—in order to show how "natural it is that the criminal fantasy of the two remains limited by their own labor conditions" (Ertl and Knepperges 75). The function of work in people's desires and object-choices, its role in formulating who they are at the most intimate level, will recur throughout his career right up through *Barbara*. Work and the prevailing economic conditions impinge on and determine the nature of individual desires, dreams, and fantasy—including how criminality expresses such fantasy.

Notably, however, this key depiction of work is not offered in a neo-realist mode—as in, for example, the Dardenne brothers—but rather in a self-consciously generic mode. Many of Petzold's films, right through *Wolfsburg, Yella,* and *Jerichow,* engage the criminal energies that pervade the everyday as well as the thin line one can easily cross from the economically productive into the utterly criminal. Karin, for instance, has already disciplined herself, calculatingly conditioning her appearance and behavior in terms of units sold and income saved. In the "happy" ending, Sophie sacrifices herself to the police (and is even depicted in a pieta composition), so Karin can unproblematically escape with their stolen money.

The film's concluding scene, a brief epilogue, successfully delivers Karin to Paris, with a panning tilt over the breakfast table to the Eiffel Tower outside the window. In most of his films, as I shall discuss with *Ghosts,* Petzold avoids landmarks like the Eiffel Tower ubiquitously deployed to establish locations in European cities, and his doing so here remains, in the film's study of desire and the sacrifice it demands, highly ambiguous and ambivalent.

Cuba Libre: Fantasies of Mobility and Faraway Places

Petzold's second feature-length work, the made-for-television *Cuba Libre* (1996), confirms his interest in genre films and his commitment to fostering an "intelligent" cinema by refunctioning them. Also made with the help of ZDF's *Das kleine Fernsehspiel,* the film opens in another, though different kind of transit space than that foregrounded in *Pilots*: a Berlin train station and its run-down café full of commuters and transients. In this rather Fassbinder-like setting and setup, one well-dressed commuter is trying to convince a homeless woman, Tina, to prostitute herself with a story about his boring domestic life. The transaction is witnessed by a homeless man, Tom, who recognizes Tina as a former lover he once robbed of her savings (debt, symbolic and literal, figures prominently in this and many of Petzold's films). When he approaches them and addresses her hopefully, she promptly knocks him down with her bag, leaving him floored and bloodied. An observer of these abrupt goings-on, Jimmy, picks Tom up and brings him back to his posh hotel room, but Tom quickly returns to the train station in search of Tina. Soon thereafter, however, Tina departs, hitchhiking to

Nice, France, in search of sea air to ease her ailing lungs. Jimmy hires Tom as his driver and offers to start off after her, with Tom searching every rest area and gas station along the autobahn for her. Jimmy, however, has been downing some kind of medicine throughout, and shortly into the trip he has a seizure and dies. Without much ado, Tom decides to bury him and take his car, his money, and his identity, apparently to resume his search for Tina.

Following *Pilots'* play on *The 39 Steps*, *Cuba Libre* extends Petzold's engagement with genre films by invoking Edgar G. Ulmer's film-noir classic, *Detour*. From its opening scene, in a train-station café with a song recalling a lost past, *Cuba Libre* cites *Detour*, which opens in a roadside diner with a similarly music-triggered flashback. It is easy to see why Ulmer might appeal to the young Petzold as a filmmaking model. Ulmer was a German-speaking émigré from Central Europe who went from codirecting one of Weimar Germany's most celebrated art films, *People on Sunday* (*Menschen am Sonntag*; 1930) to Hollywood's Poverty Row system of genre pulp. In Hollywood, Ulmer's art-frugal style included carefully framed stock footage; copious, often deliberately surreal rear projection; and ubiquitous, artful fog to obscure shoddy sets and shabby actors. *Detour* (1945) has gone down as Ulmer's B-masterpiece, celebrated by scholars and cinephiles alike—it was, for example, the first B-film to earn a place on the National Film Registry (Isenberg 9).

Despite—in part because of—these modest origins, *Detour* is usually regarded as canonical film noir, but Dana Polan argues that the film best fits a particular subset of the film noir, the "film gris." The filmmaker and film critic and scholar Thom Andersen, whom Petzold knows, initially coined the term. For Andersen, the film gris refers to a set of films noirs made after the trials of the Hollywood Ten by politically inclined directors who took the film noir in a different, more desperate direction (Maland). Such films forego the sometimes heady celebration of anarchy and rebellion in many films noirs in favor of a much bleaker vision of 1940s and 1950s America. This emphatically pessimistic, even dreary vision is realized along the mid-1940s highway in *Detour*. As he recounts in sometimes unreliable voiceover, the anguished Al Roberts heads west toward California "via the thumb route" to join his love, the singer Sue. He finally seems to enjoy some good luck in Arizona, where a well-off, congenial bookie from Miami, Charlie, offers him a ride all the way to Los Angeles. Constantly popping pills, however, Charlie later passes out in the car, and when Al opens the door to check on him, he falls to the ground, hits his head on a rock, and summarily dies. Not wanting to be accused of murder and desperate for money, Al buries Charlie's body and takes his car, clothes, and even identity. This plan seems to work until Al picks up a hitchhiker, Vera, at a gas station, whom Charlie had once picked up and probably sexually assaulted. She spitefully accuses Al of murder and starts to blackmail him into getting them Charlie's money.

In *Detour*, Polan notes, Ulmer avoids the iconographic urban aspects of noirs like *The Maltese Falcon* or *The Naked City* and favors instead "the harsh brightness of the California sun, the dreariness of the used car lot, and the nondescript blandness of the hotel room in which Al and Vera play out their duet of doom" (Polan). *Detour*'s foregoing of noir's urban and urbane settings for bleaker, yet brighter spaces of such drifters certainly serves Petzold's approach in *Cuba Libre* and his abiding interest in movement and transit spaces. As in *Pilots*, Petzold recasts the genre classic by way of well-lit transit spaces of contemporary Germany, all traversed by the movement space of the car: the scruffy looking train station; the contrastingly frictionless freeways; nondescript motel rooms and holiday apartments that Tina and Tom come to inhabit. As in *Detour*, the road, gas stations, and rest areas serve as crucial settings in the drama, in Tom's futile search for Tina and Jimmy's deliberate deception of Tom. Perhaps most telling, however, is what Petzold makes of *Detour*'s used-car lot, where Al and Vera try to cash in on Charlie's vehicular bequest. In *Detour*, the used-car lot serves as the site of unabating capitalist churning—the turning of the wealth wheel—while in *Cuba Libre*, Tom and Tina find their way to Jimmy's fortune through a series of banks, linking money to mobility, as it is throughout Petzold's cinema.

Even bleaker than *Detour*'s open road, however, is the way that these spaces host Tom's and Tina's dreams lost amidst desperation, paranoia, and mutual exploitation. Most disturbing in *Detour* is the ease with which Al buries and robs the man who showed him unprompted kindness; solidarity, as it is throughout Petzold's cinema, is tenuous and consistently short-lived. This roadside development in *Detour*—a flowing traffic in identity itself—dovetails with the willful, often desperate remaking of people Petzold investigated in *Pilots.* In *Cuba Libre,* however, it is not so much, as it is in *Pilots,* work that catalyzes this transformation in people but the material presence of cash itself. The distorting effects of money—money materialized in an almost camp prop—recur in a large number of Petzold's film, and here it galvanizes the kind of innermost transformation in people that Petzold's cinema repeatedly registers. Tom is adopted by Jimmy—by his cash, his car, his clothes—and remade almost entirely through the latter's wealth, wealth that becomes a conduit to personality.

Although suspicious of Jimmy's motives in helping him, Tom adapts himself to Jimmy out of a lack of other plans or resources, material or emotional, with which he might resist (a vaguely homoerotic remaking of a man by another, wealthier man, as in other classic noirs as well, e.g., *Gilda*). To Al's treatment of Charlie in *Detour,* Petzold makes two telling revisions. First, viewers learn that Jimmy deliberately schemes to remake Tom and send him to a Belgian bank as a decoy for the thugs seeking Jimmy, so the wealthier individual initiates the troubled traffic in identity. Jimmy is planning to exploit Tom (probably fatally so) from the moment he sees him laid low at the train station. This recasts *Detour's* desperate, low-life solidarity with even more exploitation and paranoia.

Petzold also recasts his femme fatale, perhaps not least because Ann Savage's Vera, in one of film noir's most memorable performances, would be so hard to mimic. The gap between Savage's fiery, ferocious Vera and Fleming's cool, detached Tina underscores the kind of coldness I mentioned above and foreshadows the ghostliness that preoccupies him in his later films. Echoing *Pilots,* Petzold spends more screen time in *Cuba Libre* depicting the deliberate makeover of ghostly Tina than Ulmer does. Although Vera insists on being taken shopping by Al's new "found" wealth, Ulmer does not depict many details of this illicit consumerism. *Cuba Libre* has lengthy scenes of Tina and Tom in boutiques buying dresses, shoes, and then even visiting a plastic-surgery clinic, extending the theme of cosmetics and the intimate remaking of the individual.

Yet perhaps the greatest revision to *Detour* rests in the emphatic presence of a past injury to Tina—the debt Tom owes to her, both symbolic and (increasingly) monetary. *Detour's* Vera hints at vague economic struggles and then Charlie's sexual assault, but a much more precise, and revealing, past transgression plays a central role in *Cuba Libre*. Throughout the film, Tina is obsessed with Tom's earlier theft of her savings and abandonment of her to the street. That theft and its psychological persistence underscore the theme of material exploitation interwoven with love, an inextricability that renders her permanently and perpetually paranoid. This phenomenon—the presence of a past injury by loved ones and the paranoia bred of it—becomes another of Petzold's central themes, one that Richard Sennett, for example, locates at the core of "new capitalism" (Sennett 43; see also Bauman 3). A past trauma, usually at the crossroads of love and material need, repeatedly embeds itself in his characters, who subsequently comport themselves in paranoid, spectral detachment, even as they move forward.

The increasingly ghostly westward journey of women for economic opportunity is something that Petzold reads out of U.S. Westerns (and Hitchcock's *Psycho*) and that informs his own work, not least in *Yella, Dreileben,* and *Barbara*. This topography also further illuminates this film's title, *Cuba Libre*—a mythical and geographic and emotional designation. The film's unhappy end, in/outside the café (called Cuba Libre) where Tom finds Tina working, manifests this skepticism about geographical desire as well. Whereas *Pilots* ends with a dressed-down Karin at a riverside and then realizing her dream (albeit it somewhat ambiguously) in Paris, Tom is, in fact, robbed and killed by the criminals for whom he was to serve as Jimmy's decoy. Like *Pilots*, the film ends with a pieta-like composition, but this time it is the character to whom our perspective has mostly clung who is dead. The promise of a makeover by a stranger who lends a hand—with new clothes, new cars, a well-paying job—turns out to be a ruse of (further west) criminal exploitation.

The Sex Thief (Die Beischlafdiebin): Sisters in Criminality

Another of his television films to win an Adolf-Grimme prize, *The Sex Thief* (1998) opens in medias res and in flagrante delicto. Without preparatory courtship or even an establishing shot, the first image frames a tall, blonde woman, Petra, pulling close to a man in a well-palmed tropical garden. As they embrace, Petra encourages him to "take me in your arms, Germany is so far away." As she passes his hugging line of sight, however, she looks away, somewhat bored and even scheming.

The film only then draws back to establish the setting as the German tourist scene in Morocco, where Petra frequents hotel lobbies, lounges, and bars, claiming to be a lonely hotel manager for the well-heeled men she encounters there ("I am as lonely as a pensioner on Mallorca," she intones regularly). But when she gets back to these men's hotel rooms, and before they sleep together, she administers them knockout drops or shocks them with a stun gun, relieving them of cash, valuables, and presumably no little pride.

The opening twenty minutes of *The Sex Thief* return to the traveling milieu and transit spaces of both *Pilots* and *Cuba Libre*—more precisely, they revisit and radicalize those works' critique of a mental geography of desire and its yearning for (staged) authenticity (as Dean Maccannell has analyzed among tourists [91–107]). Petra's performance of the lonely hotel manager even emphasizes the artificiality of such travel fantasies. Petra, however, soon encounters a German policeman (played by Richy Müller, Tom from *Cuba Libre*), who has been dispatched abroad to apprehend thieves like her. Only apparently knocked unconscious by Petra's spiked champagne, he follows her back to her apartment and discovers her stash of money, jewelry, and passports. Petra flees, initially to a male thief, who suggests that they head off together to another tourist destination (he says in a breathy and almost mystical way, "Bora Bora"). But she says she feels old and tired and wants to go home to Germany, and, after a fast-paced airport chase scene in which the policeman narrowly misses her, viewers see her arriving on a train in noticeably gray and industrial Cologne, Germany.

These first twenty minutes of *The Sex Thief* are similarly, if a bit more exotically, set in the sorts of transit spaces that Petzold repeatedly features: hotels, vacation apartments, and airports, with the people populating them perpetually mobilized. For the rest of *The Sex Thief*, however, he explores something that he had not yet undertaken, namely, the fantasy of an actual, long-loved and long-term home. Although she has preyed on the travel and erotic imaginary of German tourists, Petra, like Karen and Tina, falls victim to her own spatial fantasies; but, for her, they are dreams of home. Neither *Pilots* nor *Cuba Libre* offers its main characters any kind of stable domestic space; they all live, as far as viewers know, on the road or in transient transit spaces associated with it. In fact, part of *The Sex Thief*'s innovation to Petzold's feature-length work seems to be that such spatial fantasies pertain to the impossibility of arriving at either foreign destinations or at home.

When Petra informs her male thieving counterpart that she wants to return home to Germany, he ominously declares that destination farther away than Bora Bora. His insight highlights the emotional valence of places over and above their physical geography, and he is more correct than he could have realized. After arriving home and initially soaking in the familiarity and comfort of her childhood home, she begins to sense that something is amiss with her sister, Franziska, who has been maintaining the house. Most of the proceeds from her robberies have gone to Franziska back in Germany, financing her studies, not least so she could maintain the childhood home. To explain the steady stream of money, Petra told Franziska the same story that she offered the men in Morocco: she is a successful hotel manager traversing the world. Franziska's gullibility underscores how Petra's lying lifestyle infects not only her romantic but also familial relationships. This arrangement also attains the vague shape of colonialism, with (clandestine) criminal activity in the exotic south supporting a beautiful house and bourgeois lifestyle back in the metropole.

It turns out, however, that Franziska has also been leading a double life of lies and misleading performances of her own. Petra has subsidized Franziska's Ph.D. and translation business ("The Translator"), but when she goes to visit her sister at work, Petra finds, in a very contemporary office building, the ruins of an abandoned office. The long shot of her in the abandoned office foregrounds the churn of capitalism, one of the recurring themes of Petzold's cinema from its beginnings. The hypermodern office building offers a typical service-sector means of production (desk, fax machines, certificates on the wall)—part of the wider dematerialization of labor (Peck and Tickell 393)—to which the assiduous cycles of late capitalism have laid complete waste (figure 4).

This memorable image of a small, flexible company exploiting global flows in goods and services, named in English and now completely defunct, is one that recurs almost ten years later in *Yella*. When Petra confronts Franziska about the abandoned company, Franziska lies again, saying that she has become an interpreter instead. Suspicious of her own sister—professional paranoia has settled into the family, as it does elsewhere in Petzold's work—Petra follows Franziska to work, and she

Figure 4. Petra (Constanze Engelbrecht)
in ruins: creative destruction of the workplace
in *The Sex Thief* (1998).

discovers that her younger sister is, in fact, working in retail at a glass-walled department store. Petra quickly suspects that this job cannot be successfully supporting their sprawling childhood home, and it turns out that Franziska has remortgaged to the point of foreclosure. Debt, particularly in the financialization of intimate space, once again overshadows and overdetermines the characters and their lives.

Hewing close to the genre tendencies of his first two films, Petzold begins *The Sex Thief* by invoking a well-worn setup: an exotic travel milieu, a beautiful thief, and her thrilling escape from a police posse. But then he steers the film, as viewers see in the reciprocal lying of the two sisters, to a different set of themes and styles typical of an art-house film. Building on what he began with *Pilots*, he develops more precisely the ubiquitous processes of disciplining and the control function of contemporary labor. *The Sex Thief* goes considerably further than *Pilots* or *Cuba Libre* in illuminating the subtler control aspects of contemporary society by integrating, for almost ten minutes of the eighty-five-minute plot, a nonfiction film by Harun Farocki, Petzold's erstwhile instructor at the DFFB, filmmaking mentor, and, on all his feature-length works, script collaborator or cowriter. In *The Sex Thief*, after its generically provocative title and Petra's Moroccan escapades, Petzold stages scenarios derived from Farocki's *The Interview* (*Die Bewerbung*; 1997), subjecting his fictional character Franziska to the nonfiction economic processes Farocki traces therein (see Fisher, "Times of Transition"). It is a technique of subtly mixing genre and nonfiction, rendering them mutually illuminating, that recurs in more developed form nine years later in *Yella*.

At almost exactly halfway through *The Sex Thief* and for ten minutes, Petzold offers a series of three interviews that borrow explicitly from Farocki's *The Interview*. Franziska's first interview begins where Farocki's film concludes: with a fateful question on her salary requirements. When asked to self-commodify in this way, Franziska misunderstands the rules of this economic game, much as she had with the rapidly shifting economic conditions around her translation company. Seeking some security, she answers with a guaranteed (rather than commission-based) salary so high that it immediately disqualifies her from the position. Franziska's second interview subjects her to a camera recording the entire interview (figure 5). In Petzold's later, better-known films, surveillance-camera footage comes to play an important role (as I shall discuss in *The State I Am In, Wolfsburg,* and *Dreileben: Beats Being Dead*), but it is noteworthy that his first usage of it here, in *The Sex*

Figure 5. The job interview as surveillance
in *The Sex Thief* (1998).

Thief, relates directly to an overtly economic context. As Jamie Peck and Adam Tickell note, as work has changed in neoliberalism, surveillance has become more and more widespread (Peck and Tickell 393).

By the increasingly futile third interview, Petra remakes Franziska by dressing her in a fashionably cut black dress and counseling her in front of a mirror that she should change her hair and wear, "in any case, more makeup"—revisiting Petzold's recurring (economic) makeup and makeover themes in *Pilots, Cuba Libre,* and even *Barbara.* After Franziska sleeps with this third interviewer but does not get the job, Petra seeks revenge on him with her own particular expertise. She picks him up at a restaurant and manages to have herself invited back after hours to his office, where he proudly plays Petra a tape of the interview (unbeknownst to him) of her own sister. At his boorish comments about her sister's being "something for after meetings," Petra shocks him with her stun gun and steals the tape as well as his wallet, a modicum of revenge against the misogyny of the system. When, the next morning, Franziska declares that she is giving up on interviewing, Petra hands her the wallet and finally reveals that she was never actually a hotel manager.

Even as they come to recognize the deceptions underpinning their relationship, the sisters realize that they still need money to save their childhood home. So, the refunctioning of Franziska that Petra had initiated for interviewing continues apace: Franziska accedes to being trained by Petra on how to rob men. Although studying at the knee of her expertly seductive sister, Franziska is never able to control her performances as well as Petra. First, after pedantically correcting his pronunciation of Dom Perignon, Franziska sleeps with a mark who offers her very little professionally in return. Second, and more fatefully, she falls into a trap with the same policeman from Morocco—when Petra gets a call from Franziska as the latter homes in on him, it is immediately apparent to Petra that it is a trap, and she rushes to save Franziska but is too late. The policeman has already removed the batteries from Franziska's stun gun, so she flees after her failed attack. He chases her through a parking garage—another transit space in these early works—and she is hit by an oncoming car. She does manage to stumble home to Petra, but there Franziska dies as the film closes, in the arms of her sister on the stairs of the childhood home for which she refunctioned herself twice, first to interview with wealthy men and second to rob them. The narrative impact of her remaking herself first for employers and second for criminal prey emphasizes the thin line between economically minded productivity and "abnormal" criminality that Petzold explores in *Pilots* and *Cuba Libre*. In all cases, criminality courses through the veins of everyday life and interactions, a great Hitchcock theme, but throughout these early works of Petzold's, his characters are remade more explicitly for the purposes of money and especially career.

The State I Am In (*Die innere Sicherheit*): Terrorists Return as the Undead

The State I Am In (2000) won, among many others awards and accolades, the 2001 German Federal Film Prize in Gold, Germany's equivalent (at the time) of a best-film prize. The awarding of the Federal Film Prize to Petzold's first theatrical release was surprising, and momentous, on a number of accounts. For Petzold, who had directed only three feature-length works before that point, and all for television, it represented a significant breakthrough that has helped make him the most critically celebrated filmmaker in Germany (*Hollywood Reporter,* for instance, declared him "arguably the most influential of post-Reunification German filmmakers" [Young]). The award was also surprising because artistically minded films rarely receive this kind of prize. Winning the prize in 2000 was particularly unusual since, in the years preceding, the German cinematic landscape was dominated by comedies and other commercially oriented films that were part of the 1990s "cinema of consensus" (Rentschler). *The State I Am In* became, in fact, a cornerstone of the so-called Berlin School, whose abreaction to the cinema of consensus I discuss in the introduction.[9] The film and its surprise success also helped usher in a remarkable wave of German films about domestic terrorism and radical politics, including, among others, *Baader* (2002), *The Edukators* (*Die fetten Jahre sind vorbei*; 2004), *Sleeper* (*Schläfer*; 2005), *The Edge of Heaven* (*Auf der anderen Seite*; 2007), and, most spectacularly, *The Baader Meinhof Komplex* (2008).

Unlike most of these films, however, *The State I Am In* provides a provocative rumination on the inability of terrorists' political ideals to abide over time and through history. The film contemplates the historical and mnemonic dimensions to terrorism's often spectacular politics—a contemplation realized through its balance of the national particularity of German terrorism with the refunctioning of a self-conscious genre film, Kathryn Bigelow's *Near Dark*. At the level of the plot, the film traces the struggles of two parents, Hans and Clara, and their teenaged daughter Jeanne, who have been living underground after earlier, unspecified terrorist activities. Living comfortably at the beginning of the film in a vacation apartment on the Portuguese coast, the family is forced, by a robbery of their apartment, to return to Germany in order to resume contact with old comrades and to seek financial support, all while Hans and Clara cope with the challenges of an adolescent daughter. Without an obvious place to stay in Germany, Jeanne leads her parents to an abandoned villa about which she learned from Heinrich, a fellow teenaged German tourist she met in Portugal. As Jeanne has more and more doubts about living underground and about the family's planned flight to Brazil, her parents grow increasingly desperate and eventually rob a bank. Hans is wounded, and they are caught shortly afterward, perhaps due to an inadvertent betrayal by their daughter. This account of the narrative does not convey the film's stark and provocative stylistic choices, including an overarching aesthetic of silence and reduction shared with many other films of the Berlin School—an aesthetic that Petzold unusually, even uniquely, combines with selective aspects of genre films.

The popular and critical success of *The State I Am In* was interwoven with the late-1990s revival of interest in German domestic terrorism, especially in the Red Army Faction (Rote Armee Fraktion, or RAF). The German title, in fact, evokes the theme of domestic or "homeland" security: "Innere Sicherheit" refers to a country's domestic security as well as an individual's feeling of personal security or confidence. The RAF was commonly referred to (by the media and government) as the Baader-Meinhof group or gang, named so for two of its central figures, Andreas Baader and Ulrike Meinhof. The twentieth anniversary in 1997 of the infamous 1977 "German Autumn" coincided with Petzold's writing of the screenplay for *The State I Am In,* an anniversary accompanied by numerous TV documentaries and magazine features (Homewood).

The confluence of events in autumn 1977 was a culmination of several years of such political actions, largely inspired by the student generation's suspicions of the older, wartime and Holocaust generation as well as by West Germany's political proximity to the United States during the Vietnam War. The German Autumn subsequently included a series of RAF-related events that, some have argued, traumatized the whole nation (Elsaesser, *Terror und Trauma*). At that time, Baader and Gudrun Ensslin, among others of the RAF's "first generation," were being held in the Stammheim prison; the RAF kidnapped the former SS officer, industrialist, and then president of the Employers' Association, Hanns-Martin Schleyer; and an allied group, the People's Front for the Liberation of Palestine, hijacked a Lufthansa jet that landed in Mogadishu, demanding the release of the Stammheim inmates. When the negotiations failed and the jet was stormed, the kidnappers killed Schleyer, while Baader and Ensslin were found dead in their prison cells, presumably suicides, although doubts have lingered. In this tense period, when a fairly small number of radicalized individuals dominated the national news and mood, the government took swift action: the police seemed to be everywhere, civil liberties were curtailed, and paranoia prevailed on all sides. With the end of the Vietnam War and the death of some of its leading figures, RAF actions became rarer after 1977, although some of its members continued to make news into the early 1990s (Trnka). In 1998, some RAF members let it be known that they were officially disbanding.

The late 1990s reexamination of 1977, an important context for *The State I Am In*, also intersected political developments at the time. In 1998 the Social Democrats returned to power in Germany after sixteen years of conservative chancellor Helmut Kohl (CDU), bringing with them some politicians, particularly Joschka Fischer and Jürgen Trittin, who had known some of the terrorists in the 1970s. Although there was no evidence of their having been members of the RAF, their presence in the government led to much discussion of that legacy and its role in (legal) politics.[10] Assorted articles on *The State I Am In* have connected the film explicitly to this debate (Worthmann), including to the high-profile effort by Meinhof's daughter, Bettina Röhl, to draw attention to Fischer's proximity to the terrorist scene in the 1970s (Rodek, "Wer zu Lange"; Peitz and Petzold, "Nach dem Schiffbruch"; Martens). As head of the Green party and Germany's foreign minister, Fischer certainly attracted the most attention. Right around the time *The State I Am In* was released in early 2001, Fischer testified at the trial of an accused terrorist he knew earlier, Hans-Joachim Klein (Cohen). To increase the controversy and debate at this point, the media sensationalized (previously public) footage of Fischer's beating a policeman in the 1970s, not the typical résumé item for a top government minister. But he was emphatic that he had not followed some of his colleagues down the path to more radical violence, and the controversy subsided, especially after September 11 and concerns about terrorism recalibrated away from leftist, antistate extremism.

The anniversary of the German Autumn, the SPD-Green government, and the controversy about Fischer created a level of discussion in the public sphere that helped, and was helped by, Petzold's film. Although the original release was so small that only twenty-eight prints were made for its national opening, well over one hundred thousand viewers saw it domestically, which, like its best-film award, constitutes a rare feat for a German art-house film (Rodek, "Wer zu Lange"). Although, as many have noted, the RAF is never mentioned in *The State I Am In*, Petzold has explained that he had the terrorist group in mind when writing the script and directing the film. There are specific indications of this. Beyond references to the "underground" and the "family cell"—vocabulary that Petzold drew from the terrorist discussion in the 1970s—Jeanne conspicuously uses Herman Melville's *Moby Dick* to signal Klaus, a former colleague of her parents. Petzold chose *Moby Dick* because it was frequently referenced by members of the RAF, ostensibly with the state as the great white whale and the obsessively destructive Baader as Ahab (Petzold, *The State I Am In* DVD commentary; Aust 193–95). At one point, another former colleague, Achim, sarcastically refers to Hans and Clara's fleeing to Yemen, an apparent reference to the fact that some members of the RAF's second generation went underground in South Yemen after the events of the German Autumn (Scheufler 106; Aust 10).[11] Petzold has repeatedly mentioned in interviews how he was inspired in part by reading about Wolfgang Grams, an RAF member of the "third generation" who died in 1993 (under somewhat murky circumstances) during an arrest by state authorities. Petzold said that until that time, he had always imagined the RAF members like their wanted posters, in grainy black-and-white, the men menacingly unshaven, but he read that Grams, in his time in the underground, liked to write blues songs and even make jam, and so for the first time he seemed like a fuller person (Peitz and Petzold, "Nach dem Schiffbruch"; Worthmann). In terms of the film's images, Petzold also admits to studying the famous photographs of the Stammheim prison when deciding how to shoot Hans and Clara's belongings on the floor of their vacation apartment after the break-in. Petzold thought carefully about how to shoot the handgun that Hans and Clara have in their possession and recounts that the Stammheim photos gave him a model for how the former terrorists would hide their weapons (Peitz and Petzold, "Nach dem Schiffbruch").

Memory Matters Although the film's engagement with the RAF milieu cannot be seriously disputed, it is remarkable and revealing that it avoids any mention of the group. This lack is a peculiarity, I think, to be explored rather than excused. Petzold has recounted that he did not believe that a family that had been living underground for years would continue to discuss its former activities or current non-grata status (Mustroph), perhaps a veiled reference to Sidney Lumet's *Running on Empty* (1988), which does offer somewhat clunky exposition at many turns. But Petzold's deliberate lack of specific reference also underscores how he approaches the past: he has stated, and staked, his foremost interest in the present, such that *The State I Am In* addresses the past through memory, particularly the operations of memory in the present in a mode reminiscent of Walter Benjamin, one of Petzold's stated influences. Much as Petzold regularly affirms his interest in the aftershocks (*Nachbeben*) of history, the film engages with the actualization of the past in the present, a recurring theme in all three of the Ghost trilogy films (Gansera and Petzold, "Toter Mann, was nun?"). As in the later films, his primary interest is in what condition the abiding remnants of the past have left people to deal with a rapidly changing present, a present of neoliberal practices and beliefs, for which they are, as Petzold underscores, ill prepared (Abel and Petzold).

In this past-present mode, rather than retrospectively tracing the terrorists' rebellious radicalization that culminates in thrilling spasms of violence (as, for example, the 2008 *Baader Meinhof Komplex* does), *The State I Am In* engages in questions of memory, the aftershocks of political commitment, and the impact of time on (leftist) politics. The opening sequence establishes the film's recurring contrast between political memory and fantasies over time (and among the generations) that have to sustain commitment to such politics. This turn to fantasy in the opening, when read against the film's lack of political memory in the younger generation, underscores what lends the film its considerable power: how a political project has to function not only in the public sphere but also in people's memories, hopes, and fantasies, and how, subsequently, such a project can (or cannot) abide over time. This, notably, remains one of Petzold's core concerns right through the 2012 *Barbara,* his recurring interest in people's desires and fantasies in their politics. Such a constellation of themes elucidates how *The State I Am In* and *Barbara* are adamantly political even without much political exposition: through its very silence, for instance, *The State I Am In* contemplates the impact of time, history, and fantasy on politics. The film opens with Jeanne, the mid-teen daughter of Hans and Clara, on (as viewers learn later) the scenic Portuguese coast. Petzold initially shot a different beginning, with Jeanne reciting a poem of Heinrich Heine to Clara on the beach, but opted, as he often does, for the softer and quieter touch of Jeanne sitting alone and silent in a beach café. She puts a song on the café's jukebox, Tim Hardin's melancholic, and here fitting, "How Can We Hang on to a Dream?" The song's other lyrics ("She's walking away") foreshadow Jeanne's elusiveness for other characters and for viewers throughout the film (an important performative aspect of Petzold's style; see the section on *Something to Remind Me*).

Sipping on cola, Jeanne catches the eye of a young surfer, Heinrich from near Hamburg, with whom she soon makes plans to meet at night. By the nighttime seaside, Jeanne asks Heinrich to tell her about himself, and he narrates a story whose scenario then takes over the visual track of the film as his narration continues in voiceover. He tells her to close her eyes and imagine a mansion that his father would pass as a child and then bought after becoming rich, a sprawling villa with floor heating in every room (to which the image track shows Jeanne touching the floor, underscoring how her sense of touch, especially of objects of her fantasy, will be important later in the film). When Heinrich and Jeanne, in this fantasy tour of the house, reach his room, however, he divulges that they have since abandoned this villa because his mother committed suicide, her body found in the swimming pool (see Fisher and Alter). The swimming pool is visible from his window, and, as Jeanne approaches Heinrich on the window sill, they kiss for the first time. But then they come out of this shared fantasy, with a reverse angle of that kiss, rather like waking from a dream at a dramatic moment. Jeanne is jerked out of this fantasy by her parents, who, in the morning gray of the Portuguese town, are desperately seeking their missing daughter.

The diegetic status of this extended fantasy is unusually opaque, since, although the fantasy seems to unfold from Jeanne's subjective (internal diegetic) point of view, she will find precisely this house in precisely this configuration when her family reaches Hamburg. The ambiguous status of this fantasy-cum-reality confirms Petzold's abiding interest in dreams and fantasy. *The State I Am In* develops the kind of complex desire and fantasy Petzold analyzed in *Pilots, Cuba Libre,* and *The Sex Thief* and foreshadows that in *Yella* and *Ghosts*: fantasy is an even more complicated phenomenon than simple desire and/or wish-fulfillment. It represents a more extended and complex interplay of desire with lack and with defensive processes like repression and censorship, both psychological and social (Donald 138). For Petzold, very often, the confines of fantasies and its distortions of desire are defined by the economic world. Although every fantasy's impulse may be, at least in part, utopian—a yearning (pace Fredric Jameson) for a different social order that could be—such fantasies are still fundamentally confined and limited in Petzold's cinema, censored by the prevailing and penetrating economic conditions (see Prager). This sequence early in Petzold's film demonstrates the socioeconomic mechanisms of even the most intimate fantasy, with such fantasy contradictorily manifesting every individual's utopian hopes and their simultaneous, severe curtailment. Heinrich and Jeanne's fantasy of luxury domesticity contrasts to the parents' discussion, shortly before, of the family's next abode, another transient vacation spot for which they will abandon this town. Their discussion of the family's future home is a matter-of-fact accounting of variables relating to their hiding, with a photo, a map, and a quick nod—utterly lacking in any attraction for Jeanne's imagination.

Jeanne's fantasies throughout contrast to the largely lacking memory of the events that keeps the family on the road. Such an intergenerational contrast between her parents' memories and her own resonates with a distinction Avishai Margalit draws about forms of collective memory. Margalit differentiates between the "common memory" of an event as it is experienced by those present and the "shared memory," which relies on people communicating their memories to others—especially in an earlier generation's relating it to a later one (Margalit 51–52). The second, shared memory intersects Marianne Hirsch's notion of postmemory (Hirsch 106), but Margalit's notion of common memory introduces another mnemonic dimension beyond Hirsch's that features prominently in *State I Am In*. It is this underlying contrast and abiding tension between two forms of collective memory that drives much of the dramatic tension of *The State I Am In*. On the one side, there are Hans and Clara (and their once and perhaps future comrades Achim and Klaus), who represent an aging a community of memory—it is they who experienced the (terrorist) events of the past and who might, or might not, transmit them on. On the other side, with Heinrich and especially Jeanne, the film simultaneously tracks the next generation with whom the events would typically be shared.

In terms of the former, common memory, a large part of the efficacy and power of *The State I Am In* is its ability to conjure the pervasive fear and paranoia that marked the 1970s terrorist era without much explicit exposition (Petzold generally omits expository dialogue). Not only Hans and Clara but also Achim and Klaus manifest something shared in the past, an aftershock (as Petzold puts it repeatedly) that does not have to be discussed but nevertheless creates an overarching structure of remnant paranoia. Without having to flashback to the details of the events, the film revisits and reveals the remnants, aftershocks, or remains of past experiences that consistently haunt the ghostly archeology of Petzold's films.

For the younger generation and the contrasting notion of shared memory, Margalit highlights the importance of communication, which intersects one of the film's most conspicuous stylistic choices I highlighted above: the lack of discussion of the past and the remarkable silence about it that prevails between Jeanne and her parents. The perspective of the film almost always remains close to Jeanne's point of view, a point of view limited by her (generational) position in the family. For example, while viewers often see Hans and Clara discussing some issue at hand, it is frequently out of earshot, so that viewer knowledge (so central to the thrillers as well as horror films that interest Petzold) is limited to what has been communicated directly to Jeanne.[12] It is not so much that her parents do not talk with her, but that they talk to her about quotidian, most often financial, issues facing them. Typically in Petzold's cinema, in lieu of meaningful discussion (the very fabric of shared memories), silence and an expressive body convey the aftershocks and remnants of memory. As in many of his works, decisions that determine one's life are taken far away, at a definitive distance from the protagonists whose lives are in the balance. This tends to leave the words that ought to most matter unsaid or unheard, with this distance and silence registered as remnant gesture of and on the body.

This historical divergence between common and shared memory resonates with something that Petzold has discussed in his interviews and commentary, but that has gone largely unmentioned in the literature on *The State I Am In*—the fact that he was intrigued not so much what exactly happened to the RAF but rather what happens to leftist politics in the course of time (Hauser and Schroth). Farocki proves here, too, a formative influence, especially in his work on Georg Glaser, a leftist German exile who (rather like Heine) fled Germany for France in 1935 and ended up working there as a metal smith, continuing to think and write far away from his political home. In discussing the film, Petzold has cited Farocki's work on Glaser, as well as the philosopher Hans Blumenberg, who, Petzold mentions, wrote a book about shipwrecks in which he said the leftist "68ers" were like survivors of a shipwreck floating on planks (Nicodemus; Peitz and Petzold, "Nach dem Schiffbruch"). Discussing Glaser, Petzold recounted how he has the sense that while right-wing political figures retreat to a cave and await their reawakening (a reference to Barbarossa, the Holy Roman Emperor who is rumored to slumber until he awakens to reestablish the empire), leftists wander like ghosts through the landscape, present but invisible (Petzold, *The State I Am In* DVD commentary).

A little closer to home, Petzold has also often had the sense (not least in Berlin's leftist neighborhoods where he lives and works) that leftists sometimes lack a substantive connection to the world, something he repeats in the interview in this book, which suggests that the terrorist couple have a child in part to reestablish such a connection (Nicodemus). But this connection remains highly attenuated, as Hans and Clara's common memories diverge from what they can share with the next generation, particularly as that next generation fantasizes about and moves toward something else altogether. Given this lack of communication about memories of a past that haunts them, Jeanne never has a meaningful framework for her own experiences, memories, or fantasies, something Maurice Halbwachs emphasizes in his original concept of collective memory. Intergenerational communication and connection and therefore memory have broken down, leaving all three characters increasingly isolated, lonely, and ghostlike, a tendency Petzold depicts almost as soon as Hans and Clara return to Germany.

Border Crossings and the Dedramatizing of Suspense A watershed event confirms the divergence between common and shared memory—a border crossing between France and Germany, underscoring the growing obsolescence of the terrorist parents' worldview. One would expect the family's return to their homeland, after what seems an extended exile, to be a moment of existential searching or at least the subject of some conversation. Such reflection would be especially appropriate for West German terrorists because, as one critic noted, reunified Germany has never really considered, like some other European countries, an amnesty for former terrorists, dooming them in effect to their ghostly outsider and/or illegal status (Peitz and Petzold, "Nach dem Schiffbruch"). Examples of this kind of momentous border crossing and these ontological tensions abound in films, German and otherwise, about terrorism. These scenes recur so often because border sequences depict moments in which the terrorists, as non- or at least antistate actors, have direct contact with the material practices of the state terrorists (see Fisher, "Syntax of Terrorism?").

The originality of Petzold's approach to terrorism is confirmed in his variation on this recurring border scenario. After what viewers presume have been many years away, Hans and Clara, with Jeanne in tow, are crossing the border back into Germany to resume contact with old comrades from the terrorist scene. The border-crossing sequence signals the key development in the film's plot, an unwanted and presumably perilous return to Germany from life on the run abroad. Viewers are further cued to expect some tense confrontation with police at the border when Clara first informs Jeanne, "We are going to Germany. . . . We have to be careful." At the border, however, Petzold dismantles these expectations by entirely dedramatizing the setup and scenario. He cuts from a point-of-view shot from the car as it enters a tomblike tunnel in southern

Europe to a shot of the white Volvo on a river bank, with three flags—the flags of France, the European Union, and Germany—matter-of-factly signifying its northern European territorial negotiation (figure 6). The river as a transitional space is a recurring theme in Petzold's films, one that revisits its mythic importance, Petzold observes, as in the River Styx, thus invoking the capacity, even necessity, to forget to move forward (as in *Dreileben*).

In Petzold's staging of the expected showdown at the border, he contrasts the memory of the terrorists to the contemporary reality (or perhaps irreality) of European borders. The border space that formerly created delineated territory (and suspense for terrorists) has become, historically and especially in Petzold's hands, completely uprooted in an era replete with socioeconomic and now clearly political deterritorializations. Petzold dedramatizes the border crossing to emphasize the changes in the border due to the Schengen process, one presumably introduced in Europe since the family left (given the film's deliberate lack of exposition, viewers never know for certain when they left). The Schengen Agreement, which went into effect in 1995, is part of those tectonic historical events I underscored in the introduction. Schengen

Figure 6. Europe's increasingly open borders traversed by terrorists in *The State I Am In* (2000).

sought to reverse centuries of nationalistic tension, strife, and war over borders inside and outside of Europe, a reversal that contemporary anti-immigration politics bespeak and Petzold's film renegotiates. The border scene in *The State I Am In* registers the radical disjuncture between the common memory of Hans and Clara and the historic transformation of borders and politics since then—it introduces a historical dimension too often lacking in films about terrorists.

The changing character of the border as a space not of demarcation but of open traffic and continuous flows grows clearer in a seemingly tangential continuation of this understated border sequence. After arriving in Germany, the family has the standard conversation about whether they have local currency ("a little" is the answer); as noted above, their momentous return to Germany entails no discussion of what it means to be there, to have any shared memory of this national space at the border. Viewers are left unaware of whether Jeanne has ever been to Germany before. A few seconds later, at a highway rest area apparently waiting for Achim—in another watershed transit space for Petzold's cinema—Jeanne goes to the bathroom to smoke. Upon leaving the stall, she finds herself amidst a throng of immigrant women, apparently from Eastern Europe (Petzold refers to them as Albanians, although they remain unsubtitled and unidentified in the film). As Jeanne leaves the bathroom, the camera gives viewers what seems to be a point-of-view long shot of her parents and the Volvo. A police van and then police car suddenly screech to a halt, effectively boxing the Volvo in (figure 7). Viewers would assume, given the worry articulated by Clara about returning to Germany, that the police have come to apprehend the former terrorists. But the police jump out of their cars and head off in the other direction, sprinting after the fleeing immigrants. An elliptical cut then has the policemen kindly waving the family of terrorists back onto the autobahn as viewers see the immigrants arrested.

Despite the terrorists' and viewers' expectations for a confrontation with the police at the border, such state agents are more focused on contemporary issues like immigration than obsolete political dissent of these former terrorists. This historical disjuncture, between expectations and reality, is also confirmed in one of the film's most cited sequences, in another one of Petzold's recurring movement spaces (Körte; Rodek, "Wer zu Lange"; Worthmann). Soon thereafter, the family stops at an

Figure 7. Terrorists boxed in but overlooked
by the police in *The State I Am In* (2000).

empty four-way intersection, when black vehicles suddenly pull up to
the intersection from the other three directions (figure 8). The family
assumes it is the police, and Hans climbs out, hands up, while Clara and
Jeanne duck defensively. But once again, their and our expectations of
the statecraft of the police misses the historical mark—the cars all leave
without bothering them. Much as when they cross into Germany and
expect a tense confrontation, they and viewers realize they have a common memory of a West Germany now vanished. History has moved on,
even as their paranoia bred of their unarticulated and unshared common
memory has not.[13]

The border and intersection sequences demonstrate how this paranoia about the police has been internalized in the family, an aftershock
remnant of the past that the ghostly parents cannot escape. Per Fou-
cault and Deleuze, the family has internalized paranoid, disciplined
behaviors even without the direct intervention of the police. Although
the police are hardly after them, Hans and Clara nonetheless introduce
police techniques into their private lives in interrogations of their own
daughter, scenes singled out as among the film's "most brilliant" (Körte).
"Can I have a glass of water?" Jeanne asks them hoarsely at one point,
confirming that the family dinner table has replaced the police interro-

Figure 8. Paranoia at an(other) intersection
in *The State I Am In* (2000).

gation room. Jeanne in turn applies these techniques to Heinrich—this paranoia and its consequences have been passed on intergenerationally from her parents more than any shared memories or politics, the unconscious behavior of the family registering the aftershocks of years on the run.

The return to Germany, along with the apathy of the German police, foregrounds how the family, like Farocki's Georg Glaser, has fallen out of history, and the rest of the film is filled with scenes of confusion created by contemporary Germany. Petzold declared *The State I Am In* to be the first of his Ghost trilogy, and he cites all three works as films in which the protagonists are like the undead, having all fallen out of history in one way or another (Althen; Peitz and Petzold, "Nach dem Schiffbruch"). Petzold's remaking of the border scenario at a key narrative point in the film is the first indication of such an exit from history. Another example of this historical disjuncture and obsolescence is the scene in which Hans digs up hidden, but no longer valid, money, a "history lesson" (as he puts it to Jeanne) cited by many reviews at the time and analyzed in intriguing detail by Marco Abel (Abel, *Counter-Cinema*). Generally and tellingly, the police take little interest in the former terrorists until near the end, when they rob a bank. The "state" the characters are in is a radically changed state, one in which the police are more focused on immigrants than the avowed but increasingly ghostlike enemies of the state.

Ghosts, Vampires, and Bigelow's* Near Dark: *Generically Transformed Bodies Such scenes—the border and intersection sequences, the obsolete money scene, and another in which Hans digs in a graveyard, presumably also after money—serve as episodic, isolated moments that underscore how the terrorist couple functions, like Farocki's Glaser, as ghosts, remnants from an earlier historical moment. As discussed in the introduction, part of these fragmentary remnants scattered throughout the film are the bits of genre that are "there for the taking" (Abel and Petzold)—in fact, Petzold discusses in the interview herein, genre can seismically register historical change and transformation. For *The State I Am In*, Petzold has mentioned two films in particular: Lumet's *Running on Empty* and Bigelow's *Near Dark*, the latter of which features a different, more literal undead—vampires. Although Christopher Homewood has explored the metaphor of the vampire in terrorist films generally, no one has analyzed Petzold's reference to *Near Dark* in detail, a citation that the archeological approach I proposed in the introduction elucidates. As is frequently the case in his cinema, Petzold excavates and refunctions aspects of a genre film to illuminate his own context as well as the generic model. He lets moments of generic transformation—always a historical phenomenon for him—elucidate historical transformation in contemporary Germany. Such an approach, one review noted, helps keep *The State I Am In* from backsliding to merely "conceptual art," a tendency that marks Petzold's cinema generally ("Stille vor dem Schuß").

As Leo Braudy has recounted in an "appreciation" of *Near Dark* twenty years after its release—he regards it as a "genre landmark" (30)—Bigelow's film "meditates" on its genre elements to create a film that is at once elegiac and resurrecting. Arriving late in both vampire and Western cycles, the film acknowledges and tracks the fading of those two genres. Such belated fragments of *Near Dark* reappear in *State I Am In* as what Rick Altman has called its generic syntax (89): The boy (Caleb) meets girl (Mae) in a rather stereotypical opening, but almost immediately she has to hide from him a familial secret. In *Near Dark*, her secret and elusiveness turn out to be something monstrous;

in *The State I Am In*'s refashioning of this genre grammar, it is something monstrously political. In *Near Dark,* the nonconventional family within which the protagonist becomes cocooned keeps its distance from society, slinking around at night to avoid the daylight that might expose and ruin them. Their evasive maneuvers end up subverting the promise of a normal relationship and a normal family for the late-adolescent girl who finds herself increasingly fantasizing about them. The generic model thus affords scenarios for both social outsiders and the eventual resentment of their children—a basic genre trajectory invoked by *State*'s motto, "When ghosts want to be become human, then they are always protagonists of a tragedy" (Feldvoss)—a concise summary of *Near Dark* as well. Moreover, in elaborating these outsiders' distance from society, Petzold gets great mileage out of *Near Dark*'s deliberately vehicular variation on the mobility of the outsider as drifter. Whereas Stoker's and Murnau's vampires preferred ferrying by sea, the *Near Dark* vampires tend to go from motel to motel in remarkably colorful cars. It is a basic iconography—the movement image of the automobile and the transit space of the hotel—that Petzold has made a staple of his oeuvre and that he emphasizes as a link between *Near Dark* and his film in the interview herein.

If, according to Petzold, apparently hackneyed forms can register moments of social crisis and transformation, then *Near Dark*'s self-conscious deployment of genre registers precisely such moments of transition and transformation. The film opens with boredom in the western town, with cowboy Caleb harboring increasingly antiquated fantasies of glory that no longer exists. In the interview herein, Petzold also discusses his admiration for Bogdanovich's *The Last Picture Show,* a film that similarly delivers a powerful elegy for a fading western lifestyle. But just as he appreciates how *Picture Show* registers the passing of time and the loss of entire lifeworlds, Petzold, somewhat contrarily, regards such films as non-nostalgic. His reading of these late or post-Westerns aligns with his interest not in looking backward to the (western) world lost but rather in focusing on the transition from one world to the next, from the crisis to its aftermath. For Petzold, the late Western was a form that articulated a specifically political type of crisis and transition—there is a sense of afterness but not of looking back ("Stille vor dem Schuß"). It is here that one finds the surprising intersection with Farocki's Glaser that Petzold foregrounds for *The State I Am In.* In his film on Glaser, Farocki is fascinated not only by the manual labor of the book-writing metalsmith but also by the fading of his dual mode of production, both his quixotic commitment to lonely, exiled political writing as well as to an independent smithy and shop in an age of large-scale manufacturing and retail. *Near Dark, The Last Picture Show,* and Farocki's biographical homage all register the inexorability of time, the interruption of intergenerational memories, and the historical obsolescence of political fantasy, Petzold's central topics in *The State I Am In.*

Near Dark foregrounds the relationship of fantasy to the social transition it traces. In both *Near Dark* and *State I Am In,* crisis comes with the fading of older fantasies and the threatening emergence of new ones. Bigelow introduces the twilight of the conventional Western and the temptations of an alternative lifestyle not via sympathetic Native Americans, as in other revisionist Westerns like *Little Big Man* (1970), but rather in the unexpected intrusion of gothic fantasy into the small-town milieu of the Western. In the film's opening, at a late-night moment of small-town boredom, Caleb suddenly encounters Mae, his vampiric seductress, who is coded repeatedly as the product of Caleb's dreams and/or fantasies. The standard course of the Western is thereby effectively rerouted through gothic horror's supernatural and fantastical. Interrupting the genre with a sudden, even contrary fantasy offers an important and revealing point of contact with the cinema of Petzold generally.

Petzold has emphasized that one of his interests in the horror genre is the way that horror films like *Halloween* tend to blur the lines between the real and the fantastical, between the objective and subjective, and, as with *Near Dark,* his films (like *Ghosts* and *Yella*) consistently limn this thin line. It is also, he noted admiringly, a trademark of Weimar cinema, where Thomas Elsaesser has argued that individual fantasy explodes at the moment of social struggle and blockage (Abel and Petzold; Elsaesser, "Social Mobility"). In *The State I Am In,* Petzold deliberately interrupts where viewers might assume the film is headed generically with the opening explosion of fantasy—fantasy that is ultimately revealing of the film's politics.

These themes—the failed sharing of collective memories, the encroaching seduction of emergent fantasies, as well as the transformation of the body at moments of historical transition—run through the rest of

The State I Am In. After the border sequence, in which viewers recognize the family's obsolete obsessions, the film stages Jeanne's growing fantasies of conventional domesticity and contemporary corporeality. After crossing the border, the family visits Achim, an attorney and former comrade now living in a large and well-appointed house of the sort that Petzold's films often depict, but never for his protagonists (see *Yella* and *Jerichow*). Hans and Clara first ask for, then demand help from the clearly rattled Achim. When Achim declares, "I have nothing to do with this ridiculousness [*Scheiße*] anymore," Clara coolly asks, "What kind of ridiculousness?" As Petzold notes in his commentary, particularly effective here is how the three revisit their terrorist past in just a few words, a revisitation possible with such terseness because of the depth of their common (if not commonly understood) memory.

At precisely that moment, however, Jeanne is sent out by her parents, and the intergenerational sharing of memory is again short-circuited. She ascends a staircase to the room of Paulina, Achim's likewise midteen daughter. Paulina's room conjures a parallel, isolated space within the house to contrast with the downstairs confrontation of the former terrorists—the out-of-focus point-of-view introduction (in a mirror) of Paulina, set to contemporary electronic beats, creates a kind of bubble space: throughout Petzold's cinema, especially in his many cars, he depicts what he calls "bubble spaces" in which individuals willfully isolate themselves and then out of which they have trouble breaking. In Paulina's room, the fantasy of normality is also registered directly on the body—a body, as often in Petzold's cinema, in transition. As he observes, the scene depicts the confrontation of two t-shirts: Paulina's fashionable Diego Maradonna t-shirt and low-slung pants versus Jeanne's timelessly tacky surfing-bee sweatshirt. The distance between Paulina's contemporary body and Jeanne's ghostly body are starkly staged in adolescent clothes that become a theme throughout the film (as well as in *Ghosts* and *Dreileben*). It is therefore no wonder that Jeanne leads the family shortly thereafter—after Achim and Klaus fail to support them—to the villa she fantasized with Heinrich in Portugal, a choice underscoring her fantasy and longing for the conventional domesticity that her parents cannot provide.

The importance of contemporary clothes and music—and their threat to intergenerationally shared memory—recurs when Jeanne is sent from the family's refuge in the villa to shop for provisions in the city. These scenes have mostly gone undiscussed in the literature, likely because they are not obviously linked to the marquee theme of terrorism. If one has in mind, however, the way in which Petzold foregrounds the crises of leftist politics as well as the neoliberal remakings of the body, these fragmentary scenes reinforce the gap above, namely, that between collective memories of the parents and the contemporary, corporeal fantasies of their child. They begin with Jeanne crossing a bridge that seems to originate out of nowhere in the middle of the forest. The bridge, as a movement space amidst verdant nature, is an important transformational setting throughout Petzold's cinema (see the sections on *Ghosts* and *Dreileben*).

The world to which this bridge delivers Jeanne is split, like the film generally, between contemporary consumerist fantasies and the common memories of her parents, which are now inadequately shared with the younger generation. With both Paulina and Heinrich (through his love of Brian Wilson), music connects Jeanne to her peers, and the scenes after the bridge locate the viewers in musical medias res, with Jeanne shoplifting CDs. Petzold starts the sequence not with an establishing shot but with an extreme close-up of Jeanne's hand flipping through the plastic CD covers, a shot that evokes the seductive tactility of increasingly haptic neoliberal consumerism. Similarly, on another shopping trip to the city, the scene starts in extreme close-up, this time on Jeanne's face and unusually garish jogging jacket, which reverse cuts to her POV extreme close-up on the neck of a person in front of her as Jeanne waits to try on (and steal) the latest fashions in a clothing store (Petzold refers to it as H&M, the global clothing chain). With the extreme close-ups of her hand on the CD and, later, on the nape of the young woman swaying to the music in front of her—Jeanne checking, as Petzold notes, for what her peer is wearing and how she does her hair—*The State I Am In* suggests that the state in which Jeanne finds herself is increasingly becoming one of consumerist music, trendy clothes, and socially mediated taste.

Her first shopping trip, however, also underscores the fading of intergenerational shared memory foregrounded above. In her increasing search for contact with peers, Jeanne chats with a young woman outside a school. Her newly found acquaintance asks her if she is going to the film, to which she quickly assents, and viewers are left to wonder if Jeanne, who is always shot reading and studying, has ever been to school or seen a film before. Of course, this is probably not what she imagined for a matinee with other mid-adolescents. The school is screening Alain Resnais's *Night and Fog*, the landmark Holocaust documentary whose lyrical, pessimistic last sequence Petzold replays: "On the assembly courtyards [*Appellplätzen*] and all around the blocks, grass has taken root again . . . the Nazi methods are out of fashion. This landscape, the landscape of nine million dead. Which of us will keep watch here and give warning when the new henchmen arrive? Will they really look different from us? . . . We, who look past the things beside us and do not hear that the cry will never cease." The admonishing passage invokes precisely the thematic above—a political burden abiding over time and our ethical obligations to recognize and read the remnants of an earlier era rapidly receding.

Some have suggested that the sequence cites another German film about terrorism, Margarethe von Trotta's *The German Sisters* (*Die bleierne Zeit*; 1981, also translated as *Marianne and Juliane*). *The German Sisters* tracks the radicalization of Marianne, modeled on the RAF's Gudrun Ensslin, and the diverging direction of her politically leftist but not radical sister, Juliane. In one scene, Juliane has a flashback to a school-age screening of *Night and Fog*, and von Trotta's film shows how this film's stark and brutal depiction of German atrocities helped radicalize the first generation of the RAF. Despite what seems a clear citation, Petzold, as he recounts in the interview in this book, had not seen *The German Sisters* when he wrote the screenplay. He had seen Resnais's film in school, underscoring the generational divide between him and the 1960s inspiration for the film (as he also discusses in the interview herein): he remembered the experience as moving, even formative, but also confusing.

It is in this vein that he stages the scene of Jeanne watching *Night and Fog*: when the lights come up, Jeanne and her acquaintance, unlike the radical Marianne and the committed Juliane, look dazed and perplexed, at a loss for how to think or react. When the teacher of the class misrecognizes Jeanne as a regular pupil who only shows up when there is a movie—he apparently does not even realize that she is not in his class—Jeanne flees. In his commentary on the scene, Petzold describes the teacher as a "frustrated lefty," underscoring the film's overarching engagement with the breakdown of the left in shared memory. Given an opportunity to communicate and share with the young generation, the frustrated teacher only grows furious at its predictable confusion. Jeanne's time in the city shopping thus contrasts the fantasies of neoliberal body (viewers soon see her in the same Maradona t-shirt as Paulina) to the failure of shared memory of the German left.

Fading Fantasies of German Terrorists It is revealingly ironic that, at the beginning of *Near Dark*, Caleb fantasizes a femme fatale from a postpunk vampire gang to interrupt his milquetoast late-Western-genre existence, while, at the beginning of *The State I Am In*, Jeanne fantasizes a bourgeois villa in Germany. For her, having grown up in the terrorist underground but without any framework for remembering or comprehending it, such a conventional life is, indeed, only a fantasy. If fantasy negotiates between the individual's wish or desire and the (social) world around that individual, then Petzold's depicted fantasies foreground how that negotiation is indelibly affected by the economic context. Even if fantasy holds out the promise of utopian longing and its potential fulfillment, it still has to negotiate with a fallen world. Jeanne's fantasies about a conventional life are what eventually subvert her family's alternative, oppositional lifestyle—precisely the trajectory of *Near Dark*. Although their lives have their destructive charms, *Near Dark*'s vampires are encumbered by their adamant difference, an integral part of their melancholy about being eternally undead. Caleb's alternative fantasies thus have their definite downside, and eventually the fantastical pull of the normal overcomes both Mae and him.

This genre-informed depiction develops the terrorists of *The State I Am In* against the grain of the prevailing genre of terrorist films that tend to valorize the mobile ontology of the terrorists, frequently celebrating their alternative lifestyles more than their politics. For Petzold, Jeanne's fantasy manifests the longing for normality that many terrorist films emphatically overthrow. In this sobering skepticism about the burdens of the alternative, Petzold is careful, for instance, not to spectacularize violence in the film's climax: out of financial options, Hans and Clara rob a bank. A bank robbery offers another recurring scenario from films about German terrorists, but, as with his border sequence, Petzold deliberately de-dramatizes it. He excavates the fragments of the genre but also defamiliarizes them by undercutting them as fantasies for either characters or viewers. He shoots the entire robbery (money stolen, shots fired, people collapsing) through bank surveillance cameras with little audible sound, renouncing scored music to slow down and subvert these normally suspenseful events. In this antispectacularizing vein, Petzold said that he reminded the cast before shooting the scene of Marx's famous opening to the *Eighteenth Brumaire of Louis Napoleon* (1852): History repeats itself, "the first time as tragedy, the second time as farce" (Nicodemus, "Das Phantom der Linken"). As in *Near Dark*, there is above all a sense of lateness, even obsolescence, to this putatively revolutionary violence.

Even in the wake of this robbery and the growing peril to her family, Jeanne's pursuit of a conventional adolescent romance with Heinrich leads her to ultimately, if inadvertently, betray her family, much as the vampire Mae does hers in *Near Dark*. Heinrich calls the police to report the family's desperate bank robbery, and the police, in contrast to their other phantom interventions, target them specifically. Apparently a bank robbery is a crime to finally rouse police interest—in a world of global circulation, only money, not politics or transgression, elicits the response of the state. When the police catch the family on the road, surrounding the white Volvo with their black cars like antibodies fighting a virus (as Petzold recounts his mental image in Rodek and Petzold, "Der politische Beobachter"), Clara drives off the side of the road, flipping the car. Paralleling *Near Dark*'s vehicle-obliterating climax, Petzold shoots the crash from the point of view of the family as the car rolls, releasing them from their ghostly itinerancy. The camera then abruptly finds Jeanne in a long shot, thrown clear of the wreckage, her body twisted and her face covered with mud and blood, suggesting a kind of (re)birth. On an open roadside field that Petzold says should resemble an ocean—presumably the ocean around the shipwreck of the left that Blumenberg discusses in his essay—she stands up, her parents apparently dead. Petzold said that the film originally had a different ending, with police and ambulance, but he prevailed upon the producers and, as with the border and robbery, minimizes and de-dramatizes his conclusion toward an aesthetics of reduction. The same Tim Hardin song from the opening sequence forms a symmetrical sound-bridge to the end credits from a low-angle, close-up of Jeanne's face looking out into the distance. It is a close-up for which the viewers never get a reverse shot, just Hardin's melancholic lyrics about "She's walking away . . . how can we hang on to a dream?" as the film finishes by cutting from her face to black. She is now freed from her parents and their past, but if free, ambivalently so.

The film's abiding dichotomies between the conventional and the alternative, between history and fantasy, between common and shared memory, underscore how difficult it was to maintain the revolt inherent to terrorism's original milieu. The fantasies that Petzold stages in his film about terrorism are not at all what one would expect from terrorists living underground. Contrary to such action-driven and action-focused thrillers about the RAF like *The Baader Meinhof Komplex*, *The State I Am In* slowly reveals that Hans and Clara can offer no fantasy of freedom or utopia that might compete with the domestic normality held out by Heinrich—they have not, after all, even meaningfully shared their memories. In this way, with Hans and Clara never articulating any shared memories or utopian fantasy, *The State I Am In* marks the increasing absence of such hope for those living the oppositional or alternative lifestyle. The narrative prominence of Jeanne's fantasies of the luxury villa and of her transformed contemporary body, and the way in which they overwhelm the family's shared memories, underscore the intergenerational fading of political imagination. Yet Hans and Clara seem aware of this, and in that awareness that they cannot—or, at least, will no longer—share their fantasies with Jeanne, there is a sense of loss that pervades the film, much as in *Near Dark*. In emphasizing the centrality of fantasy, but rerouting it generically through Bigelow's late-Western vampires, the film charts its historical eclipse for the new millennium. For Hans, Clara, and Jeanne, the time for such utopian fantasies is over, and their melancholy marks its passing.

Something to Remind Me (Toter Mann): The Vertigo of Ghosts

Something to Remind Me (2001) came close on the heels of the surprise win of the Federal Film Prize in Gold for *The State I Am In*—apparently Petzold started shooting it just days after learning of the prize. Although *Something to Remind Me* and the subsequent *Wolfsburg* were produced for television, Petzold has emphasized that he made both of them as if they were cinema films. He was, however, especially grateful for the relatively generous shooting schedule of twenty-eight days and budget (about 1.4 million Euro) that TV financing afforded—an appreciation that underscores the modest expectations of German filmmakers.[14] Despite these humble television origins, *Something to Remind Me* was declared a masterpiece by Germany's most respected daily newspaper (Wydra) and was nominated for five German Television prizes, winning Petzold the best-director award and André M. Hennicke best actor. It also proved formative for Petzold's better-known films because it began his long and productive collaboration with Nina Hoss, an unlikely collaboration that reflects the vagaries of German cinema in recent years.

With *Something to Remind Me* and *Wolfsburg*, Petzold has admitted (also in the interview herein) that he was concerned about the pressure of the "second film"—that is, the way in which the film after a breakthrough (like *The State I Am In*) is generally regarded as "deciding the career." Given his shock at the success of *The State I Am In* and this pressure, he recounts that he was happy to retreat to television. It allowed him to "have his peace" and to "experiment, as in a laboratory," on what his approach would be in later work. In both these experiments, it is noteworthy that he undertook what he calls "B-films," or genre films of the sort now rarely seen in German cinemas. *Something to Remind Me* is a retooled film noir, and *Wolfsburg* is a self-conscious assemblage from fragments of melodrama. Both appear very much in the vein of an archeological excavation of the intelligent genre film that I charted in the introduction.

As with many of Petzold's works, *Something to Remind Me* has a key genre intertext—Hitchcock's *Vertigo* (Gansera and Petzold, "Toter Mann, was nun?"). In my analysis of his first feature-length work, *Pilots*, I mentioned how influential Hitchcock was for Petzold's cinema and his interest in genre in particular. Hitchcock would seem, as he was for the French New Wave, the paradigmatic director of the "intelligent genre film" that Petzold also admires in Dominik Graf's work. *Something to Remind Me*, like many of Hitchcock's most celebrated films, rests at the intersection of two genres, a romance and a crime thriller. The first part of the film (its first forty minutes) charts the (apparently) chance encounter and budding relationship between two lonely people in contemporary Stuttgart. They meet in a municipal pool as the film opens (the German title refers to a swimming game and means, ominously, "dead man"): Leyla climbs out of the pool and gathers her things only to drop a book, quickly retrieved by Thomas, a shy attorney.

In this opening sequence and its consequences, the influence of *Vertigo* comes into sharp focus. It turns out that this chance encounter and the subsequent romance are anything but coincidental. To follow up on this initial meeting, Thomas restages it a couple of days later. His plan unfolds apparently as desired. Only later, after Leyla disappears after their one (unconsummated) night together, does Thomas realize what lurks under the surface of the ostensibly clear pool water. It was not he who controlled their pool encounters but she, with the objective of being invited back to his apartment and then stealing his laptop full of legal files. Viewers learn later that their encounter and ostensible falling for each other was concocted, staged, and managed by Leyla, all with the coldly calculated intent for them to meet and fall in love. The coldness among people, pervasive in many of Petzold's films, reframes the romance viewers watch in the film's first half.

It turns out that she was seeking the whereabouts of one of Thomas's clients, Blum, who was convicted of raping and murdering her sister. In this way the memorable opening long-take and pan over the pool is reframed by circumstances unknown, as with Scottie's encounters with his old friend Gavin Elster and his wife Madeleine/Judy in *Vertigo*. What seems to be one fortuitous thing becomes something else altogether under the secret orchestration of another. More precisely and more sinister: when one thinks that one is the active individual—the subject—of a scenario (a mise-en-scène), it turns out that one is actually the passive, even preyed-upon object of a staging designed by another (the secret metteur-en-scène). This reframing is central to Hitchcock's (and Lang's) work and suggests another level of meaning—and menacing intentionality—of the apparently generic encounters their films stage (Elsaesser, *Weimar Cinema and After* 165–66).

Petzold excavates this generic scenario but infuses it with his own auteurist interests, leaving the genre film in deliberate fragments and ruins. If, in Hitchcock, the villain is a metteur-en-scène (Scottie's "friend" Gavin), in Petzold contemporary society itself becomes the controlling interest. Although it is Leyla who arranges their encounter and manipulates their love—she is a femme fatale with notably more agency than Hitchcock affords Madeleine/Judy in *Vertigo*—it is, in Petzold's hands, also contemporary society and especially its spaces that determine Thomas's desire. Petzold has spoken at length about the settings

Figure 9. Thomas (André M. Hennicke) pursues
Leyla (Nina Hoss) on a suspension bridge
(cf. *Vertigo*) in *Something to Remind Me* (2001).

of the film and how he was interested in how love (perhaps counterin-tuitively) requires some public space to ignite (Gansera and Petzold, "Toter Mann, was nun?"). Indeed, Thomas's pursuit of Leyla through a park and onto a bridge—a Steadicam-shot nod to what Petzold calls Scottie's somnambulist pursuit of Madeleine/Judy around *Vertigo*'s onei-ric San Francisco—puts them in a dream world of incipient love (figure 9). When scouting locations in Stuttgart, however, Petzold saw that such public spaces requisite for romance are "increasingly rolled back, taken over by banks and trusts" (Buß and Petzold).

This question of how love might function in an increasingly priva-tized world arises in a film that Petzold also cites as another major influence on *Something to Remind Me*, Helmut Käutner's *Under the Bridges* (*Unter den Brücken*; 1944/45), which foregrounds the trans-formational character of bridge settings seen in many of Petzold's films (see the sections on *State I Am In* and *Ghosts*). In *Under the Bridges*, two barge operators in and around Berlin inhabit a "bubble space" away from the late war destruction, but they, like *Something*'s Thomas, both try to break out of it by finding love. If their contem-porary circumstances (the war years 1944–45) weighed on the barge operators' efforts to break through that isolation, Thomas's obstacles in the present are quite different. The impossibility of love for Thomas arises from the way that emotional life is increasingly the object of study, planning, and manipulation. After the radical plot turn of Leyla's disappearance (paralleling the narrative breaks of a fleeing woman in *Vertigo* and in *Under the Bridges*), Thomas discovers a book Leyla used to pursue him. Entitled *Target: Man*, the manual meticulously outlines the various scenarios in which Leyla and Thomas (ostensibly) fell in spontaneous love. As in Farocki's *Leben—BRD*, Thomas's most intimate emotions are reframed as a contrived staging. This deliberately deceptive arrangement anticipates Leyla's careful construction of a secret torture chamber into which she seduces her sister's murderer in the film's Möbius-strip-like second half.

This radical interruption in the second half of the narrative is remarkably registered in the performance of Nina Hoss, a performance that established one of the most striking collaborations between director and actor in German and even European cinema. Petzold has had even longer associations with other members of his crew, especially with the cinematographer Hans Fromm and the editor Bettina Böhler, but his work with Hoss is one of the best-known and most celebrated aspects of his cinema. Hoss's mother was an actor and later director of a theater, and her father was one of the founders of the important German Green party (Corsten). After considering training as an opera singer, she studied acting at the (state-funded) Ernst Busch Acting School in Berlin, but, at the very beginning of her 1995 studies, she was "discovered" by Bernd Eichinger, Germany's most important film producer since 1970. Eichinger produced a number of seminal works of the 1970s and 1980s New German Cinema but subsequently became a driving force behind more commercially minded cinema after 1990 (see Baer). Symptomatic of that era's cinema, he cast Hoss in his TV remake of *Mädchen Rosemarie*, recycling a genre work from the 1950s, an era much vilified (including by Petzold) for its vapid cinematic product. Part of Eichinger's self-conscious attempt to foster a more commercial German cinema was staging a "discovery" of Hoss as a star, a process that could then be foregrounded in the film's marketing campaigns. Eichinger's marketing worked well: at the ages of twenty-one and twenty-two, Hoss was featured in major magazines like *Stern*, *Bunte*, and the German *Vogue* and invited to numerous TV talk shows (Corsten).

This Eichinger-fueled career seems some distance from the cinema of Petzold—although, it should be noted, Petzold did have talks with Eichinger after *The State I Am In* about making a film with him. In contemporary European cinema, however, Petzold openly admires directors like the Dardenne brothers, and it is hard to imagine their working with someone so clearly catapulted to notoriety as a (staged) star. In fact, Petzold recounts how he came to cast Hoss through one of her many talk-show appearances. He had not thought of whom to put in the crucial female lead of *Something to Remind Me,* but when he happened to be discussing the cast with his producers, he had just seen Hoss on a talk show and, at something of a loss, offered up her name. Given her established commercial profile, the producers were immediately enthusiastic (Rother 131–32). Petzold says that he was initially unsure, but, upon meeting with her, he was impressed by how seriously she took her work, writing down everything he said and then asking precise questions, with all this information coming out in her gestures—it was a pleasant shock, he recounts.

In discussing acting, Petzold repeatedly emphasizes how he rehearses with the actors to highlight the physical and the corporeal. Part of this relates to his consistent interest in depicting work in his films, work that settles into the body and at which he finds German actors generally unskilled (see the section on *Wolfsburg* below). With the 2012 film *Barbara,* for instance, he encouraged Hoss (who plays a doctor in the film) "to spend two weeks in a hospital learning how one gives a shot," a typical emphasis on manual know-how as much as attitude and psychology. Second, and perhaps more revealing, he believes that German acting in the 1950s became extremely, and unconvincingly, dialogue-driven because "Nazism has taken our bodies away from us." The celebrated German cinema of the 1920s and early 1930s was, as he sees it, a cinema of bodies and fantasy that was largely undercut by the Nazi era and its fallout.

Physicality, manual (driving) skills, and corporeal presence are, indeed, attributes that Petzold lauds in Benno Fürmann's work, and, in praising Hoss's performance in *Something to Remind Me,* he highlights how her body is able to convey the tension, the balance situation of abeyance, that he is often seeking. For example, after Leyla flees Thomas and

Stuttgart for the town where Blum is incarcerated (some of it shot in Wittenberge, where Petzold would subsequently set parts of *Yella*), she seeks an isolated abode where she can create her secret torture chamber. A rental agent shows her an out-of-the-way washhouse, which she, claiming to be an artist, declares perfect for a "studio." But then she walks away and lets the mask of her charade fall, and Petzold observes, "This leaving, these thirty-five meters to the washhouse [that she walks]—I thought: that is an absolute event [*Ereignis*]" (qtd. in Rother 74; see also Petzold and Hoss). Turning and walking away from the viewer is central to the performances in many of his films. Petzold singled out this gesture and movement in a book that he calls "fundamental" for him, Bela Balazs's *The Visible Man.* Balazs saw "cinema beginning" at the moment D. W. Griffith does not show the actor Lilian Gish's reaction to a personal tragedy. Even though the audience might expect a trademark close-up of his star, Griffith lets her walk away from the camera (Vahabzadeh, Göttler, and Petzold, "Kino ist wie ein Bankraub"). Coupled with an absence of excessive dialogue—especially from his protagonists—this recurring turning and walking away differentiates Petzold's actors from the mainstream treatment of the body and face (Naremore, *Acting in the Cinema* 37–39).

While Hitchcock was famously contemptuous of acting and most actors, Petzold, throughout his career, has credited them for contributing significantly to his work. He regards his learning how to collaborate with actors as a key development in his personal breakthrough, the 1992 short film *The Warm Money,* as well as in *Pilots* (Suchsland and Petzold, "Der Schneidetisch eines Films"). His films are indeed remarkable for how frequently he recasts actors from film to film. He does agree with Hitchcock, however, in the latter's disdain for method acting, which Petzold criticizes numerous times (Peitz and Petzold, "Wir haben Sterne ohne Himmel"; Kreist and Petzold, "Wracks mit Geschichte"; Schwenk and Petzold 90). Neither Hitchcock nor Petzold is interested in a Strasbergian investigation and insertion of the actor's psychology and self—instead, as Baron and Carnicke note of modernist acting in Bresson and Antonioni, Petzold's actors' faces and voices become less expressive in order to highlight deep-space mise-en-scène and long-take editing (38–39; something also true of Ozu, another director, like Bresson and Antonioni, whom Petzold admires). Unlike these directors, however, Petzold relocates such modernist film performance amidst the generic fragments I have been emphasizing, highlighting all the more the subdued, often "cold" (i.e., nonexpressive) face and voice in favor of a body as graphical element amidst his many movement spaces.

Given this aversion to method acting, Petzold suggests that the task at hand is not to dig deeper into the character's, or actor's, personal psychology but "rather to follow [the characters]," presumably through the socioeconomic transformation he frequently depicts (Vahabzadeh, Göttler, and Petzold, "Kino ist wie ein Bankraub"). Given his interest in genre, in the transformative corporealities of our historical moment, he thinks that actors should not be looking within themselves but deliberately studying (as they did for *Yella*) new forms of individuality and the transitional bodies housing them (Kreist and Petzold, "Wracks mit Geschichte"). His admiration for Hoss's work in this transformational manner is clear as well in his praise of the dramatic end of *Something to Remind Me*. Leyla is set to torture and kill Blum but suddenly loses her will, all conveyed and betrayed by the physicality of her body: "[Leyla] loses the rhythm. For me, it was sensational when I saw what [Hoss] had done in the shoot: how one loses the rhythm. Because she's playing somebody who wants absolutely to keep up the rhythm, her performance should hold. The body is poised, but one notices in the many small details that it is crumbling, that it is collapsing, that this is only a façade that she is maintaining—really an unbelievable accomplishment" (qtd. in Rother 133). This crumbling of one's subjectivity, the collapse of an individuality carefully cultivated, likewise transpires with Hoss's characters in *Wolfsburg* and *Yella*. Despite Leyla's losing of the rhythm and Hoss's "unbelievable" performance of it, Blum goes through with her plan, committing suicide by police by feigning an attack on her as he whispers to her not to worry. Blum may be gone, but the actors Nina Hoss, Sven Pippig, and André M. Hennicke would all be back, underscoring the importance of performance, and especially its morphing the body, throughout Petzold's cinema.

Wolfsburg: A Company-Town Melodrama

Wolfsburg (2003) was Petzold's second television-financed project after the surprise success of *The State I Am In,* although, given his rising profile at the time, it did end up with a limited theatrical release before its broadcast. While Petzold does not regard it as part of the Ghost trilogy, *Wolfsburg* foreshadows aspects of his style that reverberate throughout his later work, including his engagement with the contemporary transformation of work and social life and, as the title indicates, the central place of the automobile among the many movement and transit spaces in his cinema. The film's title refers to a city that Germans immediately associate with the car industry as well as that industry's singular place in German history. Wolfsburg is a wealthy, small city in former West Germany that happens to be the headquarters of one of Germany's (and the world's) biggest corporations, Volkswagen. In a way, Wolfsburg is one big transit space, a space that is a by-product of modern mobility and the machinery required for it. Volkswagen has completely dominated the city since the location, originally a sparsely inhabited swampland, was chosen by the Nazis to build up their car and military-vehicle industry. Petzold's setting invokes this history and West Germany's recovery from it. In fact, he says, the city's original name ("The City of the Strength-through-Joy Car") and then its (presumably unawares) renaming by the Allies with Hitler's nickname ("Wolf") mean that the Nazi past has "stuck" to the city (Uehling and Petzold). Despite this checkered history, however, the city has served as the engine of West Germany's postwar economy and its rapid resurrection. In *Wolfsburg,* automobiles illuminate how cars as movement spaces function generally in Petzold's cinema while also demonstrating how he here excavates fragments of a genre usually only in the background of his work, namely, melodrama.

The film opens with its protagonist, Philip, in his vintage, red RO 80 traversing the landscape around Wolfsburg's resonant historical setting. While driving, he is quarreling on his mobile phone with his girlfriend Katja, who is the sister of Philip's employer at a local car dealership. Visibly agitated, he drops the phone, reaches down to retrieve it, and, in that instant, hears a portentous thud as his car strikes something. Looking in the rearview mirror, he realizes he has hit a boy on a bicycle. In a few, panicked seconds, he flees the scene. Philip's abrupt actions in the opening four minutes of the film make him a hit-and-run perpetrator, committing "Fahrerflucht" in German, which has an emphasis on fleeing or flight missing in English (as well as a double entendre of fleeing driving itself). Although visibly unsettled by his own actions, Philip's intimate knowledge of cars—as director of sales at his brother-in-law's upscale dealership and with a mechanic's training—allows him to conceal his vehicular crime. But Philip decides to admit what he has done, and he goes to the hospital to do so, where he encounters Laura, the mother of the boy he has struck. His surprise at seeing her upends his plan to confess. A budding relationship with her after the boy's death draws him out of the superficial life he has built and Laura out of the isolation of hers. This surprising development allows him to atone—at least until she finds out why he suddenly took an interest in her.

Somewhat unusually for Petzold, the plot displays clear melodramatic parameters. First and foremost, there is the pathos of the lost child and the guilty quandary of a mother, both cornerstones (separation from the child and sound and fury about it) of the maternal melodrama (Doane 70–95). The film also explores the social blockage of desire on the part of the film's lead female and male, with class difference and a previous marriage coming between Laura and Philip. Even in light of more recent theories of the genre, the makings of the melodrama are largely there: melodrama's inherent moral logic in Philip's dilemma (Brooks 42); the agnition (finding out something too late and the emotional fallout of this belatedness) of Laura's discovering who Philip is even as she falls in love with him; and the identification with an innocent victim ("surprising power lay in identifying with victimhood" [Williams, "Melodrama Revisited" 48]). When asked in an interview about melodrama in *Wolfsburg*, Petzold confirmed it by comparing his work to another artist working in a popular form, the singer Helge Schneider, who, according to Petzold, uncovers in hackneyed popular songs (*Schlager*) true sentiments: "[the comedian] Stefan Raab is terrible and Helge Schneider good. Because Raab can only caricature melodramatic feelings, while Helge Schneider can open up from a *Schlager* the sadness and sentiment hidden in it. In melodrama there is material that one really has to work through— that's what I am trying to do" (Reinecke and Petzold). Petzold's work with popular genre seems deliberately archeological, an "opening up" of what is "hidden in there." He excavates existing, even hackneyed genres for resonant conflicts and scenarios that he then recasts with his own auteurist interests.

While admitting that he works with some aspects of melodrama, Petzold suggests that he deliberately creates some distance in the film that resists the strong identification with victims of Linda Williams's "melodramatic mode." Some critics, he acknowledges, term that cold, but "then one would have to call every Western and the thriller of the 1970s cold," emphasizing how he refunctions aspects of multiple genres, recombines and recasts them, even in this predominantly melodramatic milieu.[15] These kinds of "more distanced" films, he suggests, allow for a more complex form of empathy than the facile "therapeutic empathy" that most German films evoke (Reinecke and Petzold). This approach renders *Wolfsburg* an altogether different, even spectral, kind of melodrama building on that genre's remnants without its full presence.

Petzold, for instance, refunctions melodrama's domestic setting and strife in *Wolfsburg*. After the film's opening, Philip aims to put his criminal past behind him—always a dubious proposition in postwar German cinema. He plans to return home, tell no one about his crime, and conceal the incriminating dents on his car. In the wake of their fight and now his distracted detachment, Katja is packed and prepared to leave, but when he plaintively calls her name on her way out—with emotion surely bred of desperation about his crime—she turns and embraces him. One of their few moments of emotional intimacy is underpinned as a refuge from his crime. This irony is reinforced by the domestic setting itself. Petzold highlights in this scene not the house's melodramatic-emotional but rather its historical resonances. In such domiciles, he sees an attempt in postwar Germany to create "clarity and order"—with the "recognizable attempt to live hedonism and freedom." And into this world, "guilt breaks in" (Reinecke and Petzold). Such guilt breaking into the domestic is, in Petzold's hands, certainly overdetermined by the guilt surrounding the characters in an industrial city that the Nazis conjured out of nothing. The house seems architecturally girded against this guilt's breaking in or through: Petzold offers recurring shots of the almost armored windows next to the house's driveway, underscoring the social isolation and loneliness created by their car-based lives (figure 10).

This recurring shot of their armored home balanced by the driveway is revealing because the car comes to replace the home as the key private space in Petzold's most explicit melodrama. As in one of the generic intertexts that Petzold has mentioned—Walter Hill's *The Driver* (1978)—*Wolfsburg* charts the social substitution of the house for the car as the protagonist's primary private space. The private space becomes a movement space here and throughout his cinema. In both

Figure 10. The fully armored house and its driveway in *Wolfsburg* (2003).

The Driver and *Wolfsburg,* the protagonist's car(s) express his character more than any space inhabited or any words uttered. It was important to him, Petzold recounts, that all moments of "confession, despair, sin, and tenderness occur in the auto. The automobile [functions] as a pressure chamber," something that could be said of many of the cars in his films (Lenssen and Petzold). Throughout the film, the car substitutes for the melodrama's domestic space, one that routes melodrama's mechanisms through the kind of social transformations that he consistently engages and critiques.

Cars figure centrally throughout Petzold's early work, and *The State I Am In* foregrounds the car ontologically, as a mode of itinerant being, with the family's car as a "cage" (Nord and Petzold, "Das Auto ist ein reicher Ort"). After largely leaving aside the automobile in *Something to Remind Me, Wolfsburg* is Petzold's most extended rumination on the automobile and its singular place in German economy, history, and culture. Petzold has said that he had in mind how some 50 percent of German industry is related in one way or another to the automobile (Nicodemus and Petzold, "Kino als Auto-Analyse"), the most important export of the world's second biggest export economy (and that with only eighty million inhabitants). Wolfsburg interested him in particular, he recounts, because there was no other city in Germany where history was so "concentrated" (*verdichtet*) as there: on the one hand, the "traces" of the Nazis were everywhere, but, on the other hand, "when Volkswagen isn't doing well, then Germany isn't doing well," right into the present (Lenssen and Petzold). He has remarked numerous times that it is no coincidence that the person appointed in 2002 to head the commission to address persisting federal unemployment was a VW human-resources executive, Peter Hartz, such that these controversial reforms (to which Petzold makes regular critical reference) are still known as the "Hartz IV" reforms (Rodek, "Das Auto als Ort der Wahrheit"; Nicodemus and Petzold, "Kino Als Auto-Analyse"). Similarly, on sundry symbolic and cultural levels, cars have permeated the German popular imagination. For instance, Petzold has recounted how one of his parents' favorite television shows when he was growing up concerned a garage, in which the main characters were dressed like "nurses on a nightshift" treating and reviving ill automobiles (Nicodemus and Petzold, "Kino Als Auto-Analyse").

Wolfsburg's opening shot of an expansive landscape with the factory in the background is, however, the only one in which this city- and nation-dominating company is explicitly invoked. For much of the rest of the film, the massive VW factory, with its trademark chimneys, is merely in the background, glimpsed only occasionally, foreshadowing Petzold's deliberately subdued use of historically resonant spaces in *Ghosts*. In practice, Wolfsburg's Nazi past and industrial present act not so much as background but formative social and emotional foundation, even if somewhat obscured in the shifting sediments of time. The Wolfsburg-shot images hint at this past's presence but, simultaneously, its absence, at least for Petzold's preoccupied characters, such that this past's subterranean ubiquity underscores the characters' increasing obliviousness to it. Petzold's films deploy historically overdetermined places like Wolfsburg to suggest how individuals today inhabit and largely ignore such resonant spaces—contemporary capitalism, as I argued with *The State I Am In*, has other things on its mind.

After invoking but obscuring Wolfsburg's industrial past, the film's opening shot balances these multiple functions of the German car by panning to follow a single car limning this history-laden landscape (figure 11). The shot suggests the widely shared dream of traveling the open summer road in a fetishized vintage car. But such a pan also foreshadows the disengagement from the factory and a shift to the individual, following and preferring the private individual against that large corporation, factory, and the collective experience and consciousness they offer (see Sennett 37–47). The car embodies this dual drive, so to say, to dreamlike mobility but also self-focused seclusion in both leisure and labor. The car serves Petzold's work consistently as a space of contradictory social isolation in which one can inhabit one's own movement space without the struggle or stress of social life. As noted in the section on *The State I Am In*, he often terms them "bubble" or "parallel" spaces, and in *Wolfsburg* this bubble space is conspicuously the car. Given the title and topic of the film, he was frequently asked by German journalists about his understanding of the car, and, in one interview, he recounts how he watched a great many car commercials to prepare *Wolfsburg*. Petzold was particularly taken with one advertisement for Mercedes-Benz. It depicts a (presumably ethnic German) man in Cairo, where (per the Orientalist imagination) the mob is pushing closer to him—Petzold says that they simply do not maintain "the distance from one another that we [in Germany] demand—they jostle and push." But when the man climbs into his car, "it becomes completely quiet and the text appears, 'finally at home.' That is the idea of the Federal Republic of Germany: to create a living space [*Lebensraum*] that does not have anything to do with the complex outer world" (Reinecke and Petzold).

Figure 11. A lonely car in a factory town
(*Wolfsburg* [2003]).

This simultaneously anthropological and ontological understanding of the car illuminates how it functions for Germans at the most fundamental level, in their psychological navigation of the "complex outer world." Such a precise understanding of the automobile's ontological and fantasy function elucidates various (vehicular) turning points of *Wolfsburg,* including why Philip fails to leave the car when he hits Laura's son Paul, why ultimately getting out of the car to meet Laura becomes so meaningful for him, and why getting in the car becomes so fateful for Laura. These choices to enter or exit the car are, for Petzold, essential psychological and social navigations on the topography of our contemporary world. As the car does in this opening sequence when Philip fights with Katja, in dangerous detachment from the world around them, the car becomes a "filtering system" for perceptions of the outer world, as if the windshield were a movie (Nicodemus and Petzold, "Kino Als Auto-Analyse"). In many of his films (*Pilots, Cube Libre, State I Am In, Yella, Jerichow*), people are driven out of these vehicular filtering systems into a wider social world that they poorly understand and have difficulty managing. The experience of the car, getting in and out of it, navigates fundamental modes of perception and experience.

For Philip, the automobile is the basis for his professional and personal life, although, with Philip's work, Petzold is tracing another fundamental transformation in society and economy that his cinema also repeatedly tracks. Philip is the head of sales at his brother-in-law's upscale car dealership, a surprise, given that one would expect a film with the title of *Wolfsburg* to be about the city's unique manufacturing, not the quotidian selling, of cars. Petzold is pointing to the ongoing deindustrialization of formerly industrial powers like Germany, investigating, as he does even more fully in *Yella,* the kind of dematerialized work now rampant in a consumer-oriented, service-based neoliberal economy (see Sennett 133–36; and Bauman 2). His approach in *Wolfsburg* shows the influence of a nonfiction film by another of Petzold's teachers at the DFFB in Berlin, Hartmut Bitomsky. Petzold, in fact, recounts how he became more familiar with Wolfsburg through his work on Bitomsky's documentary about the architect Hans Scharoun (*An Imaginary Architecture: The Architect Hans Scharoun;* 1995). The Scharoun film crew spent time in Wolfsburg, and Petzold recounts seeing, on the drive from Berlin, crosses along the road marking vehicular deaths. A roadside cross becomes a recurring image in *Wolfsburg,* as Philip returns compulsively to the site of the accident. During the preparation for the Scharoun film, the crew also watched Bitsomsky's *VW Komplex* (1989/90), which, with its focus on Volkswagen as well as the city of Wolfsburg, is another key intertext for Petzold's own film.

While careful to historicize Volkswagen and Wolfsburg in their Nazi past, *VW Komplex* also traces the recent changes in industrial production that powered postwar Germany. Bitomsky's film alternates sequences of heavy production performed by robots with images of largely inert human workers often only inspecting the work of their automated colleagues. The film gives the bittersweet sense that the days of manual production in Germany's key industry are nearing their end; this industry that has busied so many unemployed hands since the 1930s is increasingly doing away with human labor. Bitomsky uses Volkswagen and Wolfsburg to trace the postwar history of the Federal Republic—viewers see stock images of the Nazi-heralded factory, early postwar deprivation, and the rapid rise of the 1950s "Economic Miracle"—but the film also looks to the robotics- and computer-dominated future.

In his DVD commentary on *Wolfsburg,* Petzold says that the actors were particularly interested in his script because of the details about work that Petzold wrote into it. For example, in an early scene in the "Autohaus" where Philip works, he, as sales director, coaches a new salesman on how to sell cars. From above, they look down on a couple and their young child who have just arrived in an aging, hand-painted Volkswagen. Reading these marks expertly, Philip informs his trainee that one can see that the child's car seat is worth more than their whole vehicle, so there must be a wealthy relative bankrolling their upgrade to a new Audi for the child's safety (not coincidentally, since Philip just ran over a child on a bike). Philip's masterful analysis of a sales opportunity displays a real professional skill that Petzold says they modeled on the many American films they had watched in preparation (Petzold, *Wolfsburg* DVD commentary). Philip's expert reading of a business situation provides for his longest monologue in a film that is primarily about his ultimate silence: his silence to the authorities about hitting the boy, to his girlfriend/wife about his crime and betrayal, and to Laura about who he is.

This depiction of Philip's work, ethereal as it is, contrasts to *Wolfsburg*'s (workplace) introduction of Laura. Shortly after Philip runs over her son, viewers gain their first glimpse of her through a surveillance camera at her job in a nondescript, unlocatable big-box supermarket that deterritorializes Wolfsburg's singular place in German economic history. Petzold frequently cuts to the point of view of a surveillance camera in his films, although it is somewhat unusual for him to introduce a character this way. Surveillance-tape POV serves different functions in the various films, but such images all underscore the contemporary ubiquity of surveillance as well as the disciplinary forces of control societies they manifest. This society, argues Gilles Deleuze in "Postscript on the Societies of Control" (which both Farocki and Petzold quote), conditions individuals' behavior in increasingly granular ways through noninstitutional means like surveillance. Here, in *Wolfsburg's* study of labor, the surveillance camera in the workplace underlines the pathetic, controlled character of Laura's job as a "Regalpflegerin," the equivalent of a stock person in a grocery store, though the German word euphemistically terms it something akin to a "shelf caretaker."

It is an economic irony of the first order, then, that Laura's employment situation only improves through the intervention of, and financing by, the man who killed her child. Laura actually planned to be a graphic designer, but, continuing a theme from *VW Komplex*, she was never able to find a job in the field in which she trained for years. In *VW Komplex*, this long-term preparation for disappearing positions results in the unemployed people landing at Volkswagen; by 2003, Petzold seems to be saying, the increasing problem locates these workers at the lowest rungs of retail. When Laura rejects the amorous advances of her supervisor and is fired from the discount store in a breathtakingly cruel scene, Philip finds her a job with a graphic designer and printer he knows through his work for the Autohaus. This professional trajectory—fired by one would-be paramour, hired by another—emphasizes the relative lack of power of women in the economy, as well as the entwinement of the economic and amorous. Echoing Philip's work-love for Katja's dealership-owning family, Laura continues to fall for Philip more and more as the job he supplied her grows better and better.

When Katja realizes that Philip is having an affair—not by finding the proverbial lipstick on the collar but, rather fitting for Wolfsburg, Laura's shoe in his car—he loses his job and even the loaner Audi he has been driving since hiding his RO 80. It is, in fact, the return to this fetishized, vintage accessory to his crime that ultimately betrays Philip. When they realize that Laura has a free day from her new job—the first of May, the "day of labor" of which they, as "incredibly individuated workers," seem utterly unaware[16]—they undertake an excursion to the sea. Foreshadowing the memorable use of the beach in *Jerichow,* they eventually spend the night together on open sands next to the Baltic Sea, a place away from their work, from their dysfunctional relationships, and even, temporarily at least, from cars. As in *Jerichow,* however, this potential utopian refuge is ruined, as it becomes the site of a final misunderstanding between the two. Philip says her name and seems, Petzold recounts, finally prepared to confess, but, as with Katja at the beginning of the film, his desperate, despairing articulation of a woman's name is melodramatically misunderstood as love. As he also had with Katja, he yields to the easier route of sleeping with her. On the morning after, Laura returns to Philip's car to retrieve something to drink and realizes then that the only clue that her son gave to his assailant ("Ford") referred not to the manufacturer of the car, but to Philip's license plate, which reads "FO-RD 813."

Reading these hieroglyphics of the car resolves Laura's search for the killer. It was a quest for which she had utterly remade herself (as in Chabrol's *This Man Must Die,* according to Petzold), but a quest, unlike in the Chabrol film, that is interrupted by moments of melodramatic love. The suspense of what she will do does not last long. Weeping in the passenger seat as Philip cheerfully drives away from their edenic night on the beach, Laura stabs him, and he flips the car. As Philip lies bleeding on the ground, Petzold cuts to his point of view on his assailant, a return to Paul's point of view after being struck at the film's opening. It is a low, earthbound POV ending the abeyance of the protagonist that marks most of the film. Climbing from the wreckage, Laura does, as Petzold notes, the one thing with which Philip never bothered: she calls for help. These last lines of the film, distinguishing her from him, are road directions to their location. Such concluding words are not a surprise for a film that, from beginning to end, is about the movement space of the automobile and its intimate relationship to people's professional, psychological, and (decreasingly) social lives.

Ghosts (*Gespenster*): Spectrality at the Center of Berlin

Ghosts (2005) was Petzold's second film intended (and funded) from the beginning as a theatrical release. Although the television-financed *Something to Remind Me* and *Wolfsburg* intervened between his break-through *The State I Am In* and *Ghosts*, many (including the director himself) saw this film as the crucial follow-up to the surprise success of *The State I Am In.* Petzold has mentioned that he had initially entitled *The State I Am In* "Ghosts," but that title ended up attached to the second part of his Ghost trilogy (Petzold, "*Gespenster*"). This spectral recurrence in these titles underscores the interest I located at or near the center of his work in the introduction: an abiding engagement with remnants, remains, and ghosts that emerge at, and survive, moments of historical crisis and transition. Petzold's particular depiction of rem-nants, remains, and ghosts deliberately marks the passing of time and the inexorable ravages of history in his work.

The film opens with French Pierre driving to Berlin to retrieve his wife Françoise from some kind of medical, probably psychiatric, facil-ity. Music plays on his car audio system, with Bach's cantata *Streams of Salted Tears* (*Bäche von gesalznen Zähren*) immediately lending the film an atmosphere of aching loss, mourning, and beauty. Françoise ap-parently landed in this facility because she went to Berlin and accosted a teenager as their long lost daughter Marie, who was kidnapped there at age three. These opaquely depicted events are quickly intercut with the encounter with and friendship of two young-adult German women, Nina and Toni, adrift in the middle of Berlin. Nina lives in an institution for young people while working in a low-level, likely state-subsidized job in a large city park. In that park she randomly encounters Toni, who similarly seems to have no conventional home, a "stray," as many reviews put it; the two of them become friends and have something of an amorous relationship. When Françoise observes Nina and Toni from her hotel room, she becomes convinced that Nina is her lost daughter Marie, an unlikely presumption whose veracity remains ambiguous because of a matching scar and perhaps a shared, heart-shaped birthmark between the shoulder blades. The film is set in central Berlin, a space saturated with the marquee history of twentieth-century Europe. Françoise's private suffering remains in ambiguous relation to the public history implied in the spaces of the German capital—this tension between personal loss and the remnants of public history obtains throughout the film.

In discussing the inspiration for *Ghosts*, Petzold describes the intersection—a typical intersection for him—of the fantastical-mythical with the change wrought by the contemporary world. Back in his student days, he explains, he had the idea of resetting fairy tales in the present and even bought an elaborate edition of such tales (Schenk and Petzold, "Christian Petzolds Gespenster"). Years later, he was reading some to his daughter and came across a particularly brutal fairy tale of the Brothers Grimm that he had forgotten, "The Burial Shirt" ("Das Totenhemdchen"). In the tale, a mother mourns her dead child, a boy, with such fervor that the child cannot enter heaven (Petzold, in his recounting of the tale, tellingly changes the little boy to a girl; Nord and Petzold, "Mit geschlossenen Augen Hören"). The ghost of the boy returns and informs the mother that her constant tears have so moistened his burial shirt that he cannot rest in his coffin—her excessive mourning seems to have doomed the child to remain a ghost, suspended (like so many of Petzold's characters) between this world and an unknown hereafter. The child begs the mother to cease her mourning, which the mother manages after a couple more days, and the ghost disappears for good. On one side, the tale seems an admonition about excessively mourning (private or personal) loss. On the other side, it also depicts a necessary, perhaps also desired, separation from the parents (Nord and Petzold, "Mit geschlossenen Augen Hören"). This second theme resonates, in fact, with the ambiguous and intriguing relation of Nina to *The State I Am In*'s Jeanne, played by the same actor, Julia Hummer. Nina's life in an institution adrift without parents is a fate (never clarified or confirmed) that might have befallen Jeanne, (likely) orphaned as she is at the end of *The State I Am In*.

Petzold had "The Burial Shirt" in mind when he came across what he calls "phantom pictures" in post offices in northern France: bulletin boards displaying pictures of missing children whose appearance had been re-created ("calculated," he says) by computers to adjust for the time since they were lost. He notes that the posters were produced for and hung by the children's parents, not by the police, so there was decidedly something of the Grimms' tale in this computer-aided mourning

(Nord and Petzold, "Mit geschlossenen Augen Hören"). Such a modern-mythical mélange resonates with a theme from *The Sex Thief*, the disciplinary function of modern regimes of technology, especially around contemporary visual systems. Petzold suggests that a child mocked up by machines does not have any "social age anymore, doesn't have any more experiences [*Erlebnisse*]," because he or she has to live (in) this computer picture (Nord and Petzold, "Mit geschlossenen Augen Hören"). This intersection of the mythic with the contemporary world highlights how our technologized contemporary world shapes and confines basic human behavior, especially around private loss and obsession.

Just such an intersection of the fantastical with the contemporary frames the initial encounter between Nina and Toni near the beginning of the film as well. After Pierre's arrival in Berlin in the opening sequence, the camera cuts to the film's other narrative line, introducing Nina in a long shot, her bright orange safety vest contrasting to the verdant green surrounding her. Amidst the resplendent trees and meadow of the summertime park, she is marked and reduced by her disposable work uniform over t-shirt and jeans, retrieving trash from the park meadow. Despite Petzold's typical emphasis on the beauty of nature—the sound of the wind in the trees is preternaturally audible (see Schwenk 76–79)—he entwines his recurring themes of labor and the changes it effects on and in the body. With Nina and Toni, as in *Cuba Libre* and *The Sex Thief,* Petzold foregrounds social outsiders with only marginal economic prospects.

Nina's job resonates, as in Petzold's other films, with the increasingly spectral presence of workers amidst Germany's "modernization" of its labor laws and conditions. In another description of the films' sources, Petzold recounts how he was one day sitting in the Tiergarten (the central Berlin park where the camera finds Nina working) and encountered a young person doing "a one-Euro" job and immediately thought, "Something is not right here" (Kreist and Petzold, "Irgendetwas ist nicht in Ordnung"). The one-Euro jobs were measures introduced and subsidized by the government in 2003 and 2004 to add "flexibility" to the labor market by allowing employers to hire unemployed workers for only one Euro an hour, with the rest of the worker's basic needs funded by the government (for the ubiquity of such newer norms of flexibility, see Bauman 4). The notion behind it was to bring the long-term unemployed back into the workforce, even with low-skilled work in homes for the elderly or, as here, in public parks.

Petzold struck up a conversation with this worker and learned that the individual was "not a lumpenproletarian or a skinhead . . . who was supposed to be resocialized by collecting garbage. These were people who, after high school, wanted to drift a bit, and then all of a sudden are twenty-three and too old" (Gansera and Petzold, "Über die Brücke und in den Wald"). This, for Petzold, has become a general condition in contemporary Germany: "[T]he five million unemployed we have [in Germany] today are actually also ghosts, in a bubble, that live in a parallel world" (Petzold, *"Gespenster"*). While Nina is a poster child for the struggles of low-skilled workers in the German economy, Toni, adrift at the center of the Berlin Republic, does not seem to work at all. She supports herself, as far as viewers can see, through petty theft and far-fetched dreams. As in many of his films, Petzold starts with the remnant of a fairy tale or a genre film but ends up thoroughly engaged with contemporary themes related to work, economy, and the body, offering us workers at the social margins for whom normality is, as he says, only a faraway dream (Petzold, *"Gespenster"*).

Petzold does, however, consistently balance this kind of materialist critique with remnant fairy tales and genre stories. His critical approach, as I noted in the introduction, does not tend to the realism of postwar Italian cinema or the Dardenne brothers, admiring though he is of those films. Although engaged in a deliberate critique of contemporary economy and its casualties, Petzold cultivates, following his engagement with fantasy in *The State I Am In,* a dreamlike tone throughout *Ghosts.* That makes his engagement with the contemporary economy somewhat oblique, but also uniquely arresting. If the plot line of excessive mourning is lifted from the brutal Brothers Grimm, other oneiric aspects are borrowed from genre films, especially in this film and its follow-up, *Yella,* from works of the horror genre. The original title of *Ghosts,* Petzold recounts, was actually a reference to a memorable intertitle from F. W. Murnau's 1922 silent film *Nosferatu* that describes Hutter's journey to the castle of the vampire: "And once he had crossed the bridge, the phantoms came to meet him" (the German is even more poetic: "Als er die Brücke überquert hatte, kamen ihm die Gespenster entgegen"). Petzold explains that "I found this sentence so lyrical, that's how cinema has to be. One pays at the box office, then one goes over the bridge, and then the ghosts come upon us" (Suchsland and Petzold, "Ein Roman hält uns nicht zusammen"; Rodek and Petzold, "Totenhemdchen beginnt zu leben"). Petzold has recounted in interviews his great admiration for *Nosferatu* and the fantastical tradition of Weimar cinema, something he finds lacking in contemporary German cinema (Khouloki and Petzold). Informing this link to the Weimar fantastical was the originally planned location for *Ghosts*, the studio where Joy May made *The Indian Grave* (*Das indische Grabmal*; 1921).

These genre remnants serve Petzold in his staging of the film's fateful encounter between Nina and Toni—an encounter whose "reality" remains ambiguous, as discussed below, not least because of its idyllic park setting. Shortly after Nina first sees Toni being attacked in a long, point-of-view shot, Nina is sitting with her fellow one-Euro workers, and they hear some shouting accusing the fleeing Toni of theft. All the workers start off after her, but only Nina, on her own, finds the accused thief. Much of this park pursuit is shot with POV Steadicam, which adds, especially given the surrounding path and lush greenery, to the dreamlike movement of camera and character (Petzold used Steadicam to similar effect in a park in *Something to Remind Me*). Altogether fairytale-like, Nina comes across a single, abandoned shoe on an antique bridge, reiterating the bridge as a transformational crossing over for Petzold (see the sections on *The State I Am In, Yella,* and *Dreileben*). When Nina retrieves the shoe, she hears Toni sobbing offscreen and descends to find her, again fairy-tale-like, hiding in the bush below the bridge. As in *Cinderella,* Nina gives Toni her shoe (as well as a t-shirt to pull over her torn blouse) and invites her to breakfast.

For breakfast, they come into a clearing in the forest where the camera has located them thus far, a clearing configured to the contemporary world. It is a café amidst a large and loud intersection in the middle of the park whose tumult underscores their idyllic-sylvan encounter. Leaving behind the forest for the clearing anticipates an overall trajectory for Nina, from the forest to paths that lead out of it, a trajectory repeatedly traced in fairy tales. The forest is a central, recurring space in fairy tales, as the place where abandoned children end up for the duration of the tale, only to become stronger as they emerge from it at the end (see the section on *Dreileben*'s use of the woods below). Petzold has said that he initially named Nina "the forest girl" in the script, and he thought of Toni as she who "drives Nina into the city" (Suchsland and Petzold, "Ein Roman hält uns nicht zusammen"). This is, however, a self-improving progressive logic he inverts, or rather that he regards as inverted, by the contemporary world.

The Afterness of National History and the Family   Despite the deployment of fragments of remnant forms (the fairy tale and its forest, the horror film and its bridge to ghosts), Petzold's approach entails not a naïve or nostalgic deployment of these earlier forms. Instead there is a self-conscious awareness, like Bigelow's *Near Dark* or Bogdanovich's *The Last Picture Show*, of one's own late place in the cycle, of coming at the end or after what formerly had firmly grounded individuals and their societies. This prevailing, modernist sense of afterness, as the theorist Gerhard Richter has called it, informs *Ghosts* in its basic formal approach and its themes, even if this tendency is material in all of Petzold's films (Richter, *Afterness*). In *Ghosts*, in fact, Petzold's recurring interest in remnants and the spectral is in many ways radicalized. The entire film is conceived narratively and set spatially in ways that foreground the remnant, the remain, the ghostly, as created by contemporary society. In discussing the basic approach with his former teacher and regular collaborator Farocki, Petzold asserted that he was not so much interested in a conventional plot as in narrative "Nachbeben" or aftershocks; particularly, I would emphasize how past public trauma is intertwined with private loss obtaining into the present (Kreist and Petzold, "Irgendetwas ist nicht in Ordnung"; Schwenk and Petzold 91).

   Ghosts does not tell its story by way of a conventional plot erected on clear cause-and-effect events in a protagonist's pursuing a stated goal, but rather on the aftershocks and/or remnants of such events. Viewers watch what comes after the usual marquee events of film plotting. Without conventional plot exposition, much of the film remains fallout of past events: Nina's orphanage and underemployed wandering in the forest; Toni's numerous thefts at which the plot only hints; and Françoise's long-ago but still reverberating loss of a child. These elements linger to create a sense of afterness—of their remaining, without sublating what has come before, as a ghost might. The economic subtext of the film is similarly structured by a sense of afterness, as Petzold explains: "The economic situation, the world of labor [*Arbeitswelt*] is completely at an end, but [personal] identity still depends on work. In the 1960s and 1970s there was the big narrative of the SPD [Social Democrats, about a middle-class society], but they haven't been able to articulate any new narrative. That all went through my head" (Vahabzadeh, Göttler, and Petzold, "Karneval der Seelen"; he returns to this point much later in Husman and Petzold). The gap between sociopolitical narrative about work and the socioeconomic reality, between individuals' reliance on work for identity and that work's evaporation, is precisely what creates the sense of ghosts throughout much of his work. This attenuation and dissolution of older narratives and identities constitute, as Petzold recounts, the film's prevailing sense of "posthistoire" (Kreist and Petzold, "Irgendetwas ist nicht in Ordnung"), the uneasiness (and, for him, paranoia) that intrudes as the old master narratives (here of identity through work and family) no longer carry legitimacy.

A central instance of this prevailing afterness in *Ghosts* relates to one of the most surprising aspects of the film, namely, its two Francophone actors (Marianne Basler and Aurélien Recoing) among the four principal roles. Although some critics thought that this had to do with the French cofounders of the film, Petzold recounts a number of times that this choice belonged to the initial concept of the film, to a story he had conceived back in his 1989 and 1990 time around Potsdamer Platz in central Berlin (Suchsland and Petzold, "Ein Roman hält uns nicht zusammen")—once again, the tectonic shifts in German and European history inform his cinematic interests and choices, though in subtle and oblique ways. Here, as with the RAF references in *The State I Am In,* (conventional) public history and experience undergird his cinema, even if he approaches it by way of its remains and remnants in our increasingly privately obsessed world. In explaining the French presence in *Ghosts,* he recounts how, in 1989 and 1990, he saw all sorts of people flocking to the crumbling Berlin Wall from around Europe, and he conceived a story about a French journalist from *Libération* who comes to the city to cover the world-historical developments with her family, including a young child who is kidnapped amidst the epochal events.

This story developed in part from a literary parallel. Petzold found the excitement and exuberance about the fall of the Wall—including its curious attraction for the religiously devout flocking there—reminiscent of Heinrich von Kleist's celebrated novella "The Earthquake in Chile" (Suchsland and Petzold).[17] Kleist's novella considers, in a dreamlike style and tone, the impact of the 1647 Santiago earthquake that destroyed all the city's social institutions, including the church, only to have religious fervor assert itself again in what could have been a revolutionary moment. The religious revivalism and mob mentality results in the murder of young parents and the adoption of their orphaned child by a more benevolent survivor of the earthquake and the mob.

The (surprising) grounding of *Ghost's* plot in the fall of the Berlin Wall and the Kleist novella underscores Petzold's engagement with national history and his abiding interest in sociopolitical transitions. Both Kleist and Petzold track how individuals fare in these moments of radical transformation. As Petzold does in *The State I Am In, Ghosts,* and *Yella,* Kleist's novella uses the metaphor of a family to navigate such sociopolitical transitions, although, tellingly, the family is, in all cases, in some form of dissolution and obsolescence. When asked about the family in *The State I Am In,* Petzold said that it interested him because it was becoming as obsolete—as ghostly—as the RAF. In *Ghosts,* similarly, there is within the contemporary social and economic constellation little left of the family—the child is gone, the mother institutionalized, and the father alone in a foreign country seeking to pick up the remains. Here (as in *Yella* and *Jerichow*) it is the remains and remnants of a social structure that become the means by which to explore and locate history and change. As noted above, the implicit continuity between *The State I Am In's* Jeanne and *Ghost's* Nina suggests Nina's orphanage; Toni has no family and, indeed, shows (even violent) aggression toward the mothers in the film; and, in Pierre and Françoise, Petzold offers a portrait of a couple in lonely disarray and decline.

Although Françoise does not seem to blame Pierre for the kidnapping of their daughter, she—like *Cuba Libre*'s Tina, *Something to Remind Me*'s Leyla, or *Jerichow*'s Laura—remains unable to overcome this trauma. As with those women, the past trauma comes to anchor their personalities and remake their persons, though not producing identities grounded so much in melancholic lethargy as a disconcertingly obsessive movement forward. Early in the film, shortly after Pierre retrieves Françoise from the medical facility, Petzold gives the couple a moment of gratitude, warmth, and intimacy, but tellingly, as in *Wolfsburg*, in the movement space of their car. While (typically for Petzold) they do not substantively discuss the important matters at hand, Françoise does say that she is sorry and puts her head on Pierre's shoulder as he drives her to their hotel. In the hotel, however, two scenes offer a bleaker window onto their relationship. In the first, after suspiciously observing Françoise for hints of further flight—from another uncanny, surveillance-like POV from behind a door—Pierre reveals that he has made a business appointment in Berlin with "Professor Bürger," a shadowy business contact about whom viewers never fully learn. Françoise visibly recoils at this news and then asks cryptically if he made the appointment on the way to Berlin. Yes, he answers, at which she looks decidedly unhappy. As in *Wolfsburg*, a family-melodrama scenario (husband picking up his ill wife after lost child) is suddenly reframed as an economic opportunity (business traveling eastward to discuss "printers in Poland").

In this turn in their relationship, Petzold offers yet another example of the molecular interweaving of romantic love and economic undertaking, the shifting grounds of love that subtly arc to align with economic interest. It is in resistance to this corrupting context that Françoise's attachment to her past trauma seems to function. In a second hotel scene, Pierre is preparing to go to the meeting with Bürger. Françoise informs him that she will not accompany him, closing down what seems a clear instrumentalization of her as a wife for business purposes. It is at this moment of sudden resistance and distance between the couple that Françoise glimpses Nina from the hotel window, distinctly interweaving Françoise's obsession with finding Marie with Pierre's own obsession with his business dealings. In fact, she spots Nina from the window at the very moment that Pierre says, trying to convince her to accompany him, "But you like Bürger," another entwining of personal feelings and economic interest. The past trauma, like Tina's or Laura's, is not so much psychological as emotional-economic, with an economics that exacerbates an emotional wound and locates it at the core of personal identity and behavior. As in many of his works, the economic context has compelled the principals, as Françoise does here, to depart the conventional couple or family, a fundamental transition with destinations, emotional and literal, unknown.

Spaces of Afterness: Potsdamer Platz and Environs

Petzold's explanation of *Ghosts'* French characters (and the remnants of their family) highlights the importance of location settings and space in general to the film's conceptualization. I have emphasized the significance of location settings for Petzold's style and narrative throughout his work—evident in his earliest student films like *Eastwards* [*Ostwärts*] and *South* [*Süden*]—and *Ghosts* definitively confirms the centrality of space to his cinema. The film's spaces underpin *Ghosts'* unusual narrative approach of basing a film not on plot but on the (private and public) aftershocks of a plot. For example, in answer to an interviewer's question about how one makes a film with actors but without a plot—"after the plot" would have been the more precise question—Petzold answers: "We met for a week and talked about the stories that are, in the film, already over, and then about Potsdamer Platz, whose story is also over" (Vahabzadeh, Göttler, and Petzold, "Karneval der Seelen"). As his answer implies, *Ghost's* specific locations and its manipulation of space facilitate his reducing the plot while materializing his abiding interest in remnants, remains, and ghosts. He regards space as an expressive medium for depicting the afterness of an event—an approach confirmed by his regular references to Joel Sternfeld's *On This Site: Landscape in Memoriam.* Petzold is fascinated, in the interview herein, by Sternfeld's photographs of scenes of crime after the crime has taken place. Apparently over and done with, these scenes, says Petzold, could at any time explode once again—by embodying simultaneous afterness and the promise of fantasy, such a space holds out the possibility of plot tension even in the absence of standard narrative action.

If, as Petzold suggests, the spaces of Potsdamer Platz figure in lieu of the plot, their deployment remains deliberately elusive and allusive. Almost all of the film's action takes place at or near the Platz. What is particularly unusual in Petzold's approach to Berlin's marquee spaces, however, is his studied avoidance of images that might render the Platz legible to viewers—as he recounts, he rejects postcard views of locations: "I don't like it when filmic settings are initially shot in a long shot like a postcard. The place has to have something to do with the staging! I like it when a place is shown so that one feels a certain disquiet" (Westphal and Petzold). Anyone who knows the Platz (as many Germans would, if only from other media representations) would probably recognize the general setting, but would likely have difficulty pinning down exactly where the principals are in the often-filmed area. Being uncannily lost in what seems familiar territory is a central mechanism of the horror genre that Petzold repeatedly invokes (see the section on *Yella* below). In *Ghosts*, however, the familiarity of this territory also comprises its well-known (public) history, which Petzold renders uncannily both present and absent in the film.

For the historical and present-day Germany, Potsdamer Platz is a thoroughly overdetermined space. Originally an eighteenth-century customs gate, Potsdamer Platz now rests at the geographical heart of the city, approximately halfway between east and west, and is said to have been the busiest urban intersection in the world in the 1920s—it was even host to the first European traffic light (Ladd 118). This epicenter of 1920s European metropolitan modernity and modernism is, however, also very near to where Hitler's chancellery and bunker were located, so the area was reconfigured, first, by the Führer's architects, and then more thoroughly by World War II. After the war, the area was split between the British and Soviet occupational zones, and the Berlin Wall, built in 1961, ran right through it, dividing the Platz, like the larger city, into a cold-war East and West and rendering the seventeen-acre area between Potsdamer Platz and Leipziger Platz a desolate no-man's land. Since the fall of the Wall, the area has become the center of reunified Berlin and Germany's revival. It was the largest construction site in Europe for much of the 1990s and also at the center of a number of political and cultural controversies, controversies that displaced onto architectural questions wider debates about the past and future of Germany.

In choosing Potsdamer Platz and environs as the setting for *Ghosts*, Petzold has made a provocative choice, much like his declaration that Potsdamer Platz's "story is over," such that he set a film about ghosts at a landmark destination ubiquitously hyped for contemporary Berlin. As he says, one could easily make fun of the new, reconstructed Potsdamer Platz, "like [the German comedian] Harald Schmidt, who said it looks as if [the Romanian dictator] Ceausescu, right before his death, had come into a lot of money. But in film, such a place should . . . be taken seriously. Because [this space of Potsdamer Platz] is about transitions [*Übergänge*] and paths [*Gänge*], that should interest one, and not simply as backdrop" (Nord and Petzold, "Mit geschlossenen Augen Hören"). For Petzold, of course, primary among these transitions and paths that fill his work are those that yield globalizing, neoliberal capitalism. The cold-war "void" of Potsdamer Platz served as a battleground for competing "images" of Berlin after the fall of the Wall (Huyssen 62–65). Potsdamer Platz has come to be dominated by corporate interests that bought up the intersection before the city government had even properly appraised the property (Ladd; Huyssen). If the reconstruction of the center of the city was a struggle between images of Berlin, the battle, as Petzold says, is over, with the image of a trendy, corporate contemporary global metropolis—at least at the surface of the image—winning out.

Petzold's depiction of this ground zero of German history pivots on this recent, globalizing makeover (to invoke another recurring theme throughout his work). Wealthy, BMW-driving travelers from France, Pierre and Françoise, inhabit a Potsdamer Platz hotel that is clearly marked as expensive, but also as what Marc Augé calls a "nonplace"—in no way distinct or interesting, an upscale but unidentifiable movement or transit space of the sort Petzold's cinema often invokes, here, tellingly, at the heart of Germany's very particular history. Against the historical ghosts usually invoked in discussing Potsdamer Platz (cf. Ladd)—ghosts that confirm the importance of place to collective memory (Casey 186)—Petzold conjures instead ghosts created by the processes and practices of the contemporary world. Like these nonplaces, his ghosts are oblivious to history, no matter how proximate or relevant—the private interests of these spectral characters downplay and overwhelm any engagement with Berlin's public histories. One finds in Petzold's Potsdamer Platz a deliberate staging of something that both Walter Benjamin and Alexander Kluge (another important influence on Petzold) have emphasized: the assault of the present moment on (an understanding of) the rest of time. Nina and Toni wander around these historically overburdened spaces without even acknowledging, let alone engaging, the many historical *Schaustellen* (viewing sights) that have been staged for visitors. They have, instead, other preoccupations, like food, clothes, and a coming casting call.

A characteristic sequence in this spatial manipulation and the private downgrading of public history is the narrative turning point of the film: a six-minute sequence at the exact midpoint of the eighty-minute film, when Françoise first speaks with Nina. Having caught a glimpse of Nina and Toni from her hotel window, Françoise runs to catch up with the two young women. Echoing the apparel theme of "The Burial Shirt," Nina and Toni have shoplifted some clothes (revising a scenario and setting from *The State I Am In*), and Nina runs from Françoise, thinking she is a store detective. The space in which Françoise finally confronts them is open, flat, and austere, but here this openness and flatness abuts an architecturally imposing building in a neoclassical style, with the bullet holes and shrapnel damage from the 1940s bombings and Battle of Berlin still visible (via deliberate close-up; figure 12). These shots are unusual because most of *Ghosts'* images of Potsdamer Platz feature only its rebuilt, corporate-financed architecture—this building, the Martin-Gropius-Bau, is one of the few classical buildings in the vicinity with remnant scars from Germany's wars. Even as the shot invokes this history in close-up, the building remains fragmented and elusive, like viewers' perspective on this space in general.

Despite the proximity of this prominent public history, viewers are never offered a conventional establishing shot, never afforded a vantage point on this looming building or its monumental history. Detailing the long-ago kidnapping of Marie, Françoise informs Nina that two identifying marks, a scar from a childhood accident and a mole between the shoulder blades, would identify her as her lost daughter—a powerful private memory that momentarily overwhelms Germany's most painful public history. The notion of an identifying scar from long ago seems a reference to the great chronicle of travel, history, and memory, Homer's *Odyssey*. Another Hitchcockian reframing, however, interrupts this *Odyssey*-echoing reconciliation and reunion. Toni has been observing with suspicion Françoise's emotional plea to Nina and suddenly steals Françoise's wallet, at which point both young women run. For the moment, the potentially melodramatic reunion has been reframed by Toni's economic need and criminal proclivities (when Nina asks her why she did it, she says, "Because we're hungry, and she's wearing Prada," to extend Petzold's clothing theme). The sequence is remarkable for setting the watershed encounter about Françoise's past next to a building that invokes Germany's past—the scars of the building matching the scars on Marie and Nina—but the private traumas of Françoise and Toni eclipse the public history all around them.

To comprehend Petzold's self-consciously elliptical approach to private memory and public history, it helps to clarify another vector intersecting *Ghosts*. This recasting of history and memory via space resonates with the so-called Berlin film, a staple of German cinema at

Figure 12. Nina (Julia Hummer) in front
of the Martin-Gropius building, damaged
in World War II, in *Ghosts* (2002).

least since the 1920s, and its own navigation of private interests and
public history. Since the fall of the Wall, there has been a renewed wave
of Berlin films to accompany the city's physical makeover. This included
many films that deliberately market the glamour of the renovated city, a
surfeit of quasi-advertisements about Berlin as having arrived as a global
corporate metropolis (Ganeva; Mennel, *Cities and Cinema*). Following
the 1990s cinema of consensus, many of these post-*Wende* Berlin films
downplay the complex public history and politics implied by Berlin,
opting instead to focus on the private individual and individualistic au-
tonomy (Ganeva; Clarke)—precisely these mainstream films marketing
the metropolis manifest the processes upon which Petzold reflects in
his elusive depiction of public history and its transformation.

    Much as Petzold's cinema seems to harken back to the politically
engaged New German Cinema, *Ghosts* contravenes the 1990s films by
resurrecting remnants that predate them. Petzold mentions explicitly
working against this wave of big-budget, celebratory Berlin films, declar-
ing that he would much rather make a small-budget film that seriously
engages with the city; indeed, critics took *Ghosts* as a clear cinematic
shot across the bow of the mainstream 1990s Berlin film (Suchsland and
Petzold, "Ein Roman hält uns nicht zusammen"; Kreist and Petzold,
"Irgendetwas ist nicht in Ordnung"). In this contestation of the Berlin

film, Petzold demonstrates a sustained level of savvy about, and critique of, other media and films—the various "neighborhoods" of German media, as he puts it.

In *Ghosts*, in fact, Petzold offers one of his most self-reflexive ruminations on the media environment around him. In her meandering around Berlin, Toni has been planning to attend a "casting," an audition for a television show entitled, fittingly for the themes of the film, *Friends.* Casting scenarios have played an important role in other films of the Berlin School, like Thomas Arslan's *A Fine Day* (*Der schöne Tag*; 2001), and they tend to emphasize the necessity of performance and theatricality in modern life (see Webber; Mitchell). Her initial plans to go there with an unseen woman named Susanne seem to have fallen through for unexplained reasons—another hint of afterness of other, obscured events—so Toni decides to shoplift clothes for the audition and bring Nina as a late substitute. For the show's audition, they are supposed to explain the origins of their friendship, and Toni has been preparing an outlandish story about their first encounter, because, in front of such people, she says, you have to say "the most wild [*lebendig*] things."

When they arrive at the casting after having stolen Françoise's wallet, Nina is clearly uncomfortable, even morose, first in the waiting area and then in front of the director. Nina sits with a downcast and absent gaze while Toni tries to recall her ridiculous story about their meeting on a sailboat on a Dutch lake. When his staff whispers that these two are a waste of time, the director asks to hear from Nina. After desperate encouragement from Toni and a stuttering start, she gives a long monologue—a remarkable five straight minutes, from a woman who has been almost entirely silent about herself up until this point. She recounts how, in "always the same dream," she "had dreamt of Toni before she knew her." The monologue is shot in three shots plus the occasional reaction shot of the director and his staff, who are slowly pulled into Nina's entrancing recounting of their friendship, in which making an acquaintance is emphatically after—after the fantasy and dream of that acquaintance. In her dream, Nina follows a dog she had always wanted to a car. Near the car, she hears screaming coming from a forest, where she sees Toni being raped by two men. In this repeating dream, the men do everything to Toni, but Toni just stares away, out at Nina, who, despite wanting to intervene, cannot, and this is when she wakes up.

Nina then segues (apparently) to the reality of her life, to always being sent to new foster parents, to new schools, to new classes. In each class, she says, there was always a queen who did everything just right, and "in the new class," Toni was this queen, the most beautiful Nina had ever seen and the same person of whom Nina had repeatedly dreamt. Like everyone else, Nina wanted to be Toni's friend, but Toni was never even aware of her, though once she dropped a glove and Nina returned it to her, and she smiled before turning and walking away.

This description cannot adequately convey the otherworldy character of Petzold's text and Julia Hummer's remarkable performance of it, which Petzold praises effusively, calling the scene his favorite in his films. The monologue manages, like a mise-en-abyme for the whole film, to limn the blurry boundary between dream and waking worlds, to show how behaviors in reality are contiguous with and indeed driven by dreams and fantasies. Nina might be making up the story of their friendship, as Toni had made up her own story for the director, but Nina's story nonetheless explains assorted mysterious aspects of the film. There are fragmentary links to the film thus far, especially to the forest and its function, to Nina's witnessing Toni being attacked there, to Pierre and Françoise's sun-roofed car, and even Nina's finding Toni's shoe on the bridge and returning it to her. As in Jeanne and Heinrich's fantasy of the Villa Stahl in *The State I Am In* and much of Yella's fantasy in *Yella,* Petzold explores how people's desires and fantasies become behaviorally productive—in fact, like fantasies, they serve as such a stark driving force that their diegetic status as mere dream or fantasy becomes unclear. The fact that the diegetic status of these desires and fantasies is unclear—are they "real" or not?—underscores their power and pertinence for Petzold's characters, who live the putative fantasy like reality. Living fantasy as reality is especially true of ghosts, who are often unaware of their own spectral status and strive (as Françoise, Nina, and Toni all do) to break through to normality.

As with Jeanne and Heinrich in *The State I Am In,* these fantasies and the utopian energies they indicate have political repercussions, although often in unconventional ways. The same is true of Yella, then Thomas and Laura in *Jerichow,* as well as Johannes and Ana in *Dreileben* and Barbara in *Barbara*: even as it indicates the potential for the productivity of yearning, the demonstrable power of desire and fantasy becomes corrupted, most often by economic interest and need. Nina's dream and its aftermath here surprise the viewer in part because it recalls how Nina, who has remained something of a cipher in her inscrutable desires, has her own vivid fantasy life that underscores how her relation to Toni is, in its own way, exploitative. Toni has clearly exploited Nina, in the most bald manner, from their first encounter: using her for a literal shirt off her back, a café breakfast, a shower in her room, and then as an unwilling accomplice to shoplifting and casting. But Nina's astonishing monologue underscores how Toni functions in Nina's fantasy intimately and always for Nina as well. Petzold has repeatedly emphasized this structure of mutual emotional-economic exploitation—one of Fassbinder's great themes—in discussing the film (Hitzemann and Petzold).

In the wake of the audition, the last sequence of the film suggests one of Petzold's very few happier, if not altogether happy, endings. Nina, having so impressed the director, is invited to a party at his house. In a red-lit room with a DJ, Toni invites Nina to dance, an apparent reward for her remarkable performance in the audition. Marco Abel persuasively emphasizes the physicality of this moment, with its low electronic beats and then overwhelming red (Abel, "Imaging Germany" 273). The scene recalls, I would emphasize, the scene in which Jeanne visits Achim's daughter Paulina in *The State I Am In.* Both scenes seem to hold the promise of bubble spaces, as Petzold calls them—of a space away and all to one's self, a private utopia from which departure is invariably painful. But in both cases, these spaces are reframed by the gaze of the other: in *The State I Am In,* by Jeanne's mother Clara, and here, by the director Oliver, who is watching the unlikely couple from the brightly lit room next door. Via eyeline matches, Petzold shows that Toni, even as she dances and embraces Nina, recognizes the gaze of the director and subsequently performs for him, first her desire for Nina, and then more overtly leaving Nina altogether to join him. When Nina awakens the next morning, apparently having slept with Toni—more ambiguous afterness—Toni has disappeared from their makeshift bed in order to, as Oliver's angry wife informs a perplexed Nina, fuck her husband.

Likely recognizing how Toni has used her to promote her "career," Nina boards a municipal streetcar in the middle of the forest and rides back to Potsdamer Platz. She revisits the resonant settings from earlier in the film: the corner where Françoise first observed them from her hotel, through the shopping center where Françoise put her hand on her shoulder, down the tree-lined street where she ran with the shoplifted clothes, and then back to the Martin-Gropius-Bau (although viewers still do not see it in a conventional establishing shot). Françoise is back there as well, apparently waiting for Nina to return to the scene of Toni's crime. Revisiting these spaces recalls the film's use of space to compensate how little happens plotwise. Such an approach to the afterness of space corresponds to Petzold's admiring citation of Sternfeld's *On This Site: Landscape in Memoriam*—empty spaces erupt again after the marquee crime. When Nina divulges to Françoise that she, indeed, has the heart-shaped mole, Françoise takes Nina back to her hotel for breakfast, inverting Nina's taking Toni to breakfast near the film's opening.

At this point of apparent resolution and happiness, however, Pierre suddenly intervenes. He comes to the hotel restaurant and retrieves Françoise, whose willingness to be separated from Nina seems to suggest that this use of a stranger to relive a phantasmatic reunion has happened repeatedly before. Françoise furtively asks Pierre to give Nina money, but Nina refuses, saying that she wants to go "to my mama," at which Pierre informs her huskily that Marie is dead. His intervention reveals, for Nina, that Françoise has chosen a series of teenaged girls as ersatz Maries in a desperate fantasy of maternal redemption. The Grimms' "Burial Shirt" theme returns, but only, as with many of Petzold's mythical and generic fragments, to be refunctioned. With Pierre's wallet out, Françoise's excessive mourning seems just another instance of emotional exploitation and (conspicuously monetary) exchange (figure 13). Their wealth insulates them from the renunciation of mourning that the fairy tale pedantically demands of its grieving mother, another transformation and transition realized in, and due to, contemporary capitalism. Their money funds the repetition of this joyful reunion, no matter its toll on the emotionally exploited young women.

In its concluding moments, *Ghosts* also revisits many fairy tales' trajectory of the child leaving the forest, recasting the recurring story to register historical change. Once she has refused Pierre's paying her to play in Françoise's fantasy, Nina, the "forest-girl," as Petzold called her, returns to the wooded Tiergarten. There she happens upon the same garbage can into which Toni had discarded Françoise's wallet. In the wallet, Nina finds a mockup of what Marie would look like as she aged

Figure 13. Pierre (Aurélien Recoing) with his wallet out to pay Nina (Julia Hummer) in *Ghosts* (2002).

"naturally"—the computer-aided "phantom pictures" that Petzold came across in northern French post offices. Upon seeing the resemblance between the computer-calculated adolescent Marie and Nina, viewers could well imagine, even fantasize, a sentimental ending in which Nina convinces Pierre that she might indeed be Marie, an ending that would conform to a mainstream, lost-child melodrama formula. But instead, Nina simply and quickly throws the wallet and its pictures back in the garbage can and walks away into the verdant plenitude of the park. It is an act of liberation, as Petzold calls it (Schenk and Petzold, "Christian Petzolds *Gespenster*"). Revealingly, *Ghosts* is the only film of the trilogy (or, indeed, of a string of seven of his films) not to offer a vehicular conclusion. Schooled in the emotional exploitation that Petzold emphasizes above, Nina rejects this late-capitalist fantasy of the redemptive encounter with the random stranger: she rejects the cash it might bring, the luxury-car ride it might offer, and walks instead back into the forest. Petzold, in fact, compares it, in yet another fragmentary deployment of genre, to the Westerns he often cites—everything is lost, and yet she goes on, walking off alone and silent (Suchsland and Petzold, "Ein Roman hält uns nicht zusammen"). Nina's quiet gesture of turning away, in an eerily quiet park at the center of Germany's most boisterous metropolis, is one of refusal—refusal to get in the car, to accept compensatory cash, or to vest the stranger with a misplaced, inevitably exploitative fantasy. And, with that refusal, she stays within the fairy-tale forest of self-discovery and fantasy, rebuffing Berlin's recent transitions and transformations.

Yella: Love and Failure in the Age of Neobliberalism

The final film of the Ghost trilogy, *Yella* (2007) opens with a scene and scenario similar to one I highlighted in *The State I Am In*: the crossing of a border, likewise near a river, that marks a boundary rapidly fading. As in *The State I Am In,* the waning physical border hints at both a transformative historical context and the boundary between fantasy and reality. In a medium shot, viewers see the eponymous heroine of the film, played by Petzold regular Nina Hoss, on a speeding train. Yella/Hoss, who won a Silver Bear at the Berlin Film Festival for her performance, is changing out of a more formal red blouse and skirt into a plain pullover and jeans. Yella, viewers soon learn, is returning from a job interview in the former West Germany to her former–East German hometown of Wittenberge. Like the border crossing itself, this small-city setting revisits an earlier moment in Petzold's cinema, resurfacing after the fact: in *Something to Remind Me,* Hoss's Leyla—a notable anagram of Yella—crosses from western Stuttgart through Wittenberge. In *Yella,* however, the overall direction and the protagonist's trajectory are the opposite. Yella may be returning east, but only temporarily, as she is in the midst of migrating westward, for economic opportunities no longer on offer in her hometown.

Yella's return to this geography, to this town, and even, in some form, to this character indicates Petzold's decision to focus in more deliberate fashion on the fallout of the 1989–90 end of East Germany. As with his work in general, however, the engagement with a national event opens onto a more fundamental examination of how contemporary economy, society, and culture are remaking individuals at the most intimate level of desire and fantasy. If *Pilots* and *The Sex Thief* foreground women workers who cannot stop moving, *Yella* focuses on a more directed, if likewise familiar, economic migratory pattern: a young bookkeeper fleeing her hometown in the former East for the West—fleeing, viewers soon discover, both a failed business and failing marriage. Yella has landed, she informs her father, a "job—in a good firm," but her former romantic and business partner, Ben, insists on driving her to the train for the first day of her western work. Soon, in a scene I examine below, he drives them off a bridge and into a river. Yella apparently drags herself from the water and continues to the train and on to her job, on which the rest of the film then focuses.

The basic parameters of this story are modeled on the horror cult-classic *Carnival of Souls* (dir. Herk Harvey; 1961), which also follows a female economic migrant, Mary, in the wake of a vehicular plunge off a bridge. *Carnival of Souls* is based in turn on a short story by Ambrose Bierce, "An Occurrence at Owl Creek Bridge," set in a very different (U.S. Civil War) milieu that likewise traces desire and delusion in the moments before death. As in "Owl Creek" or *Carnival,* Petzold's Yella does not realize that she has been fatally injured, and so most of all three narratives unfold as a final fantasy of the expiring. In the interview in this volume, Petzold discusses his long-term interest in *Carnival of Souls,* starting in the late 1980s and reaffirmed in the mid-1990s, and *Yella* follows even more closely the parameters of its generic model than *The State I Am In* and *Ghosts,* both of which also reflect the influence of the horror genre.

It is remarkable that Petzold's third film of the trilogy is the one that is closest to its generic model, confirming his abiding interest in what genre films can offer art-house cinema. Here, again, one finds a non-nostalgic archeology of genre, in which Petzold excavates fragments, mechanisms, and effects for his own ends. This recurring and sustained interest in genre keeps him at some distance from the other films of the Berlin School, at whose forefront Petzold is usually regarded. In *Yella,* he exhumes aspects of horror's generic grammar as well as some of its most efficacious methods, but with a different purpose. Compared to *Carnival,* the horror in *Yella* is the degree to which contemporary capitalism infiltrates the individual such that his or her most intimate desires, dreams, and fantasies are consistently interwoven with the economic—another sort of boundary crossing in this film full of them. While Petzold has previously explored how economy can impinge on desire (from *Pilots* on) and fantasy (*The State I Am In, Ghosts*), *Yella* radicalizes this insight by showing how even the most intimate, dying wishes of its protagonist express themselves primarily economically.

Although Petzold was born and raised in western West Germany, his parents were refugees from points much farther east. As a child, in fact, he made regular trips with them to East Germany to visit relatives and for vacation (Nord and Petzold, "Ich wollte, dass die DDR Farben Hat"). Moreover, his 1980s West Berlin residence made him, as the Potsdamer-Platz basis for *Ghosts* makes clear, a front-row observer to the momentous 1989 fall of the Wall and the 1990 "unification" of Germany, world-historical events that, within days, irrevocably changed Berlin, Germany, and Europe. In the interview in this volume, Petzold provocatively declares that, for him, the failure of East Germany was the failure of all of Germany—the "complete failure" of the notion of a counter-state to the Nazi period and a leftist counter-idea for all of Germany, an economic and political failure with which Petzold has been thoroughly engaged in his more recent work.

Within the context of his career, *Yella* thus seems a milestone. It marks a systematic engagement with these watershed events of Petzold's life: the fall of the Wall and the rapid, often painful fusion of the two Germanys. He has continued to explore the former East and former West in his three more recent films, *Jerichow, Dreileben: Beats Being Dead*, and *Barbara.* Given his abiding interest in afterness—in remnants, ruins, and ghosts—it is fitting that he turned to these topics over a decade after they transpired. In the interview herein, Petzold speaks about the confusing time in which he and his colleagues (including his friend, the fellow Berlin School director Thomas Arslan) struggled to come to terms with the epochal events of 1989–90. (Petzold's own short film *Ostwärts* [*Eastwards*] was, he recounts, an early nonfiction attempt.) But in the end, he says, he felt that one had to live with this confusion, with this "balance situation," rather than run out and rerecord the stereotypical images of people celebrating on the crumbling Wall. The inklings in *Something to Remind Me* and then the more sustained engagement of *Yella* underscore how Petzold lived in this "balance situation" for many years, although it is notable that *The State I Am In* is also about the failure of leftist discourses and the wide wake they leave for individuals who live these utopian impulses after their time seems to have passed. *Yella,* as he recounts herein, takes up the events at which they only had an inkling at that 1989–90 moment: the transformation of a socialist state that (officially) manifests such utopian impulses into a neoliberal state. It is another passage and transformation in a cinema replete with them, one realized in the migration and longing of a young woman heading westward.

When the eastern German Democratic Republic was absorbed by the western Federal Republic of Germany, it was the first time in history that a capitalist country merged with a socialist country. Although East Germany had been a model economy for the Soviet-dominated Warsaw Pact, it was geographically and culturally closest to the West, and many of its citizens, not least through western television reaching across its border and regular visitors between East and West, had a strong sense of West German capitalism and consumerism, some of it doubtless illusionary. The heady euphoria of those days in 1989 and 1990 quickly gave way to economic and social despair in much of the former East Germany. While the other former Warsaw Pact countries rebuilt their economies (primarily) on their own, East Germany's was (largely) taken over by West Germany. The Treuhand Anstalt, charged with privatizing East German assets, sold some 85 percent of the businesses it privatized to West German companies (Petzold has mentioned his low opinion of the Treuhand Anstalt in interviews; see Peitz and Petzold, "Wir haben Sterne ohne Himmel"). The tremendous inflow of western capital and labor led to the rapid physical renovation of many East German cities and towns, but it simultaneously resulted in extremely high local unemployment. For instance, of the roughly four million jobs the Treuhand controlled (in a country of only around eighteen million residents, including high numbers of retirees and children), nearly three million were cut.

Such economic devastation resulted, predictably, in massive migration westward, as unemployment in former West Germany remained much lower than in the former East. Petzold recounts how an industrial town like Wittenberge typified these trends: partially renovated, it had, by Petzold's estimate, a real unemployment rate over 50 percent and its population shrunk by over a third (Göttler). In *Yella*, he takes up this socioeconomic constellation by engaging a related phenomenon, the migration of women from the former East into former West Germany. Unemployment in East Germany hit women workers disproportionately hard (see Biendarra 467), and, for Petzold, this was one of the key occasions for revisiting his late 1980s and early 1990s interest in *Carnival of Souls*:

> [W]hen I started making films in [the former East Germany] . . . I discovered the mythological location of so many German legends—the

river landscapes, etc.—as a place abandoned by the women who used to live there. All the women gone: this was the first moment when I thought, this is movement, this is an image, and I can make a film about this! Then I watched Fritz Lang's *The Blue Gardenia* (1953), for I was always curious about these women who, in the 1930s in the U.S., live together in large urban environments. . . . And I thought: where did all the girls from the former East Germany go? Which dreams do they have? . . . And when you watch John Ford films, you notice how women always seem to sit in the front of the stagecoaches. Of course it is the men on whom the films focus—they fight, shoot, scream—but it is the women who are the real agents of movement. . . . And this was the starting point for Yella. (Abel and Petzold; cf. Kreist and Petzold, "Wracks Mit Geschichte")

The passage is telling for Petzold's cinema because it connects a socioeconomic observation about the contemporary moment to both the "mythological location of so many German legends" (see the sections on *Ghosts* and *Dreileben*) as well as to Hollywood genre films (the crime thriller/noir and the Western). With *Yella,* his archeological excavation of *Carnival of Souls* includes the image of a female protagonist who becomes increasingly spectral in her economic migration to the (U.S.) West. Although made with low production values that frequently tend to camp—the acting is at many points painful to watch—*Carnival* has become a favorite among cinephiles because it maps, in remarkable location settings in Salt Lake City, a familiar story onto the socioeconomic phenomenon that Petzold foregrounds. The young woman on the road, an "agent of movement," seeks a job and eludes some men while falling into the arms of a largely fantastical, ghostly other.

As discussed in *The Sex Thief, Ghosts*, and *The State I Am In,* Petzold's characters are often described as psychologically and spatially adrift—or sleepwalking, as one critic put it (Zander). But, especially in his work after *Ghosts,* this drift of his characters is also deliberately mapped over carefully charted settings of economic unevenness. Indeed, many of these films engage with what the geographers Neil Smith and David Harvey have termed "uneven geographical development," the phrase with which they analyze those processes usually called "globalization" (Smith; Fisher, "Globalization as Uneven Geographical Development"). Smith and Harvey regard globalization not as a qualitatively different phenomenon but rather as the accelerated remaking of space by capital flows. Harvey argues, for instance, that concentrating on unevenness in geographical development—attending to how these capital flows unevenly remake spaces and the individuals within them—illuminates fundamental aspects of our contemporary world, including un- and underemployment and increasing migration (Harvey, *Spaces of Hope* 64–65). In the films since *Ghosts*, Petzold's characters move in deliberate and revealing ways over this uneven geography. In an interview about *Yella*, for instance, he foregrounds the gap between East German cities (expensively renovated with capital from western Germany—"lighthouses," in the parlance of Germany's unification) and the depressed, dilapidated suburbs around them; it is precisely this sort of gap the film explores (Kreist and Petzold, "Wracks mit Geschichte").

The remarkable opening ten minutes of *Yella* depict this uneven geographical development and the migration it galvanizes by way of the ruins of both spaces and people. While many mainstream films might start with the protagonist waking and dressing for the day, *Yella* starts (typically for Petzold) in medias res, with Yella's dressing down in the opening sequence as the landscape blurs by her train window, another of his many shallow-focus movement spaces. She changes into her nondescript, casual clothes to blend into Wittenberge's depressed economic condition. In earlier Petzold works (*The Sex Thief, The State I Am In, Ghosts*), the changing of clothes—its implied self-promoting makeover—underscores how economy remakes the body of individuals, but in the opening moments of *Yella*, viewers see a woman self-consciously concealing the transformative neoliberal body that Petzold emphasizes; later, when she returns for her new western job, she will don her distinguishing red blouse and professional skirt again. Yella's self-conscious manipulation of her body highlights what David Harvey, following Donna Haraway, has called the deployment of a new kind of laboring body, namely, the body itself as an accumulation strategy (Harvey, *Spaces of Hope* 97–116). Individuals are increasingly aware of the body as a key interface with capital, thus the ubiquitous obsession with resume-padding capabilities and muscle-toning exercise. Like much of Hitchcock's *Marnie*, which Petzold cites as another important influence (Peitz and Petzold, "Wir haben Sterne ohne Himmel"), Yella's changing of clothes recasts a potentially voyeuristic view upon the body into an economic one. The gaze upon this female body witnesses its transformation into an appendage of capital itself (Harvey, *Spaces of Hope* 97–99).

Yella's new beginning and reinvention of (her)self, typically for Petzold, transpires in an emphatic afterness, built on the ruins and remnants of a shattered dream. Viewers learn on her walk home from the train station that she has an estranged husband, Ben, from whom she is at pains to keep her distance. He says, as he stalks her on a dilapidated street, that he can see from her walk that she has a new job, "indeed, a good one," underscoring the economic recasting of her body (as well as the repeated importance of walking in Petzold's films; see the section on *Something to Remind Me*). At one point, he has to draw closer to Yella due to a construction site on his side of the street; to his pleas shortly thereafter, however, she answers curtly that the "construction site is over." Beyond banishing Ben, the declaration seems a clear reference to the stuttering reconstruction of East Germany, which, for her in her westward trajectory, is indeed over.

Petzold has commented that, with *Yella*, he had in mind the destruction of a collective existence and essence (*Gemeinwesen*), uprooting entire social worlds (Kreist and Petzold, "Wracks mit Geschichte"). This kind of transformation and destruction is vividly conveyed in the rest of the film's first fifteen minutes, in which viewers see the newly employed Yella interact with Ben and with her father, including in her childhood home. Despite the ubiquity of movement and transit spaces in his films—as in Yella's opening train ride and train station, respectively—it is frequently overlooked how many of Petzold's films feature such emotionally vested places on the precipice of destruction (*The Sex Thief, Jerichow*, even *The State I Am In*). Many of his films offer childhood homes shot and staged to emphasize their meaning for a protagonist who is about to depart it, literally and emotionally. Upon returning home, Yella finds her father outside in warm, hazy summer sun. The openness of their house, the verdant landscape surrounding it, and a lingering hug with her father all emphasize the contiguity of intimate place with her inner emotional life. In the morning before she is to depart to the former West, perhaps for good, Petzold shoots her father peeling an orange for her in an extreme close-up that suggests, given the acting, that the father has done this for her many times. The personal meaning of these details is confirmed throughout the rest of the film because these quiet, poignant images of home and family serve as what Freud called the *Tagesreste* (fragmentary remains from the day) for Yella's fatal flashback. Petzold recounts that the Freudian dreamwork hung over his desk while he was writing, emphasizing the *Tagesreste* elements that Yella's expiring mind transforms in her dreams and fantasies (Kreist and Petzold, "Wracks mit Geschichte").

Throughout the flashback-fantasy that takes over the film after this opening, Petzold has emphasized that he was fascinated by hewing not only close to Yella's visual perspective, but also even sticking close to her subjective perceptions (Kilb). A notable exception to Yella's perspective in this opening of the film, however, hints at the fragments of genre Petzold excavates for *Yella,* particularly those of horror. One of the key aspects of horror that informs *Yella* builds on the genre's consistent manipulation of the interplay between gender and point of view. Horror functions, as a number of scholars have observed, as a "body genre," one that deliberately spectacularizes the body under extreme duress and subsequent sensations (Clover; Williams, "Film Bodies"). It is the body of a soon-to-be-victimized woman, frequently depicted in the convulsive throes of terror, that anticipates horror (Williams, "Film Bodies" 142–44). This privileging of the female body intersects horror's normally male-gendered monsters (Neale, *Genre* 61; Jancovich).

Petzold foregrounds the body of Yella, transforming it into an accumulation strategy, but he also subjects it to many of these horror-genre mechanisms. When Yella arrives in her hometown, the film abruptly cuts to a handheld shot that emphasizes the point of view of someone viewers do not see or know yet, observing Yella menacingly from afar (figure 14). The point of view is that of her estranged husband, Ben, in a deliberate point-of-view shot from the male predator's perspective. This familiar gendering is a threat from the earliest horror films—one critic identifies it as a crucial technical marker of the horror film in general (Jancovich 5). Petzold has discussed how this effect, a fragment of the horror genre, was formative for him:

> When I was eighteen I saw John Carpenter's *Halloween* (1978). That was a major filmic event for me, which left its mark on me to this day. It's a film with mental, subjective images as well as objective ones; their alternation creates the sensation of horror. You never really know

whether what is on screen is objective or subjective. And sometimes the possessor of the gaze suddenly steps into what appears as a point-of-view shot, thus appearing as an object, not subject, in front of the camera. This comes as a shock every time anew. I think this really formed me. Hitchcock does this frequently as well. (Abel and Petzold)

After locating Yella's husband within the general grammar of horror, Petzold turns him into even more of a monster. Following the somewhat sentimental scene of her father peeling a farewell orange, Yella hears what she thinks is the taxi, which turns out to be—another horror cliché—her stalker-husband in its place. Ben insists on driving her to the train, but this ostensible kindness turns quickly cruel. The failure of a business they had started together has led her to leave him. He grows increasingly agitated and aggressive as he recounts the dizzying devaluation of the bankrupt business's assets. When she resists reading a new business plan he offers, he grabs her hair and wrenches her head back and forth ("When there's no more money, the pretty Yella wants out, goes to Hannover, interviews, shows the pretty legs, and dumb Ben sits on the ruins"). In short order, in the most terrifying of the many car scenes Petzold has shot, Ben then drives her off the bridge in an (apparent) murder-suicide.

In their openings, *The State I Am In* and *Ghosts* offer serene idyllic spaces—the lovely Portuguese coast and the verdant Berlin park, respectively—that are then interrupted by robberies, economic desperation wrecking an idyll fleetingly depicted. In *Yella,* as in *Jerichow,* it is the details of failed businesses that reframe and revoke the idyllic opening. The estranged husband-monster reminds how the story of Yella's reinvention of herself is built on the rubble of a past failure. The triumph of Yella's new position—"indeed, a good one" and "in a good firm"—is recontextualized within the larger mechanisms of the economy, which, in the former East Germany, dovetail with the world-historical events detailed above. Petzold's interest in remnants and remains intersects here with the kind of creative destruction that David Harvey, following classical economic theorists like Joseph Schumpeter, also highlight as central to capitalism (Harvey, *Spaces of Hope* 69). Petzold depicts this economic volatility with the fragments of the horror genre: in *Yella*'s carnival of bankrupt souls, the horror-film monster

Figure 14. A horror-film point-of-view shot
from Ben's Range Rover in *Yella* (2007).

is a destructive ghost generated by the cycles of dizzying boom and
ultimate bust. Ben's failure dramatically—and scarily—contextualizes
Yella's reinvention of herself. In the front seats of an aging Range
Rover, the horror genre is mapped onto globalization, with *Yella's*
haunting specter turning out to be a ghost in the machine of contemporary capitalism.

Given this creative destruction, it is not a surprise that Yella's fantasy
after their fatal plunge begins with a first day of work. The "good" job,
at "a good firm," lands her at the evocatively named Alpha Wings, at
the Hanover Expo grounds (as Petzold notes, this is where capitalism
built "its own Documenta," referring to the enormous German art show,
"with an aesthetic of glass and steel ruins" [Peitz and Petzold, "Wir haben
Sterne ohne Himmel"]). But, in line with such a creative-destructive
aesthetic, the company is already being dismantled at the very moment
of her arrival: laborers remove computers, a walkie-talkie–wielding security guard prowls the premises, and her supervisor is left to loiter outside
near symmetrically parked luxury cars. He is calling a taxi because he
has been banned from the building and banished from his company
car, an ontologically consequent car-ejection familiar from *Wolfsburg*.
Petzold's pointed use of the movement spaces of the car becomes all
the starker when one has to walk.

These images of the rubble of a contemporary office recall the ruins of Franziska's translation company ("The Translator") that Petzold offered viewers in *The Sex Thief* and even in the sale of the Blue Eyes cosmetics firm in *Pilots*. All focus on the constant creative-destructive churn of capital, labor, and entire companies in capitalism. In these films, the economic foundations under the feet of a female protagonist crumble, leaving her scrambling to traverse a remade economic landscape, not least because, as Petzold has observed, "the men still own the companies, and the women have to do the work" (Abel and Petzold).

Housed in the Hotel Yella had been warned about the crumbling condition of her future employer, Alpha Wings, the evening before when she met another business traveler, Philip. As Yella sits alone in an eerily (under)lit hotel restaurant/bar—a portrait in neoliberal loneliness—Philip is working on his laptop nearby. He suddenly asks her if she is interested in financial statements, certainly one of the more memorable pickup lines in German cinema history. Petzold's films are full of this kind of obliquely erotic encounters with strangers, especially toward the beginnings of the plots, from Tom's with Jimmy in *Cuba Libre* to Nina's with Toni in *Ghosts* and Thomas's with Ali in *Jerichow*. The relationships that grow out of these chance encounters become the most important in the films and usually result in a kind of a noir-like alliance around money.

These unexpected encounters consistently result in a similarly fantastical negotiation of Petzold's many resonant spaces. The spaces of Petzold's films are often symptomatic of the creative destruction detailed above, of capitalism's remaking of space to render it more open and, as far as socioeconomic flows go, frictionless (Fisher, "Globalization as Uneven Geographical Development"). Such open and frictionless movement spaces are key aspects of many of the spaces in these films, contrasting to a second type of more conventional space that the films sketch, namely, the many forests (see the sections on *Ghosts* and *Dreileben*) as well as the private house. The most important of the former, frictionless spaces for Petzold's cinema is that of the road and the car on it, each a monad for how capitalism recasts space in its own image to allow for the free flow of capital (Fisher, "Globalization as Uneven Geographical Development"). Beyond the road, however, there is another transit space symptomatic of this frictionless contrast to the private house, one that recurs in many other films of the Berlin School and that comes up as early as *Pilots* in Petzold's work: the hotel.

Although some have discussed the hotel as a liminal space between public and private (Matthias; Biendarra), the hotels of the Berlin School films tend to manifest instead an abiding tension between personally meaningful place and what theorists have termed "abstract space," the kind of open and frictionless space discussed above (see Fisher, "Hotels"). Another key influence that Petzold has mentioned for *Yella*— even after he had *Carnival of Souls* and Bierce in mind—was reading Marc Augé's book on "nonplaces" of the contemporary world, including the global proliferation of nondescript, unlocatable spaces like airport lounges. At the core of this notion is the manner in which largely abstract and abstracting economic processes increasingly dominate the planning and living of human spaces, as Henri Lefebvre has influentially argued (Lefebvre 104). The question for Petzold's films, however, is how mobile characters negotiate such abstract spaces, and it is here that the space of the hotel serves these films particularly well. The intersections of transportation, traffic, and nonplaces are perfectly reflected in the transit space of the hotel, which houses travelers not in chaotic guest-house charm, but organizes them in fastidiously numbered rooms (depicted in many deep-space shots).

While the hotel is based upon the abstract functions and flows of late-capitalist mobility, it is also, emotionally speaking, a hermetic world in which individuals desire one another outside the home, all without mediating back (as Siegfried Kracauer recognized) to any larger-scale collective. They are another example of what Petzold frequently describes as "bubble" spaces in contemporary society—socially isolating but also personally seductive (see the sections on *The State I Am In, Ghosts*, and *Wolfsburg*). As in all of his films, Petzold depicts contemporary social reality not so much through gritty realism of urban poverty but rather through such fantasized bubble spaces and the desires that generate them. In Petzold's films, the hotel serves ambiguously, not only as a space of estrangement, of deformed experience and maimed humanity, but also emancipatorily as a place vested and producing personal meaning amidst the ruins of the home.

The basic trajectory of Yella's stay at the hotel manifests this duality and contradiction in the hotel as both a socially isolated and emancipatory space. On the one, alienating hand, Yella has a tense exchange at check-in, where she fumbles with the means to pay for her stay, and then she places a subdued call home as a migrant worker alone in her room. This is a hotel-set migratory experience that Petzold discusses in one of his own published pieces: he details a scene in *The Face behind the Mask* in which an immigrant, played by Peter Lorre, writes a letter home from a New York hotel (Petzold, "Das Gesicht hinter der Maske"). On the other, emancipatory hand, her fantasy then begins to take over as she imagines the upside of the many open doors in the long corridor. Yella fantasizes Philip visiting her room and then herself fatefully visiting him. Hotels are not simply alienating amidst and via estranged spaces—they are fantasized as something quite the opposite, as a modern substitution for the personally vested place that she departed when she left Wittenberge.

Both of these tensions—between the hotel as meaningful place and abstract space as well as between fantasy and social isolation—are in operation in the two genres that regularly visit the hotel, the so-called hotel film (like *Grand Hotel*) as well as horror films like Hitchcock's *Psycho* (1960) or Kubrick's *The Shining* (1980). The hotel film builds on the kind of chance encounters that Petzold often exploits in his films, the simultaneous promise and threat of modern encounters with the stranger, encounters facilitated by capitalism's ubiquitous spaces. In his films, such hotel encounters transpire on a topography of simultaneous isolation and desire (for example, *Ghosts* and *Dreileben*). Horror films set in hotels invariably build on fears of economic desperation and the inherent seriality of modern life housed in the hotel. In a society where everyone, or at least their labor, is fundamentally replaceable, the hotel manifests the anxiety of our (sometimes violent) substitution by others. Both *Psycho* and *The Shining* associate the hotel with economic desperation—*Psycho* even foregrounds a female protagonist (at least initially) on the economic run westward.

In such films, the interplay of hotel encounters, seriality, and tenuous privacy becomes highly menacing—thus the power of the uncanny open hotel-room door in all the films. On the one, fantasy-fulfilling hand, the hotel's open doors allow Philip to enter even when Yella has collapsed on her bed (in her work clothes) after her disastrous first day at Alpha Wings. He does so to offer her a job with him, underscoring how the attenuated privacy of the hotel room is open to economy. But, on the other hand, these same perpetually open doors allow Ben to enter and terrify her when her new position with Philip is about to carry her off to a vaunted venture-capitalist future. The phantom Ben chasing her, she is soon dashing down the hotel corridor, sprinting past the identical doors, and running to Philip's rooms to embrace and kiss him. It is a fear, a longing, a consummation bred of the hotel's abstract spaces.

Not without Risk: **Yella's *Images of Finance***   For its detailed depiction of contemporary society and economy, *Yella* returns to a method that Petzold had developed almost ten years before in *The Sex Thief*: basing a series of scenes explicitly on a nonfiction film by Petzold's mentor and collaborator Harun Farocki. Petzold based three sequences in *The Sex Thief* on Farocki's *The Interview* (1996), sequences that take up almost ten minutes of Petzold's eighty-minute film (see Fisher, "Times of Transition and Transformation"). In *Yella*, Petzold presents a total of five business meetings, each of which is kept quite short (usually two to four minutes), but together they offer the plot an overarching structure. As with *The Sex Thief,* both the general setup and the specific dialogue build on what Farocki uncovered in one of his challenging nonfiction films. Farocki's fifty-two-minute *Nothing Ventured* (*Nicht ohne Risiko* [Not without risk]; 2004) offers an extended negotiation, over two meetings and a lunch, between a small, apparently predominantly family-owned company, NCTE, and a venture-capital firm, Buchanan Industrial Technologies. Petzold divides Farocki's single negotiation into five meetings with multiple clients, a range of scenarios whose repetition and variation help mark the trajectory of Yella and her relationship with Philip.

Among other themes, Farocki's film investigates how venture-capital firms aim to intervene in and "monetize" ambitious people's plans, fantasies, and dreams (Fisher, "Times of Transition and Transformation"). In *Yella*'s first meeting about planned (or dreamt) versus real production, in fact, viewers have one of their first hints that Yella is fantasizing the entire post-plunge episode. Midway through the meeting, the film's audio track tunes out the dialogue and gives viewers Yella's audio point of view of gurgling water, wind, and a raven— precisely those uncanny sounds that envelop her on the river bank where she is dying. But in this first meeting, she is able to overcome this soundtrack harbinger of her own murder. Hesitatingly at first and then with increasing confidence, she recycles for the meeting some details Ben offered of the dizzying depreciation of computer assets in the film's first ten minutes. With the advantage of insider knowledge—another fantasy of the contemporary economy—she demonstrates to Philip and their opposing negotiators that she can see through financial statements and uncover exaggerated assets.

The second meeting underscores another recurring theme of many of Petzold's films—the relation of the body to contemporary economy—here with a touch of rare humor between Philip and Yella. Such humor is not common in Petzold's usually controlled and even cold films, but sometimes he does allow for lighter moments, particularly to affirm the encounter and partnership of strangers detailed above (for example, between Jeanne and Heinrich in *The State I Am In*). While driving to the first meeting, Philip has prepared Yella by discussing how she should behave in these meetings. He has her try glasses on, coaches her on where to look during the meeting, and then preps her on "broker posing," from any number of "crappy John Grisham films," in which one puts one's hands behind one's head and then leans casually back in a chair. This posture of contemporary society recalls Petzold's interest in what he characterized as the transformative bodies of neoliberalism (here striking another balanced position, like that he highlights in *My Darling Clementine*, as discussed in the introduction). Should he strike this pose, Philip instructs Yella, she should lean over and whisper something, anything, in his ear, just to keep the opposition off balance. This advice returns in the very brief second meeting, when the opposing team tries this trick, and Yella and Philip burst out laughing.

The repetition and variation of these business meetings registers change not only in Yella and Philip's relationship but also in the recurring *Tagesreste* remnants from the film's opening minutes. After these initial meetings, for instance, the scene in which they first spend the night together recycles but also recasts such remnants. After being terrified in the hotel by Ben, Yella sprints down the corridor and into the arms of Philip, emphasizing the two men's contrasting definition. When she awakens in Philip's room the next morning, Yella does so slowly, luxuriating in the bright morning and only half opening her eyes, a stark contrast to the way she has awoken in the film to this point. As Nina Hoss and

Petzold note in a joint interview, they worked specifically on how Yella would wake up throughout the film and agreed that she should usually do so with a startle, as if (not coincidentally) waking from a dream of drowning (Petzold and Hoss). In Philip's room the morning after, however, she wakes up altogether differently, deliberately registering these sequences as the blissful zenith of her final fantasy. As she slowly awakens, Philip brings Yella breakfast in bed and then revealingly peels an orange in exactly the same manner—with what seems precisely the same implement—as her father at the beginning of the film. In this hotel fantasy, she has re-created the comfort, place, and emotional cathexes of her former East German home, underscoring the seductive power of abstract space for modern individuals, here in the contemporary hotel room of a relative stranger.

These narrative changes are confirmed in the cut from this morning-after fantasy to Yella driving Philip's car for the first time as he naps. This altogether new level of their romantic-economic partnership is confirmed in the following sequence, when Philip divulges to Yella his most intimate investment plan. The importance of the scene is under-scored again by the redeployment of remnant elements from the opening sequence. The film returns to Yella's muted sound point of view to suggest that the portents of her death (water, trees, raven) are drawing ever closer. Indeed, viewers see, in extreme long shot, the bridge from which Ben drives them as well as the river into which they plunge. But, at this point at least, the Freudian dreamwork is able to refunction these menacing omens, for Yella, into the heights of neoliberal fantasy. Philip reveals on the riverbank that he has located an Irish company that is able to repackage simple hardware parts into a safety system for deep-digging oil drills, systems costing near nothing but worth some eight hundred thousand Euro to oil companies. Philip gives her the financial details by passing her a leather-bound notebook from his left breast pocket, a gesture recalling not only his heart but also Schmitt-Ott's petty cash wallet and, more importantly, the paper-bound business plan with which Ben tried to convince Yella to take him back. Yella fatefully refused to read Ben's business plan relating to heating and ventilation, but she em-braces Philip's proposal to exploit the transnational network of resource extraction. Yella compliments him earnestly: "That is magnificent." After dismissing her mundane domestic dreams (the suburban home, the green Jaguar), Philip then makes the most heartfelt proposal one can in this era of hard-fought equity positions and perfectly timed investment exits: "Are you going to help me?" ("Machst du mit?"—implying more complicity than the English). They embrace on it. Petzold cuts to the river's gentle undulation: the menacing river, that terrible *Tagesreste* signifying her murder, has been remade by the most romantic proposal she could imagine, one founded on the enormous profit margins to be had by gaming the global oil industry.

Hurtling toward a Horror End Yella and Philip's fourth meeting depicts how their partnership attains a new equality (and equity), but, at that very moment, Philip learns that he is to lose his job. This abrupt development serves as a sudden, even paranoid return of the repressed, presumably Yella's remnant anxiety from Ben's fate. The last fifteen minutes of the film, in the wake of this news, restage her response to a lover's sudden unemployment, another repetition and variation that yields the film's pessimistic conclusion. Cinematically, in these last fifteen minutes, the (horror-) generic manipulation of perspective returns with a vengeance. In the opening sequences, as I describe above, Petzold deliberately refunctions this central aspect of the horror film: the menacing male (monster) perspective on the female victim is retooled such that the male monster is a ghost generated by contemporary economy. This generic logic of a monster's perspective is, over the final twenty minutes of the film, reversed and yields its downbeat ending.

After Philip reveals that he has lost his job—becoming all too Ben-like at the very moment Yella raises the prospect of going shopping—they pull into a more modest hotel, another repetition (hotel) and variation (emphatically a "motel," as the backside of a large sign indicates). Despite his bad employment news, Philip gives Yella some cash and the car keys to purchase some new (work) clothes, putting her entirely in the driver's seat of the film's key movement space, as this whole end section does. As she pulls out in his red Audi station wagon, Petzold cuts to an unusual point-of-view shot from the window of the motel—the shot is unusual because the long fantasy sequence hardly leaves Yella's perspective (figure 15). An echo of Ben's early point of view on Yella in Wittenberge, this shot has all the makings of a horror perspective—handheld, slightly obscured by a curtain, set in a *Psycho*-like motel—but

Figure 15. The recurring horror point of view relocated in Philip in *Yella* (2007).

the viewers know that the now-unemployed Philip hardly qualifies as a monster. The monster's perspective has been remade by Yella's fantasy and altogether defanged by the economy—she is driving now.

Yella drives not to buy clothes, as she had told Philip, but instead to the company of Dr. Gunthen and then waits for his green Jaguar to depart so she can follow him home. The transformation of the body through clothes at the film's opening has been overthrown for more malevolent methods. The close-up on her wide-open, emotionless eyes as she watches him leave is the first indication that she is assuming the role of the monster: she is watching and planning something both highly calculated and disturbingly sinister (figures 16 and 17).

The next shot is an abrupt point-of-view shot of Dr. Gunthen's house, one particularly startling because Petzold so often avoids establishing shots (figure 18). As Hitchcock noted about his own cinema, the long shot is often saved for very dramatic purposes (Truffaut and Scott 18). This sudden perspective of a would-be predator revisits the point-of-view shots that Petzold has used since the beginning to signify the monster observing his, now her, prey. This turn seems particularly powerful because viewers will recall that they have seen this Jaguar, this house, and this couple before, earlier in the film, when Yella first arrives for her fantastical first day of work in Hanover. At that earlier point, however, her perspective seems to admire the well-appointed domestic life,

Figures 16–17. Yella (Nina Hoss) turned car-based
predator in *Yella* (2007).

the luxury car, and child. By the film's closing moments, however, this
admiring perspective has turned predatory—Petzold has relocated the
horror genre's point of view and its aggression in his largely sympathetic
protagonist.

Soon Yella gains entrance to Dr. Gunthen's house and attempts to
blackmail him into giving her and Philip the two hundred thousand
Euro they need for their (now shared) dream investment. One of the

Figure 18. Yella's horror-film point-of-view
now located in *Yella* (2007).

surprising aspects of Farocki's *Nothing Ventured* is the overt talk of "blackmailing" the engineer May's company—*Yella* literalizes this talk of blackmail in this climactic sequence. Dr. Gunthen offers thirty thousand Euro from a life-insurance policy—a foreshadow of his own as well as Yella's mortality—but Yella wants more. She observes flatly, coldly that he does have the house, as her eyes rove around it calculatingly and altogether horrorlike (rather like a monster casing the unsuspecting house before attacking). This turn seems a powerful reversal indeed, given the sentimental coding of her own home at the beginning and her initial admiration of this home, its family, and its luxury car. By the end, now a dedicated denizen of hotels, she has made the house that she admired upon arrival in Hanover into the grist for her own capitalist creative destruction.

The fifth and final business meeting and its resolution confirm the monster that these horror-genre techniques show her to have become. Although the parties convene, the final business meeting never transpires. Yella, Philip, and Dr. Gunthen's negotiating team are hanging about the same conference room as the fourth meeting, but they are desperately seeking the missing Dr. Gunthen. As they wait, Philip nuzzles up to Yella and whispers that he loves her, a declaration unusual for the middle of a business meeting. But at that moment—perhaps because

"I love you" were also Ben's last words to her before he drove them off of the bridge—her sound point of view again registers water, and she suddenly sees Dr. Gunthen's ghost, drenched and covered in leaves, through the glass door of the conference room. She rushes to Dr. Gunthen's house, only to find him behind the house, having drowned himself, making her, if not a direct murderer, part of the capitalist machinery that killed the entrepreneur-engineer. This realization seems to jolt her out of layers of (un)consciousness in a telling series of movement spaces: first to a taxi, like the taxi she should have taken rather than accepting Ben's ride, and then to Ben's Range Rover, bringing viewers back to the seconds before their fatal plunge.

Yella's ending provides for a notable contrast to the endings of the other two films of the Ghost trilogy. As noted in the sections on *The State I Am In* and *Ghosts*, Jeanne and Nina (both played by Julia Hummer) assume a concluding posture of some defiance, having in both cases survived the films' cars. In *Yella*, however, viewers witness the most pessimistic vehicular ending of Petzold's cinema, again with the technique of repetition and variation that has ruled the film. When *Yella* acceleratingly moves back through her fantasy, to the taxi, and finally back to Ben's Range Rover, Yella is visibly weeping. In the second staging of Ben's murder-suicide, the most noticeable difference are these tears and the sad resignation they signify; the most remarkable variation is Yella's more passive posture as she realizes Ben intends to kill them both.

If the entire film was about her economic transformation, her growing neoliberal agency, and her personal satisfaction at it—charted largely through a series (and the serial nature) of hotel rooms and business meetings—her end registers a new recognition of what she has become in the film's horror-genre logic. In the first staging of her murder, ten minutes into the film, Yella understandably tries to seize the steering wheel when she realizes that Ben is driving them to a watery death. But, having lived through her expiring fantasy, she has grown more passive and apparently pessimistic. In this second staging of Ben's murder-suicide, she does not attempt to grab the steering wheel as Ben wrenches it, and the whole vehicle, off the bridge. She sits weeping, (typically for Petzold) turned away to the window, apparently now accepting her end. The better the villain, the better the film, Hitchcock once cited as "the cardinal rule," and the villain here, these concluding fragments of the horror genre affirm, is Yella herself (Truffaut and Scott 191)—or at least the infiltration of her most intimate self by the economically minded fantasies of mobility, hotels, and assorted business negotiations.

Jerichow: Guest Worker turned Hometown Host

The scene from *Jerichow* (2009) described in the introduction—that of the German war veteran Thomas and the Turkish entrepreneur Ali sitting in a work van and discussing a snack bar—confirms that this 2008 feature continues Petzold's investigation of people who are "becoming economic," particularly in the movement spaces that fill his films. As with *Yella* and its generic model *Carnival of Souls*, however, Petzold undertakes this exploration by basing his work on a genre classic, here *The Postman Always Rings Twice*. With both *Carnival* and *Postman*, his favored genres seem to be those that stage a conflict arising from historical changes with significant socioeconomic consequences. With *Jerichow*, he recounts discussing the relative absence of class struggle in U.S. cinema with his former teacher and frequent collaborator Harun Farocki. Farocki offered up *The Postman Always Rings Twice*, which subsequently became the basis of the plot (Lim). In *Jerichow*, Petzold relocates *Postman* to the provinces of the former East Germany with Thomas, who has tried his luck in the former West but then failed and returned. It is another genre-based story of ghostly afterness—having suffered the socioeconomic death of a failed business, Thomas gains a second chance, however haunted, to live (Uehling and Petzold). The film also seems quite influenced by Rainer Werner Fassbinder's *Merchant of Four Seasons* (*Händler der vier Jahreszeiten*, 1971; see Kothenschult and Petzold), itself a reflection of Fassbinder's engagement with the genre films of the German émigré Douglas Sirk.

Besides confirming his tendency to excavate the remnants of genre, however, *Jerichow* extends Petzold's auteurist interests considerably by taking up immigration and integration in Germany. Given that I have explored in other sections how economics recast love (certainly manifest in *Jerichow*'s memorable and oft-quoted line, "You can't be in love if you don't have money"), I focus herein more on ethnicity and immigration, particularly on places away from the movement and transit spaces that viewers so often see in Petzold's work. Although some may regard his cinema as political primarily in its alternative film aesthetics (Abel, *Counter-Cinema*; Kopp; Schwenk), *Jerichow* also makes clear Petzold's more overt political engagement with his troubling contemporary context. In a way that consistently brushes against the grain of viewer expectation, ethnic Germans and ethnic Turks in *Jerichow* are depicted, together and apart, in new ways. The film deliberately moves beyond the conventional, German-host-versus-Turkish-guest relation into one of reciprocal interaction and influence. This shift from a conventionally vertical to a more horizontal relationship, away from a hierarchal binaristic/oppositional relation to one of interchange and exchange, parallels an evolution tracked by scholars like Stuart Hall and others in postcolonial theory.

Jerichow takes its title from a real but relocated town that invokes the verdant, prosperous oasis of the biblical Jericho. This fictional hometown of the film's protagonist, Thomas, parodies that almost edenic association. The setting also seems to cite that of Uwe Johnson's multivolume novel *Anniversaries: From the Life of Gesine Cresspahl* (*Jahrestage: Aus dem Leben Gesine Cresspahl*; 1970–74), not a surprise given Petzold's literary training (see Miller). Petzold's Jerichow of contemporary Germany is a moribund town in the former East in which money is scarce, work disappearing, and people desperate. The film follows Thomas, who served in Afghanistan but was dishonorably discharged, as he struggles to find his emotional and professional bearings after the failure of his business and the death of his mother. Committed to renovating his childhood home, which he has now inherited, but running out of funds to do so, Thomas turns to the local unemployment office. He eventually finds better-paying work via a surprising encounter with Ali, an ethnic Turkish entrepreneur who owns some forty-five snack bars in and around Jerichow. Walking home from the supermarket one afternoon, Thomas happens upon and helps Ali after the latter has drunkenly driven his Range Rover off the road. When Ali loses his license, he hires Thomas as his chauffeur (rather like Jimmy hiring Tom in *Cuba Libre*), but then also employs him increasingly as his assistant in deliveries to his many snack bars. The film then follows the basic parameters of James M. Cain's *The Postman Always Rings Twice*, which Petzold has called his favorite novel (Kothenschulte and Petzold). Despite Ali's growing trust in and dependence on him, Thomas has an affair with Ali's ethnic German wife, Laura, whom Ali has also saved/employed. In discussing this intersection of work and desire in a love triangle, Petzold says that he thought immediately of *Ossessione,* Luchino Visconti's unauthorized, neorealist adaptation of *Postman* for 1940s Italy that Petzold declares "important to me."[18] Echoing both *Ossessione* and *Postman,* Thomas and Laura conspire to kill Ali and take over his lucrative business, with love driving economics and economics driving love.

In the interview herein, Petzold makes clear that although he is excavating fragments from *Ossessione* and *Postman,* he also wrote and made *Jerichow* with German films about immigrants in mind. He had long been concerned about Germans' attitudes toward "foreigners," especially in the former East Germany (see the interview herein). He was struck, when traveling for *Yella,* by the large number of Turkish people who had made lives for themselves in this region of the former East (Kothenschulte and Petzold). But, he confesses, he was not satisfied with the prevailing German films about immigration and ethnicity. In fact, I would suggest that *Jerichow* contrasts, on the one hand, to the kind of "cinema-of-duty" approach to ethnicity that dominated 1970s and 1980s depictions of Turkish people in Germany, known as the *Gastarbeiterfilme* (guest-worker films) (Malik). "Gastarbeiter" refers to "guest workers" who immigrated to Germany starting in the 1950s from various points mostly south, including Italy, the former Yugoslavia, and especially Turkey. During the 1970s and 1980s, guest-worker films like *Shirin's Wedding* (1975), *40m² Germany* (1986), and *Yasemin* (1988) focused on the victimization of immigrants in German society, particularly by racism, social alienation, and economic marginalization. On the other hand, by the 1990s, there was a marked departure from this politically pedantic approach in Germany (Göktürk; Burns). For example, of another stripe altogether are the Turkish-German "ghetto" films, which seem influenced by early 1990s U.S. films about African Americans like *Boyz n the Hood* and *Menace II Society* (Mennel, "Bruce Lee in Kreuzberg").

Both of these modes for depicting German multiculturalism, the guest-worker cinema and the ghetto film, tend to what Stuart Hall has termed a "binary form of narrativization" in terms of Germany's (alleged) ethnic "Others." The lines between Germans and nonethnic Germans are clearly and firmly drawn and usually structure the conflict built into the plot, whether it be the (German) social-work intervention in the victimization of migrants or the (German) police interdiction in crimes committed by migrants or their children. Even if, as in the guest-worker films, there is cross-ethnic empathy, it is based on the thematized differences between Turkish and German cultures, located specifically with Turkish guest workers in Germany as the (apparent) host country. Of course, these sorts of depictions and their differences are, as Stuart Hall suggests, entirely constructed (Hall 252). Hall advocates against this binarism with a conceptual shift in what had been called the postcolonial to transculturation and transnationalism. Rather than the presumed and apparently stable binaries, Hall lobbies for a model that emphasizes the reciprocal influence and intertwinement of the presumed poles of colonized and colonizers. Such a model foregrounds circulation and interchange instead of mere political and economic hierarchy. He does not intend to deny the inherent hierarchies and power relations but rather to regard them as operating within a larger and more complex field.

Petzold's *Jerichow* demonstrates how a film can move beyond binaristic forms of narrative to treat such wider and more complex fields of ethnic diversity in modern-day Europe.[19] The usual binary of Turkish guests versus German hosts is dismantled in favor of such transcultural formations. With his (art-house) neo-noir, Petzold offers a portrait of mutual influences, reversed and surprising interchanges and interactions, particularly in new spaces for such cross-ethnic encounters. In terms of such novel spaces, the mainstream genres of the guest-worker and ghetto films, like many genres, have a particular spatial logic—that is, they almost always transpire in the city. The guest-worker films often construct a revealing contiguity from the victimizing conditions to the city that "hosts" the guest workers: cramped and crowded workplaces and living quarters spill over into cramped and crowded city streets. The city, however, also provides the setting for the narrative's central encounters between ethnic Germans and ethnic Turks that lead to greater awareness on the German side and a modicum of amelioration on the Turkish side.

Much as it avoids simple ethnic binaries, *Jerichow* avoids the simplistic perspectives of the guest-worker and the ghetto films by relocating its ethnic encounters to the countryside. Petzold builds in this way upon an intriguing innovation found in *The Postman Always Rings Twice*—it displaces ethnic tensions out of the urban milieu of most films noirs, steering clear of ethnic enclaves and the stereotypical cross-ethnic encounters they might engender. Parallel to *Postman*, *Jerichow* unfolds how nonethnic Germans are not limited to Germany's global cities but inhabit even the smallest, most modest, and dearest hometown, or what Germans call the individual's *Heimat*. (For details on *Jerichow*'s relation to *Heimat* and the *Heimat* genre of the 1950s, see King 11–16.) This alternative representation of space and diversity underscores how important a spatial imaginary and spatial practices are to comprehending how immigration, ethnic diversity, and so-called globalization function.

Asked why he set *Jerichow* in a rural region in former East Germany, known as the Prignitz, Petzold answers: "If one can tell the story of the American in Germany, it should be set in the Prignitz. This is where people drive pickups and SUVs, malls shoot up, and freeways and parking lots are of American dimensions, while the local industry is on its last legs. It is all the rubble of an American dream" (Uehling and Petozld). Petzold's remarks underscore the framework within which he approaches ethnicity and diversity in Germany, one that reflects on economic promises and frustrations as well as the psychological processing of them. Elsewhere as well, Petzold discusses how he knows "no place as American" as this deindustrialized, dilapidated corner of East Germany, which he also regards as "America-addicted" (Demmerle and Petzold). He links this sort of deluded deindustrialization to the television series *The Wire* and *The Deer Hunter* (dir. Michael Cimino, 1978), the latter of which his crew for *Jerichow* watched in preparation.

Part of what the countryside affords both *Postman* and *Jerichow*— one of Petzold's auteurist themes—is business's conspicuous interface with nature and landscape. *Pilots, Wolfsburg,* and *Yella* offer assorted long shots of business people amidst lovely if eerie landscapes, underlining the unnatural and contingent character of all economic activities, even as they become all-consuming. Besides the proliferation of movement and transit spaces, part of this tension between nature and the artificial are the recurring spaces of the characters' houses, therefore of the domestic in his films. In the country, with its single-family homes set on roads, yards, and/or near forests, the shape and condition of the house become more conspicuously expressive of the personality of the owner. As Petzold observes in the interview herein, they resemble "spaceships" or "moon stations," built by their owners as if they exist in a vacuum. *Jerichow* is no exception: the homes of Thomas and Ali both play central roles in the film and are featured prominently in its iconography. Petzold also recounts, however, that he is particularly interested in the moment such isolated houses "become social" when confronted by another house next door or individuals outside peering in.

In Cain's novel, in Visconti's *Ossessione,* and then in the various noir versions, it is hard to imagine that readers or viewers would learn much about the childhood home of the drifter character. This drifter's disruptive narrative force derives in large part from his status as a rootless outsider, an external force threatening the home of the wealthy husband and lonely wife. But in Petzold's hands, the narrative, as in some of his other films (*The Sex Thief* and *Yella*), starts with the drifter's commitment to the place of home and memory. After Thomas's failed foray to a foreign war and his mother's death, he decides to renovate the house and remain in the town in which he grew up. Petzold has emphasized in interviews about *Jerichow* how he is fascinated by "*Heimat*-building" in this part of Germany—how especially men expend endless time and money on elaborate renovations of their homes, which they might (in the age of the Hartz IV labor reforms) have to leave anyway (Uehling and Petzold). Petzold's film foregrounds in this way individual people's drive to establish domesticity, even as they live in an increasingly mobile era.

To emphasize these contradictions of domesticity and capitalism, even as Petzold gives *Postman*'s drifter a home, he avoids sentimentalizing the domestic sensibilities of which the home is symptomatic. From the first moment viewers see Thomas's childhood home, *Jerichow* foregrounds the creative destruction of place that I discussed in *The Sex Thief* and *Yella.* Thomas has been driven from his mother's funeral to her home by Leon because Thomas owes him from a failed business venture. Viewers learn from Leon that Thomas borrowed money but that the venture for which he did so, an urban café, is bankrupt and has now been liquidated, with ice maker, espresso machine, and stereo system all removed (a recounting recalling images of neoliberal creative-destruction in *The Sex Thief* and *Yella*). In the background of Thomas's plan to renovate his childhood home is not a sentimental dedication to *Heimat* but rather the remnants and ruins of an entrepreneurial dream, contextualizing what one might regard as a nostalgic reconstruction of his mother's house within the framework of capitalist turnover and assiduous afterness.

The encounter and eventual alliance with Ali further complicates Thomas's relationship with his childhood home by emphasizing how the presumed foundations of German individuals and society more generally (home, the hometown) are shifting—viewers find themselves amid Petzold's telltale transitions and transformations. Thomas finds his hometown now dominated, it seems, by the immigrant entrepreneur, who prowls its rural roads in an enormous Range Rover while Thomas is left to walk, images that map these contrasting movement spaces of car and walking onto immigration and ethnic assimilation. In this variation on conventional ethnic hierarchy in Germany, the distance from the guest-worker cinema and the ghetto film is palpable. The ethnic Turk is not someone to be paternalistically helped by the film's ethnic Germans, as he would be in the cinema of duty, nor is he to be (merely) policed by the ethnic Germans, as in the ghetto film. Indeed, Ali is the only source of wealth in Petzold's meticulously drawn socioeconomic desolation of the former East. The iconography of his depiction—his fine clothes, expensive Range Rover, and perfectly appointed house—suggest a 1990s/2000s Berliner Republic yuppie rather than a 1970s West German guest worker.

Jerichow sketches a new kind of society in a new kind of space, at least ethnically speaking. The rethinking of ethnicity required by the film is occasioned perhaps more than anything by contrasting Thomas's childhood home, foregrounded in the film's first ten minutes, to that of Ali, foregrounded for much of the rest of the plot (figure 19). In depicting Thomas's relationship to Ali's affluent home, the film once again intersects one of Petzold's recurring, auteurist interests: the image of the late-capitalist wanderer standing, almost mesmerized, in front of (and fantasizing about) the luxury house, the very moment of the "social" Petzold foregrounded above. In all the works of Petzold's Ghost trilogy and then here, there is a moment when the drifting protagonist—usually after the chance and fateful encounter described above—stands before a wealthy home to which he or she does not or cannot have access. The homes in front of the drifter also serve the fantasy purpose I have emphasized throughout his work. They symbolize the better lives imagined by the drifter, an almost utopian yearning for domestic plenitude, but they do so, I would emphasize, spatially, in a postlapsarian return to the emotionally vested place destroyed at the start (as in *The Sex Thief*, *Wolfsburg*, and *Yella*).

These complex depictions of the domestic underscore how Petzold is once again working against the binaristic forms of narrativization that have tended to dominate the representations of ethnic Turkish people in German cinema, representations that Petzold explicitly critiques in *Jerichow*. In earlier cinema-of-duty guest-worker films, there was a tendency to depict the homes of ethnic Turks as socially, and sexually, oppressive spaces of confinement, perhaps most famously in *40m² Germany*. The domestic sphere of ethnic Turks often stood in even more than individual immigrants for a general sense of "foreignness." Even in relatively late films, like Thomas Arslan's *Siblings* (*Geschwister*; 1997) and Fatih Akın's *Head On*, the home of the ethnic Turkish family frequently becomes the site of confinement, especially for ethnic Turkish women. If the goal of the guest-worker films was to raise awareness for ethnic German audiences about the hardships for ethnic Turks in Germany, then the protagonists were often on a trajectory from "conventional" Turkish homes into German society. In *Jerichow*, quite remarkably, the house

Figure 19. The dilapidated house of Thomas (Benno Fürmann) in *Jerichow* (2009).

confines not the Turkish woman but the ethnic German woman, and the liberation of her planned by the German male is utterly criminal.

These spatial aspects of the film (the setting in the countryside, the foregrounded homes of the main characters) help to subvert the notion of ethnic Germans hosting ethnic Turks in Germany. Given his well-established and resourced presence and his offering Thomas a job, it is Ali who is hosting Thomas. In this way, Thomas's return to his hometown after his unsuccessful ventures abroad (Afghanistan) and in the city (the failed café) resonates with migration. It underscores how Thomas himself is a migrant trying to find a place in an increasingly unfamiliar world, even if it happens to be the place where he grew up. Late capitalism has rendered the ethnic German a drifter-migrant, the itinerant of *Ossessione* or *The Postman Always Rings Twice,* even in his own hometown, his own *Heimat.*

This sense of Thomas and Ali's shared status as migrants—as mutually drifting amidst late capitalism's spatial practices—comes through in a scene that is among the film's most discussed, that of a beach picnic during which Ali becomes drunk and sings to the music of his homeland. As King notes, the beach scene stands out stylistically by offering some of the only unmotivated long shots of the films (15). I would emphasize, however, a notable shift in these scenes from economic remakings (the key theme in Fassbinder's *Merchant of Four Season*) to ethnicity and belonging in *Postman.* Up until this beach scene, the characters offer no comment on Ali's ethnicity—there is not one remark on his being Turkish or on ethnicity in general. Viewers are certainly cued to be aware of Ali's ethnicity by his snack bars and, even more conspicuously, by the name ("Özkan") on his delivery truck, but there is none of the usual thematizing of ethnic diversity: nothing on the social struggles of migrants, or on the ethnic nature of underworld crime (as would be common in the guest-worker films or the ghetto films). This is a world, as Petzold suggested in his comment on "the American" in the Prignitz, remade by late capitalism, in which people relate to each other primarily through economic interests—a trope underscored by Petzold's own observation that every scene in *Jerichow* is about money (Hoch).

Contrary to Petzold's comment, however, is this first beach scene, in which money moves into the background and ethnic difference to the foreground. The beach provides a space at a revealing remove from the contrasting homes I emphasized above. Here, the principals (and viewers' sympathies) are not held in the crucible of a poor man staring in envy at a rich man's house nor in the rich man's slumming visit to the poor man's domicile. Further, *Jerichow*'s beach scenes recast the generic fragments that Petzold is excavating. If *Postman*'s beach focuses on the dangerous side of the desire between Frank and Cora—at one point, he considers murdering her there—Petzold's excavation of the genre classic deemphasizes the romantic relationship and highlights a more complex ethnic dynamic at the beach. In this space emphatically away from both home and business, Petzold's recasts *Postman*'s beach scene such that it now includes Ali—a revision engaging more deeply in questions of solidarity with the ethnic other.

Jerichow's beach scene would seem to evoke what Edward Soja has termed a third space beyond existing social contradictions, here between the ethnic German veteran's decaying house and the ethnic Turkish entrepreneur's luxurious villa (Soja 8–10). As with earlier films about ethnic Turks in Germany, the space away from the houses becomes the crucial one to the narrative trajectory, particularly because the film will conclude by returning to the same beach setting. But, contrary to most of those films and in a distinctly noirish mode, this third space away does not hold out the promise of a redemptive place of ethnic reconciliation. The potentially redemptive space away from the uneven geography of late capitalism—a non-domestic third space that could have joined Laura, Ali, and Thomas in a new, diverse solidarity—ends up noirishly destroyed by greed and passion and the inextricable intertwinement of the two.

In this first of two beach sequences, some twenty-seven minutes into the film, the initial shot frames Ali singing and dancing, silhouetted by sunlight sparkling off the Baltic Sea's mild undulations (figure 20). The iconography of the scene transpires at a bright remove from film noir and matches instead the happier deployment of the Mediterranean or Black Sea in any number of German films about Turks—for example, the recurring images of the Bosphorus in Akın's *Head On* or the memorable Black Sea closing image of his *The Edge of Heaven* (*Auf der anderen Seite*; 2007). But Petzold manipulates social stereotypes and genre conventions by relocating the dancing/singing ethnic Turk on the Baltic. In these ways, the Turkish song "Nazar de Mesin" (King 9) as well as Ali's

Figure 20. Ali (Hilmi Sözer) dances on the deterritorialized beach in *Jerichow* (2009).

humming, singing, and dancing all suddenly reterritorialize this space, in Germany, as belonging to an alternate geography, one of and remade by immigrants. This drive to reterritorialization—manifest as well in Thomas's renovations after his time away—underscores how Petzold's films address not so much movement and spaces but rather the tension in which they stand to reterritorializing impulses. Ali's behavior recalls Hans's mixture of celebration at economic success and self-destructive sadness in *Merchant of Four Seasons* as well as the abrupt attacks of homesickness for Ali's namesake in Fassbinder's *Fear Eats the Soul* (*Angst essen Seele auf*; 1973).

This scene also recalls, but simultaneously contrasts with, Bob Rafelson's 1981 *Postman Always Rings Twice*, in which downtown Los Angeles is reterritorialized by ethnic singing and dancing in a Greek immigrant community center. *Jerichow*'s immigrant space is not, as in Rafelson's, a confining domesticity or gritty cityscape but one of the most beautiful views in Germany. Here, lonely Ali is not part of any larger ethnic community. In fact, his romanticizing misrecognition of the Baltic seems not all that far from Thomas's romanticizing misrecognition of his childhood home. While loss of and longing for home are central to the migrant experience (Jones 79), Petzold emphasizes how that kind of loss is shared by both ethnic Turks and ethnic Germans due to late capitalism. In his reading and recasting of his generic forebears, the beach would seem

Figure 21. Interethnic harmony on beach
in *Jerichow* (2009).

to point to a distinct solidarity between the migrant and the hometown boy—both, in their own ways, drifters due to late capitalism. Ali initiates this potentially redemptive reterritorialization (in song and dance), but Petzold emphasizes how Thomas will ruin this potential solidarity, the ephemerally redemptive space held out by the beach.

After Ali complains that he is dancing alone, Thomas jokes with him that Ali dances like a Greek, a knowing provocation given Turkey's long-standing tensions with Greece. Less angry than disappointed, Ali encourages them to "dance like Germans" and convinces them to stand up ("come, German Thomas!") and start to dance. He nudges them closer and closer, to dance together as Germans do, and dances next to them in his own style, a three-shot of apparent harmony (figure 21). But when Ali heads back to his SUV, presumably to get more alcohol, Thomas takes the opportunity to kiss Laura. For now, she resists his advances, asks what kind of friend he is, and tells him to go help Ali, as the latter is completely drunk. Thomas literally follows in Ali's footsteps to the top of the cliff above the sea and finds him there looking down at Laura. It is not clear to viewers if Ali has witnessed them kissing. When he abruptly slips off the cliff, Thomas saves him after a short hesitation, an action Laura will come to regret and the one deliberately revisited at the end of the film.

The viewer is left wondering why Ali seems to encourage Laura and Thomas to dance together, and dance close, if he already had observed, as he did on Thomas's first day of work, Thomas ogling Laura. Part of this is doubtless also Ali's own shortcomings, which Petzold is careful to depict, including his braggadocio about his wife (he shows her off like a car, Petzold says in the interview herein) and the hint that he has been physically abusive to her (another complicating commonality with Hans in *Merchant of Four Seasons*). But Ali's likely motivations for bringing them together—perhaps also for hiring Thomas at all—become clear in the second beach scene, the climactic and concluding scene of the film some forty minutes later. Ali has returned from his mysterious trip, during which Thomas and Laura realize a full-blown affair and plot to kill him at the very same beach where Ali first brought them together. After Laura picks Ali up from the airport and suggests another beach picnic, he reveals to her the truth about his trip. It was not a return to Turkey to plan their later, permanent return—another cliché of the Turkish-German film (as in *Head On* and *The Edge of Heaven*)—but rather to have his irregular heartbeat checked at a clinic in Leipzig (a cardiological narrative device shared with *Merchant of Four Seasons*). He has only two, maybe three months to live. Laura cries in guilt at her plan to kill him, and the couple ends up on the beach, with her head on Ali's shoulder as he outlines his financial plans for after his death.

It is at this moment that he suggests to the grieving Laura that "Thomas will help you, he's okay," which reveals that his plan all along was to bring someone into their lives whom he could trust. His earlier encouragement that Thomas look admiringly at Laura (twice) and his exhortations of their close dancing suddenly make sense, as does his likely having seen them from the cliff above when Thomas kissed her. Ali seems the kind of metteur-en-scène well known from the noir genre, the puppet master who controls things both economic and emotional, but it is of course a shock that the ethnic Germans might have been put in this position by an ethnic Turk.

This being a Petzold film, however, hovering up on the cliff with the metteur-en-scène is the Range Rover that has been an important prop throughout the film—the natural space of the beach, a potential ethnic third space, is converted into a movement space. As noted above, all of Petzold's films feature automobiles in important scenes (see the section on *Wolfsburg* above), so the domestic/geographical unevenness detailed in *Yella* is likewise met, typically for him, by a vehicular contrast. The film contrasts Ali's Range Rover as movement space to Thomas's little red race-car lighter, which Ali finds on the cliff, as a materialization of mere movement fantasy. With the noirish clue of the lighter, Ali quickly surmises that Thomas is hiding and planning to kill him. The carless Thomas planned to kill the man who hired him, gave him a vehicle, and even encouraged him to pursue his wife. In the end, as Ali financially plans for his own death, viewers realize that he was likely planning to hand his business over to Laura and Thomas all along. In another telling revision to *Postman*, they would have received from the immigrant that of which they dreamed without murdering him.

Although Ali knows that he inhabits "a country that doesn't want me with a wife I bought," he is nonetheless shocked that those closest to him would murder him to get what he was going to give them anyway. This line, the second most quoted of the film, underscores the utter lack of solidarity that Thomas and Laura show toward Ali. It is a shocking lack of solidarity that (archeologically) evokes the era of noir, in which demobilizing veterans found no place to call home and so felt little or no empathy for the postwar society to which they returned. The noirish lack of social solidarity in *Jerichow* functions as a generic fragment that Petzold recasts in the familiar lack of empathy with the ethnic Turk who is ready to give immeasurably to Germans and to Germany, as any migrant gives to the society to which he or she immigrates. But it is the "natives," wrecked by neoliberal capitalist remakings and ruins, who have rejected and thwarted this potential solidarity. In the fateful absence of any substantive empathy, Ali drives his Range Rover over the cliff, compressing the verticality and horizontality of the film's first beach sequence and, one senses, leaving his wife Laura and employee Thomas to contemplate their fatal lack of solidarity and sympathy amid Germany's rewritten ethnic and economic landscapes.

Dreileben: Beats Being Dead (*Dreileben: Etwas Besseres als den Tod*): Generic Experiments

Petzold's ninety-minute television film *Dreileben: Beats Being Dead* (2011) underscores his professional flexibility and his personal commitment to film as a fundamentally collaborative undertaking. As noted above, Petzold tends to work with many of the same actors across his films, in addition to the same cinematographer, Hans Fromm, and editor, Bettina Böhler, as well as much of his other crew. The *Dreileben* project was a collaboration among three directors: it grew out of the email exchange ("Mailwechsel"), discussed in the introduction, among Petzold, Christoph Hochhäusler, and Dominik Graf, that explores the status of the Berlin School and its approach to filmmaking. In the wake of the exchange—and symptomatic of the greater collective effort he had sought for the Berlin School—Petzold suggested that the three of them realize a project together. They agreed to use one of Petzold's stories as the foundation, with each of the three then developing a feature-length "episode" based on it. Despite the involvement of three of Germany's best-known film directors, it quickly became clear that, in Germany at least, only television could support such an ambitious project. ARD (the "first" public-television station in Germany) took the lead in a TV coproduction, which opened on the film-festival circuit in winter-summer 2011 and then was broadcast to widespread acclaim—if to a modest audience for TV—at the end of August 2011 (Haupt).

Given that he initiated the collaboration and offered the founding material for it—he is also the only one of the three directors not to have a cowriter—the highly unusual project underscores Petzold's ongoing negotiation between art-house/auteurist and genre cinema. In discussing the genesis and gestation of *Dreileben*, Hochhäusler recounts how the model for the collaboration was the phrase that Petzold had coined to characterize genre—the idea of genre as a "neighborhood without fences" (Graf, Hochhäusler, and Petzold, "Die Welt zur Kenntlichkeit entstellen"). This kind of a genre as neighborhood is precisely what he, Hochhäusler, and Graf found in the making of *Dreileben*. As Petzold recounts, one of the most gratifying aspects of the project was shooting in the same place with the same parameters and coming across colleagues with whom one could share ideas, compare notes, and contrast approaches (Graf, Hochhäusler, and Petzold, "Die Welt zur Kenntlichkeit entstellen"). If, as Petzold and Hochhäusler had complained in the email exchange, German cinema generally lacks the potential of genre as an enriching community, the three filmmakers sought to create this nourishing neighborhood for cinema themselves.

In the story at the heart of *Dreileben*, Petzold develops a somewhat familiar thriller-genre premise: a convicted murderer escapes and terrorizes a small town and its rapidly overmatched police. In his contribution, *Beats Being Dead*, Petzold follows a young Johannes, who is doing his civil service at a rural hospital. He accidentally releases the murderer Molesch while the latter visits his mother in the hospital. In Petzold's film, Molesch's menace fades into the background as Johannes meets and falls for a young Bosnian immigrant, Ana. This unusual romance, and the project as a whole, is set in the town of Dreileben, meaning, literally, "three lives"—an apt title for a work by three directors. Dreileben refers to an actual town in the former East Germany (near Magdeburg), but Petzold, as he had with *Jerichow*, resituates it to a fictional and symbolic location. Dreileben is relocated near (and shot in) Suhl and Oberhof, small towns known for hiking and winter sports on the edge of the Thuringian forest near Erfurt and Weimar (Peitz). A number of myths and fairy tales are set in this forest, though the link to Weimar is also telling. As Hochhäusler's recounts, Petzold's idea for the story was initially based (so he thought) on a crime story by Friedrich Schiller, the classical German author and Weimar's second-most-famous resident behind his contemporary, colleague, and friend Goethe (Graf, Hochhäusler, and Petzold, "Die Welt zur Kenntlichkeit entstellen"). This intersection between German classical culture and a landscape of myth and fairy tales underscores how Petzold, as with film genre, consistently returns to recurring stories to register historical change.

It is difficult to know where to start with such a long, rich, and varied work, and I will limit myself here to Petzold's contribution. From its opening seconds, *Beats Being Dead* invokes another recurring story, the myth and/or tale of Ondine ("Undine" in German). In German mythology, Ondine is a water nymph who falls in love with a mortal man; by having a child with him, she herself becomes mortal. As she begins to age, however, he loses interest in her, and she soon finds him sleeping with another woman. Ondine curses him so that, should he fall asleep again, he will die (thus the origin of "Ondine's curse," a sleep-apnea disorder). In an almost abstract first image, gentle waves—the name "Ondine/Undine" is based on the Latin word for wave—are matched to a woman's body, turned, as in so many of Petzold's films, away from the viewer.

The Ondine myth explores the boundary between fantasy (of immortal water nymphs) and reality (becoming mortal and the subsequent banality of a cheating man), as in much of Petzold's cinema. In *Beats Being Dead,* the opening sequence invokes this boundary as viewers see Johannes asleep and slowly waking. Images of a protagonist waking in pivotal moments recur in many of Petzold's films, from *Pilots* right through *Yella* and *Jerichow*, and allow in all of them for the possibility that much of the plot is dreamt. Here, Johannes groggily waking is linked to another recurring technique in Petzold's films, surveillance monitors—he is actually returning to consciousness in front of a bank of such monitors in a hospital office. These monitors serve, as always with Petzold, a more-than-professional function, as they show his former girlfriend, Sara, arriving with her father, the head doctor of the hospital where Johannes works.[20]

The film's second wakening of Johannes also comes from a nap, this time on the shore of an idyllic forest lake that delivers to him his modern Ondine, Ana. Having fallen asleep after skinny dipping, he is awoken at night as a group of motorcyclists pull up. He had actually encountered them earlier at a gas station (one of Petzold's favorite transit spaces, this one used in all three directors' parts of *Dreileben*). Here, at night, Ana retreats from the group to the forest with one motorcyclist, all observed by the naked Johannes, whose clothes and shoes are stranded over by the group. Ana's partner photographs her with his phone in the middle of a sex act, and, when he shows his friends the picture, she angrily heaves his offending iPhone into the lake. It is the second time, in the film's opening minutes, that a modern visual technology is abused as a means of illicit surveillance, revisiting Petzold's critique of ubiquitous cameras and the mentalities they symptomatize. When she throws the phone into the water, her lover slaps her, and the motorcycle group then abandons her, leaving her topless between the shore and woods, altogether nymphlike for Johannes to rescue.

The sylvan setting of this meeting, another random encounter in Petzold's cinema, underscores the repeated importance of the forest in his work. The forest hosts the beginning of Ana and Johannes's relationship and then much of the rest of the film, as a space away from the pressures of contemporary life. Petzold and the other directors have discussed how setting and shooting *Dreileben* in the Thuringian Forest was central to the project. As noted with both *State I Am In* and *Ghosts*, the forest has long been an important location for Petzold's engagement with fairy tales and myths. This particular forest, Petzold has observed, had been little depicted in German cinema despite its hosting many myths and tales, like that of Rübezahl. In *Beats Being Dead,* as it does in many of his films, the forest is initially fantasized as a forgotten refuge from everyday life, a space away from the movement and transit spaces of cars, roads, and gas stations. For Ana, it is a space removed from an unhappy and impoverished home life and, for Johannes, a place away from the affluent doctor friends of his (presumably also doctor) mother. Here, as in *Ghosts* and arguably *Yella* and *Jerichow* as well, Petzold's reading of the fairy-tale forest echoes Bruno Bettelheim's in his classic study of the fairy tale, *The Uses of Enchantment: The Meaning and Importance of Fairy Tales.* For Bettelheim, the forest is the place suspended between the (literal or metaphorical) loss of parents and the finding of self (94). Bettelheim sees the forest as a space to be navigated and eventually mastered. Referencing Dante's use of the forest in the *Divine Comedy* ("Where the straight way was lost" before he finds his guide Virgil), Bettelheim suggests that this forest of "an as yet undeveloped personality" will give way to a "more highly developed humanity" with the child's departure from the woods (94).

Such a psychological development in the fairy-tale woods would normally correspond well to mainstream character arc, but this developmental optimism is entirely refigured in Petzold's forest. His forests resist their fairy-tale function by serving simultaneously as the socioeconomic "ghost zone" or zone of crisis, one of abeyance, that Petzold has consistently foregrounded. In *Dreileben,* Petzold deploys these fairy-tale fragments of the forest to explore Ana's potential navigation of an economic ghost zone. Underemployed and unhappy at home, she does find a guide when she is lost in the woods, but Johannes is no Virgil, and their departure from the forest for the contemporary world is highly ambiguous. She begins to believe that her forest encounter with him, and especially his plan to study medicine in Los Angeles, will lead her out of the confusing thicket of her life. In Ana, Petzold offers one of many examples of a woman set on improving her lot who mistakenly places her fantasies of neoliberal self-improvement in a stranger she meets (see also *Wolfsburg, Yella, Jerichow,* and *Barbara*).

Perhaps more than any other of his works, *Beats Being Dead* makes clear Petzold's antiromantic tendencies. In an interview on *Something to Remind Me,* for example, he distinguishes his sensibility from Tom Tykwer's *Heaven* because, he says, watching Tykwer's film, he recognized that love will not save us (Gansera and Petzold, "Toter Mann was nun?"). *Beats Being Dead* builds on this antiromantic insight with a doomed summer love affair, one that is particularly unusual for Petzold's cinema for how much physical intimacy it depicts. In his DVD commentary to *The State I Am In,* in which Jeanne hears her parents having sex off-screen, Petzold comments that he would be too embarrassed to stage a sex scene between his actors, and his cinema generally avoids much explicit depiction of sexual contact—another way in which his work distinguishes itself, despite its consistent excavation of genre films, from mainstream cinema. Notwithstanding its pointed title, for example, *The Sex Thief* pivots on the interruptus of Petra's shocking and/or knocking out her would-be lovers just before they have sex, not least so she can rob them. And, although Petzold does show more physical contact in *Jerichow,* the first time Thomas and Laura have sex, the staging is cold, mechanical, even brutal in their hallway setting upon each other.

The depiction of physical intimacy in *Beats Being Dead* is the most explicit in Petzold's cinema, but it is nonetheless refigured in the direction of his recurring themes of the seriality of modern world and the neoliberal transformation of the body. If Ana's performing oral sex on the motorcyclist is unusually detailed for Petzold's work, in both image and sound, then it is primarily utilized to demonstrate the grotesqueness of the phone photo and to show how Johannes is later disturbed when, with him, she uses the same techniques and words that he had witnessed and heard in the forest. Even more telling is a sequence after Ana has promised Johannes sex to go along with her English lessons and his studying for his medical exams. Under the covers on his bed, she quizzes him on English terms for all parts of his as well as her body, illustrating each with a touch. The scene, in its mixture of physical intimacy with English lessons, echoes Fassbinder's *Marriage of Maria Braun* (*Die Ehe der Maria Braun*; 1979), also about a postwar woman committed to improving her lot by way of English and the United States. For Fassbinder and Petzold, as well as for Ana and Johannes, self-improvement is mapped directly onto sexuality, fantasy, and the body in emphatic economic transformation.

In his commentary on *Wolfsburg,* Petzold notes that, despite many romantic comedies to the contrary, people invariably stay within their own socioeconomic stratum when finding love. In that film, Philip has already jumped a class by marrying Katja, the sister of his employer, and his unmeditated socioeconomic backslide to Laura seems doomed. In *Dreileben*, similarly, Johannes never appears likely to stay with Ana, particularly when her fantasies for self- and social promotion become more manifest. When she hears that they have been invited to "the golf club" by Johannes's ex-girlfriend Sara and her doctor dad—an invitation proffered from an Audi convertible while Ana and Johannes walk in the forest—Ana insists that Johannes introduce her to this upscale social scene. She apparently does not understand her forest function as a space away from the world that Johannes, at least temporarily, wants to escape. When, at the climactic golf-club party, Ana finds Johannes dancing with Sara—with her well-heeled friends and family clapping collective, almost ritualic encouragement—Ana burns Sara's back with a lit cigarette, graphically fulfilling the legend of Ondine's revenge on her cheating lover.

With this dramatic vengeance, Ana is banished back to the forest, her effort to leave the ghost zone in ruins. Encountering her for the last time in the woods, Johannes uses the opportunity to break from her, blaming her for a decision he was sure to make all along. When she flashes a knife and hints at a failed effort at suicide, he talks down to her, querying pedantically if she will grab a knife every time she does not like something (an echo of the therapist's pedantic condescension toward Laura's suicide attempt in *Wolfsburg*). Ana is not aware of the plans he has already made to accompany Sara to Berlin, where her father has secured her admission to the university despite her poor high-school performance. The film concludes with what viewers once again realize might or might not be a dream. After sleeping on the familiar lake shore, Ana is on the way home through the forest, but the escaped murderer Molesch is pursuing her, as viewers see in the unsteady handheld POV that has haunted the film's forest from the beginning (like the *Halloween*-influenced POV in *Yella*). It is notable how Molesch is absent from most of Petzold's contribution and only seems to draw close when Johannes has abandoned Ana to the ghost zone of the forest. But at the moment Molesch moves to slash her, Johannes wakes up—awakening, as he did multiple times at the beginning of the film, but now he is in one of Petzold's movement spaces, in the passenger seat of Sara's luxury Audi en route to Berlin. After he suggests that he drive, Sara turns on music that Johannes has given her, and he hears a song that he also, either in reality or in a dream, shared with Ana (another key diegetic use of music, the song "Cry Me a River" driving home Petzold's recurring aquatic-mnemonic themes). The film concludes with Sara's car decelerating to a stop, with Johannes apparently hesitating about his vehicular and existential push forward. It is another vehicular ending for Petzold, another movement space unexpectedly and suddenly transformed. In *Dreileben*, however, Petzold offers not the bang of his many concluding car crashes bur rather a fading, fatal whimper of forest fantasy.

Barbara: Looking Awry at East Germany

In a scene near the beginning of Petzold's award-winning, surprise Oscar nominee *Barbara* (2012), one doctor, André, hosts another, Barbara, in his lab and points to a print of a painting by Rembrandt.[21] Rembrandt's *Anatomy Lesson of Dr. Nicolaes Tulp* (1632) depicts a public autopsy in an anatomical theater; it is actually a group portrait of seven surgeons and their guild's "reader," or leader, Dr. Tulp, as he engages in the dissection of the corpse of a recently executed thief, Adriaen het Kint. André asks Barbara if she notices anything in the painting: the hand that Tulp is currently exposing is the wrong one for that side of Kint's body, right rather than the correct left, and is altogether too large for the thief's frame. André says he doubts that Rembrandt would make such a mistake and that, if one looks carefully, one notices that the audience of seven surgeons is actually looking not so much to the exposed body but to the anatomical atlas next to it—they are looking not to the corpse, where the (painting's) viewers' gaze is guided, but rather to a book representation of the body. In this way, and reminiscent of Lacan's analysis of Hans Holbein's *The Ambassadors,* as well as W.G. Sebald's of this same Rembrandt, the viewers of this painting look against the grain of viewership staged within the painting and in the anatomical theater itself. Contravening the looks of the seven surgeons whose portrait he is painting, Rembrandt guides the gaze of his viewers, André observes, from the apparent focus on anatomy to, instead, a human victim of state violence—the Dutch master has depicted divergent modes of spectatorship, coexisting yet contrasting, to empathize with a marginal figure now dead but, here, not forgotten.

Besides offering another remarkable example of cinematic ekphrasis in Petzold's work (as with the paintings of Gerhard Richter discussed above), André's citation of Rembrandt suggests a revealing mise-en-abyme for *Barbara* (with its interwoven medical-political themes) and for Petzold's cinema more generally. While most movie viewers might look in one, obvious direction—not least due to Petzold's retooling of the remnants and ruins of genre that I have been foregrounding throughout—his work allows viewers to observe individuals subtly depicted, allows them to, as Zizek puts it, look awry at individuals in transition and transformation, sometimes, as here, reduced to mere material. The painting's recognition, even Christlike apotheosis, of the thief Kint is an engagement and empathy with the marginal figures that Petzold's cinema consistently depicts. Much as Rembrandt excavates out of this anatomy lesson a sympathy for a victim otherwise overlooked, Petzold excavates out of genre cinema a sensitivity to and sensibility for individuals at the fringes of society. Often he terms such marginal individuals, those rendered spectral by continuous and fundamental socioeconomic change, ghosts, and here the ghost he archaeologically exhumes might be the GDR itself, an entire "collective existence and essence" (*Gemeinwesen*) now lost (as he discussed with the Wittenberge setting of *Yella*; see Kreist and Petzold, "Wracks Mit Geschichte"). But *Barbara* undertakes these themes not via horror, as in *Yella*, but in an entirely new, and intriguing, generic framework for Petzold's cinema.

Barbara is based loosely on a novella by Hermann Broch, but Petzold relocates Broch's post–World War I plot to 1980 East Germany (Prot). The film follows its protagonist as she is transferred from (East) Berlin and its famous Charité hospital to a small-town clinic—*Barbara*'s title recalls *Yella* in its eponymous foregrounding of a woman in transition and even on a personal and social precipice, a determined woman on the move navigating different professional and therefore political systems. The film hints initially and briefly at Barbara's recent imprisonment by East German authorities, apparently due to her application to leave the Warsaw Pact country, an imprisonment that has left her lonely, suspicious, and now reassigned to the "provinces." In this sleepy clinic, however, she is befriended and then starts to fall for André. At first (and not incorrectly), she regards André as complicit with the Stasi

(East German secret police) that not only monitors her but subjects her to humiliating house and strip searches. She does escape the Stasi's surveillance when she rendezvouses with a boyfriend, Jörg, from West Germany, who delivers to her not only the consumer goods (cigarettes, panty hose) often unavailable to East Germans but also cash and a plan to escape to the West. Once more, the physical props of makeup, money, and the presence and promise of mobility play prominently. But despite her antipathy to East Germany and its state violence visited upon its dissenters—she says at one point that "one cannot be happy in this country"—she finds herself hesitating about leaving her work and André, apparently in that order.

Barbara irrevocably changes the prevailing perception that the Berlin School and Petzold himself deliberately avoid one of the key genres of post-Wall German cinema, historical drama—here again Petzold engages with, deploys, and critiques elements of an existing and dominant genre of post-1989 German cinema. *Barbara*'s (generically) critical approach to contemporary trends in German cinema recalls the way in which *Ghosts* both cites and critiques the recently rampant genre of the "Berlin film," and *Jerichow* does likewise with the "guest-worker film." Discussing *Barbara*, Petzold implies that he was responding to the recent poster child for this historical or "heritage" trend, the work dominant in the representation of the GDR and especially Stasi, *The Lives of Others* (dir. Florian Henckel von Donnersmarck, 2006; see Fisher, "German Historical Film as Production Trend"). *The Lives of Others* follows a fictional East German playwright and the Stasi officer charged with monitoring him and tells the optimistic (and historically distorting) story of the Stasi officer lying to protect the playwright's dissident activities. Among other things, the film was celebrated for its stylistic choices, particularly its narrow and drab color palette that reflected (the memories of) a socialist world bereft of much consumerist advertising.[22]

Petzold emphasized that, with *Barbara*, he wanted to make a film in which East Germany was, by contrast, colorful (Nord and Petzold, "Ich wollte, dass die DDR Farben Hat"; and interview herein)—he himself remembered East Germany as such, as he had been there often as a child, when his parents would vacation there (he recounts that his father apparently considered returning to the East after the mid-1970s oil crisis). Given Barbara's hesitation about her planned flight from East Germany, the color is not only literal—including *Barbara*'s many shots of lovely summer landscapes and of the remarkable beauty of decaying buildings—but also psychological and political. Petzold is exploring the many forms of living under corrupt regimes, the personal colors (shot in vivid thirty-five millimeter) that could convince one to remain in countries clearly criminal in much of their behavior. As I noted with *Yella*, Petzold regards the failure of the GDR as the failure of Germany in general—that is, the failure of a state founded in principles directed explicitly against Nazi Germany. If the GDR was a forty-year project on behalf of a better Germany, what allowed it to survive so long and what ultimately led to its failure? As in *State I Am In*, Petzold investigates the key role of fantasy in this political failure, how a political system and its ideals can capture (or not) the imagination and how, over time, such a political system of beliefs can maintain or lose a hold on individuals.

If *The Lives of Others* succeeds primarily as melodrama, with its moral lines between good and bad self-servingly clear and distinct, *Barbara* excavates out of similar historical drama the moment of ambiguous abeyance that is central to Petzold's cinema in general. The film, like Broch's novella, explores the moment of decision Barbara faces between realizing her personally driven politics, her growing love for her colleague, and her commitment to her work as a doctor. Notably, however, Petzold inverts the politics of Broch's work: it is not, as in Broch's post–World War I milieu, Barbara's commitment to communism that keeps her from her colleague's love but rather her plans to flee, as in most of Petzold's work, to an economically richer West, which promises an interwoven professional and personal plenitude. Here, too, as has been the case since his 1995 *Pilots*, the relation of his characters to work is central, especially for women in a country (the GDR) that Petzold sees as more supportive of women's careers than West Germany (Husman and Petzold).

The watershed moment comes, unsurprisingly, in a hotel room, a crucial setting for Petzold's cinema from *Pilots* through *Ghosts* to *Yella* and on. As Petzold notes, Barbara's relationship with her boyfriend, Jörg, from the West has transpired in the transit spaces (*Transiträume*) that are central to many of his films: in a forest and then in an "Inter-hotel," whose name signifies the interstitial ontology of hotel settings generally (Nord and Petzold, "Ich wollte, dass die DDR Farben Hat"). This is indeed Barbara's "interspace," a hotel room housing her transformational individuality where she will learn the details of her escape from East Germany, but will also begin to rethink her commitment to fleeing. When Jörg suddenly offers to immigrate to the GDR to be with her, she declares him crazy and asserts that "one cannot be happy in this country." But then he offers to her what Petzold regards as the key sentence to the whole film (Schwenk and Petzold; see also Rodek, "*Barbara* Hat Keine Oscar-Chance"): she will be able to sleep late once she is in West Germany—since he earns enough for both of them, she will not need to work anymore.

With that, Barbara begins to realize that traversing political systems and states will irrevocably change her professional life, her relationship to work that the film, as in many of Petzold's films, so deliberately details. Seconds later, when Jörg is called to a meeting, their hotel room is visited by the newly minted East German girlfriend of Jörg's likewise West German colleague. Steffi (one of the film's only characters to speak in a regional East German dialect) wanders into the room, unaware that another, older woman finds herself likewise waiting for her western businessman-lover. The conversation between two strangers in similar situations recalls the transformative interactions between Karin and Sophie in *Pilots*, two women of different generations reflecting on their socioeconomic prospects, although here, rather than the Ruhr area versus Paris, they reflect on their chances of traversing East and West Germany. When Steffi shows Barbara a massive mail-order *Quelle* catalog with goods unavailable in East Germany and asks her what she would choose from the breathtaking plenitude of western products, one senses Barbara's reassessment of her interest in the West.

If, in *The State I Am In*, the duality between politics and haptic consumerism is generational, in *Barbara*, the more ambiguous split resides instead within a highly accomplished professional woman. Although Petzold is careful to depict the East German security apparatus's unapologetic use of violence against its dissidents—the police actions visited upon Barbara and the younger Stella are brutal indeed—in her moment of abeyance, Barbara hesitates to abandon her work and the relationships—both professional and personal—it has offered. As Petzold has noted, he was interested in how the love between André and

Barbara emerges at and through work, in how their love derives not only from (biological) reproduction but also (workplace) production (Petzold, *Barbara* Press Conference). On the one hand, this extends his recurring entwinement of work conditions and personal relationships, from *Pilots* to *Yella* and *Jerichow*. On the other hand, a love based on and growing out of production is a revealing development in a post-1989 film about the (putative) worker's state, one that nonetheless ultimately failed to capture the imagination of its people. As in *State I Am In,* love and work intersect the (in)ability of a political project to abide over time, in people's hearts and minds.

Notes

1. There is a massive literature on neoliberalism, but a succinct definition is offered by David Harvey in *A Brief History of Neoliberalism*: "a theory of political economic practices that proposes that human well-being can best be advanced by liberating individual entrepreneurial freedoms and skills within an institutional framework characterized by strong private property rights, free markets, and free trade" (2). Sennett confirms these mechanism in his volume, *The Culture of New Capitalism.*

2. I take this notion of refunctioning from Bertolt Brecht, whose plays, for example, *Mann ist Mann,* explore a similar refunctioning of people due to their changing socioeconomic contexts. See Lyons, "Brecht's *Mann ist Mann* and the Death of Tragedy."

3. The first part is in *Revolver* 16 (2007); part two is available online at http://www.revolver-film.de/Inhalte/Rev16/html/Berliner.htm (accessed February 5, 2013).

4. Petzold compares his cinema to Graf's on a number of occasions, although Petzold's films are more oriented toward art-house cinema. See, for example, Suchsland, "Geister im Thüringischen Wald."

5. See, for instance, Petzold's commentary on the *Jerichow* DVD, in which he speaks at length about "Restenergien" and "Restgesten."

6. In a short, unpublished piece on method, Benjamin writes that one "must not be afraid to return again and again to the same matter, to scatter it as one scatters earth, to turn it over as one turns over soil. . . . those images . . . severed from all earlier associations, reside as treasures in the sober rooms of our later insight." Benjamin, "Excavation and Memory" 576.

7. The budgets of Petzold's films are extremely modest compared to most U.S. and even many high-profile European productions. Schramm Film's Florian Koener von Gustorf, who has, usually along with Michael Weber, produced most of Petzold's films, estimates that *Cuba Libre*'s budget was 250,000 Euro,

and *The Sex Thief*'s was 700,000 Euros. The more elaborate theatrical releases like *Ghosts*, *Yella*, and *Jerichow* still only cost around two million Euros with thirty days of shooting, while *Barbara* had a budget of 2.9 million Euros and a thirty-five-day shoot. Author's correspondence with Florian Koerner von Gustorf, December 26, 2011.

8. For a discussion of the use of female leads in New German Cinema, see von Moltke, "Terrains Vagues."

9. Petzold, for example, said that he imagined the crew like the lonely vampires in the film, outsiders to the mainstream 1990s German cinema.

10. In one interview, when asked why the theme of the RAF reemerged around 2000–2001, Petzold suggests that it has to do with the end of, and turn away from, the Kohl years (Buck and Petzold).

11. I thank Tina Gerhardt for clarifying this reference.

12. One of the only times it leaves her perspective (aside from the end, when Heinrich surreptitiously calls the police) is when Klaus is arrested.

13. It is not an accident that the nondiegetic musical score starts—for the first time in the film—only at the approach to the border, when the family is leaving Portugal and returning to Germany. As Petzold notes, it is a ghostlike score, emphasizing their spectral nature.

14. Petzold recounts in the interview herein that *Something to Remind Me* would have had a theatrical release, were it not for (unaffordable) rights for the music. *Wolfsburg* did have a limited theatrical release.

15. The same may be said of the moral legibility of the melodrama that Brooks has foregrounded: although Petzold admits there is a strong moral element in the film, he said that he was more interested in studying the kind of "moral work" people do, rather than, as a melodrama might pathetically do, taking sides and emotionally exploiting that side taking (Lenssen and Petzold).

16. In the DVD commentary, Petzold recounts how they deleted the dialogue reference to the first of May from the script because it was too pedantic, but that "for the actors, it was still there" and "important." Without a "union or some group" to which they belong, and being so "individuated" in their work, Laura and Philip are ignorant of the date and its meaning for worker rights. Petzold's interest in workers and workers' collectives in the film is confirmed by his visual reference to Farocki's *Workers Leave the Factory* (1995), which collects references to labor actions outside factories throughout the history of cinema.

17. Petzold mentions other literary sources as well, though in a more general way, including Cesare Pavese's *The Beautiful Summer* (1949) and the 1998 novel *Rave* by Rainald Goetz.

18. Vahabzadeh, Göttler, and Petzold, "Kino ist wie ein Bankraub." See King, "Province Always Rings Twice," for more detail on *Jerichow*'s relation to *Ossessione* (3).

19. This is true of other recent films as well, like Thomas Arslan's *Siblings* (*Geschwister*; 1997), in which the three eponymous siblings are ethnically

Turkish-German (with German mother and Turkish father) and negotiate between German and Turkish society in three different ways, while Fatih Akın's recent films offer ethnic Turks self-identifying with aspects of German culture in surprising ways (*Head On*'s Cahit with German punk culture, *The Edge of Heaven*'s Nejat with Goethe, as a German professor in Bremen and then German bookshop owner in Istanbul).

20. In *The Sex Thief* and *Wolfsburg*, surveillance camera images are similarly framed with erotic impulses.

21. For the surprise around, and even controversy about, *Barbara* being named Germany's 2012 submission to the competition for the Oscar for best foreign-language film, see Rodek, "*Barbara* hat keine Oscar-Chance." The Rembrandt painting, Petzold informed me, was placed in the film in part as an homage to W. G. Sebald's *The Rings of Saturn,* which also reproduces this painting in one of its intriguing visuals.

22. It is notable how Petzold avoids the kind of fetishizing preciousness many historical drama/heritage films manifest in their treatment of mise-en-scène. Andrew Higson, in his groundbreaking work on the heritage film, criticizes the way in which the spectacularization of period sets, props, and costumes/makeup overwhelm the narrative, and Petzold has criticized this aspect of historical dramas explicitly (Rampetreiter). *Barbara* tends, deliberately I would argue, to avoid the lingering shots of clothes, interiors, or lengthy musical interludes that draw attention to the specific historical moment.

Interview with Christian Petzold |

This interview mainly took place in July 2011, with a shorter follow-up in October 2012, at Petzold's office in Berlin. It was conducted in German, so I include a number of original words or phrases that seem important to his cinema.

JAIMEY FISHER: Places and spaces, especially in small cities and towns, are consistently important in your films. Where did you grow up? Can you describe the region, the particular place, where you are from?

CHRISTIAN PETZOLD: That has to do with my parents, who grew up during the Nazi period. At the end of World War II, they were children—actually, they were refugees, so children of migration. My father is from Saxony [in the former East Germany], and my mother is from what is now the Czech Republic. They met, then, as refugees in a small town in the southern Ruhr region near Dortmund and Düsseldorf [in far western West Germany]. So, we always lived in transit spaces

[*Transitorte*], often in something like a bungalow. So where I grew up was a bit like a "trailer park" [said in English].

There were so many buildings that had been destroyed in Germany during the war that there was a significant lack of houses and apartments. So, for the first couple of years, I was really a refugee child in the city where I grew up and also always a bit on the margins. Since that time, when I arrive in a new city, for example in Milan or Madrid, I always go for walks in places far away from the tourist sights; instead I always end up at the trailer parks. I do not know what attracts me to such places. For me, those are the interesting spaces, always kinds of transitional spaces [*Durchgangsorte*]. I guess I do not have a true home [*Heimat*].

JF: What was the first film you can remember seeing in a movie theater? I ask because I always think that clarifies the time, the moment, in film history when one is growing up.

CP: That was an interesting moment. I was six or seven and in a small town where I went to the cinema with my friends and without our parents—that's probably why I can remember it. That is why cinema will never die out: it is a place without parents. We went to see *The Jungle Book*, and there was a trailer beforehand for a film called *Liane, the Girl from the Jungle* [*Liane, das Mädchen aus dem Urwald*; 1956]. Liane was rather like Tarzan, and there was a scene with her, this young woman probably twenty-one or twenty-two years old, very beautiful and with hardly any clothes on, and she was being roasted in a cage over an open fire by cannibals. She was screaming for help, and, from that moment on, cinema has always been for me a sexual space. Godard wrote a text about *Liane* because, for him, this was finally an intriguing film from Germany. Later, Harun Farocki met the woman who played Liane, Marion Michael. Even though he is older than I, it was an important film for him, too, because suddenly, in the middle of all these terrible German movies full of literary adaptations and theatrical styles, there was something out of 1920s and 1930s German cinema—suddenly a cinema of bodies, the erotic, secrets, and forests. That's really something I can remember, this Liane.

JF: So there were not any film societies, clubs, or anything similar for noncommercial or older films?

CP: Yes, once a week, there was a film evening. Then, when I was eighteen, I did mandatory civil service instead of military service in the army. I was in social work [at the German version of the YMCA] that also allowed me to work with film some—I organized a little film club for the young people there. According to the teacher there, I always had to organize a double program, so as to include a film for those who were not as educated. I never liked this kind of division between, for instance, a literary film and then a Bud Spencer film. I really never liked that at all, so I just mixed the program up, which was really fun. It was all on sixteen-millimeter, and we had to do everything ourselves, pick it up at the train station, write the texts about it. That was really a great time of my life. And then, of course, I would also watch the films alone at night—I really saw an unbelievable number of films in that time and decided to pursue film then.

JF: You came to Berlin to study literature? Berlin was pretty different at that point than it is now. Could you describe the atmosphere then when you got to Berlin?

CP: Back then Berlin was simply *the* city, as it is now, I think, where one wanted to be. Besides Berlin, there were maybe two or three other centers, maybe Munich, Cologne, Düsseldorf, and Hamburg. But the politicos, the leftists, and the anarchists all went to Berlin—in Berlin, there were no parents, and there were subsidies for the city [laughs]. In Hamburg, et cetera, one already had to find a job, earn money, as the rents were quite high. I liked everything about Berlin. Berlin was the exact opposite of the place I grew up, the exact opposite—politically, but also in terms of the rhythm, the light, everything. And since my parents were refugees from East Germany, I knew they would never come to visit me in Berlin. They would have had to pass through East Germany, so I was, in a certain sense, free.

JF: So you began your literary studies in Berlin?

CP: Yes, but I really only went to the cinema. And all my writings at first were about the relationship of literature to cinema.

JF: So you were always oriented in the direction of cinema?

CP: Yes, always in the direction of cinema, but it is also funny to think back and realize that the best times in my studies were not really when I was writing about the relationship of cinema to literature, but rather about structuralism—that and maybe Middle High German lyric poetry. So what I liked about my literary studies was precisely where there was no cinema. I was not very convinced when they tried to introduce cinema into literary studies, where education [*Bildung*] tried to become popular.

JF: And then you transferred to the German Film and Television Academy in Berlin [DFFB]?

CP: I wanted to finish my literary studies and then ended up applying to the DFFB in 1987, but was rejected. I thought I would certainly be accepted, as I had already been an auditor with [Hartmut] Bitomsky, [Harun] Farocki, and [Dominik] Graf for like two years, and I really found it all great and was clear that this is what I wanted. And they rejected me, and I'm still indignant when I think about it [laughs].

JF: Of course, Fassbinder was rejected, too, no?

CP: Yes, and they told me that, something like, "Fassbinder was also rejected, and you'll make it too." But I said that's total nonsense! So in 1988 I applied again, and in 1989 I started my studies. And my experience as I started studying there was a total shock because I had written many short stories beforehand and wanted to make feature films immediately, but then you are sitting there with seventeen, eighteen other people, young and all. One sits there and talks the whole day, watches films, and suddenly I did not understand how cinema works at all. Looking back, confusion and contemplation are great and all, but, at the time, it was a total crisis for me. It was similar to the crisis I had when I first heard the Sex Pistols and then heard the *Talking Heads 77* album. With those two albums, I suddenly did not know what to do anymore. I did not do anything for a whole year. I just watched films with my friends at the editing table, watched Griffith and all of Stroheim. I would see three films a day and so, I would guess, at least a thousand films in that year.

JF: Of course you had already seen a lot when you were working at your civil-service job, no?

CP: I knew about New Hollywood and the New Wave, found them great, but, with all the works from film history, I really watched very different films and began to think about actors. By the end of my studies there, I really was a failure because I had not produced anything. I made some short films, but some of the other students were already going to festivals and winning prizes.

JF: I saw some of the films from this period, like *Ostwärts* [*Eastwards*], *Süden* [*South*], and *Weiber* [*Women*].

CP: Yes, exactly, I managed to make those kinds of films, but I really did not know what I should be doing, so I traveled and read literature, especially American literature, Anglo-American literature. I have to admit that that literature really influenced me the most. And then I began to read [Anton] Chekhov and [Georges] Simenon, and I thought, okay, let's try to make a feature film. I made a twenty- or twenty-five-minute film [*Das warme Geld*], and then I had the courage to write a whole script. When I was done, I went to Harun [Farocki]. I always thought that he hated fiction and feature films, but he read it, and he was really taken with it, and we talked about it for weeks and what could be changed in it. That was maybe the most important moment for me—I thought: yes, this is it. And so then I made *Pilots,* my first film, as my graduation film.

JF: And so you have worked with Harun Farocki from that time on. I have a few questions about your collaboration, but I would be happy to hear about it now, if you prefer.

CP: Yeah, it is kind of like when one is happily in love, and then someone asks, why are you in love? And it is uncannily difficult to say. One can only respond, "I love her" [laughs]. Yes, I was just at Harun's the day before yesterday, as I had a problem with a scene that we are supposed to shoot next week [for *Barbara*]. As I explained the problem to him, I just was not clear on what the scene is really about, what the suspense of the scene is supposed to be. I explained the problem, we smoked and had coffee, and even as I explained it, the problem solved itself. I could not have managed that with anybody else; he just says one or two things. Kleist calls it, "On the gradual formation of thought in speaking" [*Über die allmähliche Verfertigung der Gedanken beim Reden*]. One should add to the Kleist quote that the space for articulation matters, too, the social and intellectual or emotional and mental space. And Harun, well, he is precisely such a space for me.

JF: How do you find Farocki's nonfiction films? For example, you have mentioned his film about Georg Glaser and how it relates to history, particularly how Glaser fell out of history.

CP: Yes, exactly. As I was working on *The State I Am In,* Harun gave me some writings of Glaser's, including some biographical material that is not in the film. I find his Glaser film fantastic—one really has to say that Harun really found something with it. With his films, Harun is searching for a certain type of place, sort of transit spaces [*Transitorte*], where something fundamental undergoes transformation. For example, how the working class is transformed in its representations of itself, or how life itself is fundamentally transformed in a school. And sometimes I sit there as I might in front of a feature or fiction film, and I think cinema is not at its end, that there is still so much to uncover.

JF: You were enrolled at the DFFB during the *Wende* [the fall of the Berlin Wall in 1989 and the reunification of Germany in 1990]. Did these events make a strong impression on you? I am thinking of your [short film] *Eastwards*, for example, and was wondering if there is a certain continuity in your work from this time—for example, *Yella* and *Jerichow* both unfold in the former East Germany.

CP: Yes, it came up again for me over ten years later.

JF: So a certain belatedness [*Nachträglichkeit*] was in play?

CP: Exactly, I think that this belatedness is important. We had the *Wende*, and then the Soviet Union collapsed—or rather, it was transformed into a neoliberal state [laughs], partially with oligarchies and such things. It was an absolute crime. And we saw all that. We saw, for instance, films from the Moscow Film School, which had been a totally subsidized space in the university, and suddenly it received no more money. I saw two films from that school at that point, and they were fantastic, but they had not really found a language to express what had happened in that country, and I thought, that is what we also have to do. Then Peter Nestler also came for a seminar and said exactly the same thing to us: You have to take your cameras and have to look at what is happening. That's how *Ostwärts* came to be. Thomas [Arslan] also made a very, very beautiful film about how the Wall was dismantled. But mostly people shot things as if they were downloaded from the Internet, the images that we all knew. And I myself could not manage it—I did not really find any images, at that point, for the *Wende*. I realize that I should have directed the camera at myself as well. I saw the same problem with September 11 in the U.S., when the very next day in Germany, there were exactly the pieces you would expect on King Kong in Manhattan, et cetera, as if they had already been written.

I think one really has to live with the confusion a while. And with the *Wende*, I was totally confused, as were my parents—they came from East Germany, and they really did not know what to think. This state of balance just was not maintained. And then I thought, this has always preoccupied me, so after *The State I Am In*, which was really a matter of working through the 1970s, I was able to finally address what happened: the transformation of a state-socialist system into a neoliberal system. In particular, I wanted to explore what happened to the people in the process of this transformation—and what kinds of films could be made about that.

JF: Did these events have a personal meaning because of your parents?

CP: My parents, in so far as they are refugees, were anti-Communists. I was of course a Communist just to provoke my parents, but I did not really know what that is. Of course, I had read everything, Marx and everything, but right up to today, I do not know how to explain all that to my children. But for me the failure of East Germany was the failure of [all of] Germany, the utter failure, particularly as a counter-idea to the Nazis, as a leftist counter-idea. But one just cannot base socialism on a single country. One ends up with a nationalist socialism, as in North Korea, which of course is a complete disaster. For example, my wife is Turkish, and we were at a party three days after November 9, 1989, and there were some young people from the GDR there. And the first thing they said was, "There are so many foreigners here!" And I thought, uh-oh. I knew then that this isolation of the GDR allowed for no connection to, for no engagement with others, and realized then that the former GDR would have a problem with racism.

JF: I would like to ask you a couple of questions about film genre, as I think it is worth noting that you frequently mention genre films, although it is clear that you do not find the [German] consensus cinema of the 1990s very productive. You often mention genre films as an influence on your own films, for example *Detour* on *Cuba Libre*, *Near Dark* on *The State I Am In*, *Driver* on *Wolfsburg*, *Carnival of Souls* on *Yella*, and *The Postman Always Rings Twice* on *Jerichow*. What influence have such genre films had on you? Is it much different than in New German Cinema, for example, with Fassbinder, or than in the New Wave with Godard, who both worked with genre films from the U.S.?

CP: I think the difference is that we are twenty years on. [These directors] took genre as a grammar, and they used that grammar to destroy genre and to unleash a new kind of energy—they quoted, destroyed, deconstructed genre, no? But as we began to make films, there was not any cinema anymore, no genre cinema at all. When you go to the cinema today, one does not see police films; they are all on television. One does not see melodrama; it is all on television now, in the afternoons. It is simply not there anymore. Maybe a few comedies, but in general it is mostly mythic adaptations, like comics. So we had to approach it differently. It was more the case that I wanted to rediscover genre; I did not want to destroy it, therefore not *de*construct it, rather *re*construct it. I guess that is the way one can put it. It is a kind of archaeology. And therefore we, with the Berlin School and such, wanted to build it back up again.

A film that I find really excellent in this regard is *The Last Picture Show,* as it achieves something in this direction. It not a conservative or sentimental film—it is a historical film, yet the viewer is aware very precisely that it unfolds today. And it is a film about love, about the love of cinema, the love of images, the love of America, but, also simultaneously, the poisoning of all this. I really found that great. And with the last film, *Dreileben,* I showed all the actors *The Last Picture Show.* They really are not familiar with films anymore—one can buy films everywhere, but no one really watches them. Godard said that, too. Everybody copies books but no one reads them.

JF: So just a kind of consumption of the media.

CP: Yes, exactly. I do not think one needs to be familiar with that many films; sometimes thirty is enough. I do that with my shoots, I hold little film seminars for the actors. For example, before beginning the shoot [for *Barbara*], I just tried to find an image for the male leading role. A friend of mine, Alexander Horwath, wrote a piece about *My Darling Clementine,* a film that really left a deep impression on me. The piece is about a scene with this image of Henry Fonda in a chair on a porch [shows me an image from large binder that shows Fonda tipped back on his chair on a wide porch with a western landscape in the background]. He brought the scene into a balance, and the film is exactly like that: The town has not yet fully formed, America is not yet settled, everything is in the balance. And as long as there is this kind of balance, one can tell a story, one can make a film.

JF: So, it is what you have elsewhere termed an abeyance [*Schwebezustand*]?

CP: Yes, precisely. That's really the only interesting approach. Anyone who demands films that are not in such an abeyance, not in a crisis (as crisis is also an abeyance), anyone who would upend such a balance—

they destroy cinema. The sales people in Hollywood and at the TV stations here in Europe, they all demand the same stuff. They demand secure box-office receipts, and such an approach just leads to decline and collapse.

JF: But I find it really fascinating that you so often mention American genre films, like old Westerns and horror films. This is something very unusual, even unique, among contemporary European auteurist directors.

CP: I always wondered about that as well. I thought all [directors] have to think in this way, because I worked in theater, and ancient Greek theater is, fundamentally, the beginning of democracy. In the *Oresteia*, one learns that it is no longer the gods who issue judgments, but rather the people. And the American Western is the ancient drama of the modern, especially for America. How many court cases are there in Westerns? In the saloon there are constantly hearings and negotiations: courts, lynch justice, and so forth, really just constantly in those works. And that is all fictional. These towns do not make any sense—there's a ranch there, but how could even eighty people live from it? Nothing is growing there at all. Such a community is really just an abstract idea. It is like a stage, and yet somehow there is always something new emerging there. There is always some new negotiation. And that, for me, is genre.

Film noir is also a genre. There the question is how can one, as an individual, live in a shitty and corrupt world, how can the individual go on?

JF: And these films contemplate the questions you mentioned about transformation and transition?

CP: Yes, they contemplate them. How can one manage it? Philip Marlow is not a good man, but he is trying not to be a bad one. That is also a balance situation, and I find that intriguing. And New Hollywood understood that, not least in the crisis at the end of the Vietnam War. Like Robert Altman in *The Long Goodbye*—they took these figures and made them new.

JF: As in *Chinatown*?

CP: Yes, *Chinatown*, too. And they do not make fun of their genre models. That is something many Europeans directors do—they make parodies of these genre films. I hate that like the plague. That's really the cheapest shot: The parodist says, "I actually know more than this, I am just parodying." That really disgusts me. One sees with *Chinatown* or *The Long Goodbye* that they really love these films, that they have great respect for them.

JF: Do you know the thesis of Thomas Elsaesser in his book about New German Cinema? One of his theses was that New German Cinema lacked, and was searching for, an audience—it had critical success, but never really popular success or even interest. I wonder if the interest in genre for you is also partially this concern and this search.

CP: I do not really think so, because there's simply not an audience anymore for such films.

I experienced something once, at the beginning of the 1990s or at the end of the 1980s, when *Pretty Woman* was showing in Berlin. As students of the DFFB, as film students, we could go into any cinema in the city for free, so for four years I went to see everything. That was a wonderful education, of course. One day, at 3:30 in the afternoon or something, I went to see *Pretty Woman* on the KuDamm [the former main commercial street of West Berlin], and there were all these secretaries [*sic*] in there, all these women who were watching Richard Gere, not Julia Roberts. And I was amazed: They were screaming, "What a man!" He had been sitting in a bathtub for about two hours, and then he turned on the hot water again—with his big toe. One could see that Richard Gere had really been sitting in the bathtub for at least two hours, as they showed his skin in a close-up. And the women in the audience just screamed.

And then I realized: This is American cinema, which has a certain physicality [*Physis*]. And that is for me also genre. That they do not just rummage through material but really discover something new in it. And what recurs all the time in these genre films is how men look at that particular historical moment. In *Pretty Woman*, Richard Gere is a neoliberal ass, he destroys companies or whatever, but he represents a new kind of body. Neoliberalism brings out a new kind of masculine body. That comes right out of F. Scott Fitzgerald, runs from the southern states directly to Richard Gere—and the German audiences see that and realize that they are seeing something new on the screen. I always realized that and thought, This is sexy, and this is dangerous. But we can only understand this newness when we tell the old stories and tales—*Pretty Women* is, after all, just *Cinderella.* And I find that all so interesting.

JF: Two things in particular are really interesting in what you just said. First, that you often depict such physicalities in your film and that you leave time for the viewer to perceive it. Second, that you frequently seek this corporeality with the actors, with Benno Fürmann, for example. It reminds me of David Harvey, the theorist of, among other things, neoliberalism, and of what he has written about such corporeality. He describes the neoliberal body as a strategy of accumulation [see the section on *Yella* above]. That had me thinking of Yella as she crosses over the border, and it is clear that this, too, is a form of the body as accumulation strategy.

CP: Yes, precisely. But the actors really have to work that out—it is not just there already; they have to actually develop it. We're starting to shoot [*Barbara*] next week, and, as I said, I offer a kind of seminar in a room where we watch films and read—but not psychological material. And then we go to the locations with the actors—we go walking where we are going to shoot. And that's the exact opposite of theater: Go there and really look at the location. Then they see what there is, how it smells, how it tastes, and they do that themselves. I hate theater—I mean theater not as a form, but in film.[1]

JF: I have some questions about individual films. Can you describe how you came to the political themes of *The State I Am In* after your three feature-length films for television [*Pilots, Cuba Libre,* and *The Sex Thief*], which are not, at least not as conspicuously, political.

CP: The RAF was dead; really no one was interested in them anymore. Then [Wolfgang] Grams was shot to death in Bad Kleinen, and I wondered: Where did he come from? Where have they been the whole time? What did they do the whole time? Then I started to write a screenplay about it. At the beginning, it was to be about a son of the terrorists, and the son was supposed to be me, with Harun, so to say, as my father. But then I thought that was too autobiographical, so I introduced a daughter instead, and it immediately became different. This history of domestic terrorism really permeated West Germany, in which the guilt of the father's [generation] was supposed to be worked out. With the anti-Semitism, too, that was deep in there—it was all so complicated and complex—and then came [Chancellor] Helmut Kohl and said, "We are not talking about it anymore."

So I wrote the screenplay and thought it was really pretty good, but then I only received government grants for it, not television support, and one really needs one-third TV support. But they said no. They said, "The story is good, but why not just make it with bank robbers who have a child?" But I thought that was complete nonsense.

The funny thing is that I wrote the story in the U.S., with Harun, in Berkeley and Los Angeles. That really helped me, this distance from Germany, to be in the U.S., to have to drive around in a car. In Los Angeles, I went to the villa where Brecht had been [in exile], to the Feuchtwanger villa, so I really was in a land of exiles, which fit the script. Then I finally got a bit of money from a television station and could shoot it on a really small budget.

JF: And you have said Biegelow's *Near Dark* is important for the film, no?

CP: Yes, for the way in which the actors could find a metaphor—ghosts are one metaphor, but then that does not help so much with the physicality of the characters. I thought the vampire metaphor was actually pretty good: They drive all over the country, cannot really die, but also not really live, living in the dark, hanging around transit spaces, in bars, in campers, in trailer parks, et cetera [as they do in *Near Dark*]. And I said, The vampire is also something German, was really invented in Germany. And then I thought, the Nazis have caves, Hitler in his bunker and everything, but where were the terrorists the whole time? They were everywhere in pictures, on wanted posters, et cetera, so not in a cave, but rather they were everywhere and nowhere, thus transparent.

Otherwise, I asked myself, what are terrorists, really? They are people who want to simplify a complex world. They do not want to wait, they do not want to work, they want the end and want it immediately. And so I thought, They are people who want to abbreviate history, so they were thrown off track and end up next to or outside of history. No one needed them anymore.

JF: Many critics at the time said they found it regrettable that *Something to Remind Me* was made for television. Michael Haneke, for instance, has emphasized that there are real differences, even a gap, between

TV films and cinema films. What do you think about this distinction? Do you see TV films as essentially different than cinema films?

CP: When I was making *Something to Remind Me* and *Wolfsburg*, which was also financed by television, I just pushed the whole discussion away from me, not to have to think about it. I made the film exactly as if it were for the cinema. But the consciousness that the film would at some point run during prime time and would then have a different "neighborhood" [said in English], that was clear to me, and that, of course, changes some things. I knew, for instance, that one has fewer means with which to produce a film. For example, for *Something to Remind Me*, I did not have the money to buy the rights for the Burt Bacharach song ["What the World Needs Now Is Love"]; otherwise, the film would actually have made it into theaters. The people at the television station and the producers, they would definitely have given the film a theatrical release. But that song alone would have cost, for the seven or eight minutes it plays, like three hundred thousand dollars.

JF: Yeah, and so with a budget of around $1.4 million, that would be impossible.

CP: Yes, exactly. It was dumb of me, pretty unclever of me, but maybe I did not want to be clever. I was so shocked by the success of *The State I Am In* that I did not know what to do. I wanted to make two films in two years, one right after the other, so retreated a little bit to television to have my quiet, rather like in a laboratory, where you can experiment with different things. There is always the dictum that the second film decides one's career—after every big success, people say the next one will really tell. I wanted to hold myself out of it for a bit and so made two "B" films.

JF: I wanted to ask about *Yella* and its relationship to *Carnival of Souls,* as it seems to play an important role in the conceptualization and realization of your film.

CP: Yes, the Herk Harvey was my point of departure—I always wanted to make something based on *Carnival of Souls*, but with unemployed workers. I had a project with Harun Farocki, who made a film in which the unemployed are being trained on how to present themselves. Nowadays, the worker is an individual and has to know how to present him- or herself—the whole world is a big casting call and audition. When

I saw the film of Farocki's, I thought, these are just ghosts who have to act as if they are people, having to sell themselves as something else. In *Carnival of Souls*, she dies but does not even notice she is dead. At first I thought this was too much of a student idea, but then I made *Something to Remind Me* with Nina Hoss and then saw *Nothing Ventured* [*Nicht ohne Risiko*; 2004] and thought, that's it! Not someone who is a victim, but rather a perpetrator. She takes off from the East and wants to head west; her destination is simply neoliberalism. To get there, she wants and achieves a new body.

I did, however, forbid the actors from seeing *Carnival of Souls*, and I myself did not look at it again during production, but when I was done, I saw it. There is really so much from the film in *Yella*. It really stayed in my memory, even though I did not re-see it before shooting *Yella*—I still remembered almost every shot. It is really one of the most modern films that I know.

JF: I also wanted to ask about *Jerichow* and ethnicity in the film. With Ali, a Turkish-German who lives in the country in former East Germany, I immediately thought of Fassbinder.

CP: Yes, exactly, that's why he is named Ali in the film, and we watched *Merchant of Four Seasons* [*Händler der Vierjahreszeiten*; 1971] in preparations.[2] My wife is Turkish, and migration stories are quite personal for us. I always thought that all these films in which Turks in Germany seem like victims—such films are just not very convincing. It is racist as well to say that they are all nice people and just treated badly by society. I thought I would represent someone who did everything right, like so many immigrants who come to a country and do everything right—they are attentive and friendly, and yet no one likes them. The more they try to assimilate, the more they are excluded from society. And I find that tragic, and this immigrant a tragic figure. Ali could not be more German: he has bought himself a blonde wife, a Range Rover, and a house in the forest. And this German veteran, a complete failure, and this wife, who is totally in debt—they want to kill him. I found that just really brutal. On the other hand, Ali can be a total jerk—he is so masculine, so oriented to what other men think of him, that he handles his wife like a car. He says, "Go ahead, touch it, take it for a test drive." At the end, they are all totally lost. I like it in films when characters realize things too late, and then the moviegoers, with this late recognition, leave the cinema and go out into the world.

JF: With your contribution to the three-part *Dreileben*, you return, as you did with *The State I Am In* and *Ghosts*, to a plot featuring adolescent protagonists. What do you find interesting about this age in particular, and how does your return to this constellation in *Dreileben: Beats Being Dead* fit into your work in general?

CP: There was a time in my life, between eighteen and twenty-two, when I was on the move all the time, in Italy and elsewhere, and in this time I discovered the cultural as well as the political underground. Now that I'm over fifty and take a bit of a retrospective look back to this time, I guess it also must have something to do with my parents always being on the move, always fleeing and never actually arriving anywhere. So this condition of being on the move and seeking a place in the world—that really interested me in the terrorism story that became *The State I Am In*. Similarly, in *Dreileben*, it is a young woman who is also on the move, fleeing from Bosnia and working in a hotel, thus in search of something. On the other hand, in this same small town, there are the longtime inhabitants, the ones who have big houses, who work in the hospital, who are educating their children in the schools that have always been there. But then, in times of crisis like that depicted in the film, the social relations loosen up temporarily, and, all of a sudden, maybe a homeless person can be taken into the fold, or, as in Pasolini's *Teorama* (1968), someone who does not belong there suddenly shows up . Or, inversely, a rich person (as with the young medical student in *Dreileben*) ends up abruptly in some poor neighborhood. In horror films (like *Dreileben,* in its way), such things are worked through in the plots, like high-school students visiting some place in the countryside.

In any case, if you think about how I took up such themes in *Ghosts*, it seems that, for me, it comes up every five years or so—every five years, I have to go back and analyze my youth, when I discovered so much.

JF: You have emphasized how, in *Barbara*, you set out to make the DDR colorful, something one notices immediately in the broad color palette of the film, in the vivid colors of its lovely thirty-five-millimeter photography. Why was this approach, one full of remarkable color, so important to a film about East Germany?

CP: It is related, I think, to things I saw when I still living in Cologne, where there was this group filmclub813, the name for which they got from Truffaut films. They would show musicals from East Germany, like *Heißer Sommer* with Frank Schöbel [*Hot Summer*, dir. Joachim Hasler, 1968], and, as I was remembering those films, I thought to myself: East Germany had to regard itself as colorful, too. The U.S. had Technicolor, but they in the East had certain Agfa processes, where the reds are like those in Nicholas Ray's films or in Douglas Sirk's melodramas from the 1950s. Today, almost like propaganda, we tend to imagine that East Germany had no color at all, that it was all just gray—as if a sunflower that grows in the West somehow reaches up to the sun with much more brilliant color!

Since *Barbara* is not trying to make some kind of accusation, not some kind of propagandistic message from the West, the film tries to show what beliefs, what dreams, people had in this country. A country does not survive forty years unless there is some substance, some core to it, even if that substance was growing more attenuated at the end, its dreams more faded and empty. But it was a nation that had proudly proclaimed about itself: we, more than the West, offer peace, security, nourishment and will never again turn to fascism. The romances of such a country, many influenced by Soviet literature, always took place after the summer, after the harvest. There was a certain kind of dancing and kissing—of course, that culture has its own conservative longing for the countryside, for manual labor, for hands and bodies.

And I thought: We have to work into the film these kinds of dreams that the GDR had of itself. But we also have to show how this dream was, simultaneously, beginning to fade more and more. People were starting to say that we just don't believe these messages, these claims, anymore. Just as in New Hollywood films, when Robert Altman in *The Long Goodbye* (1973) uses CinemaScope and vivid colors to show that the society is decaying and rotten—that is the message, even when the images are so beautiful.

JF: A few final questions about certain continuities and recurrences in your cinema. Can you describe what you understand as a ghost or phantom? Why has it become such a central figure for your cinema, such that you base many of your films on it?

CP: I find that, fundamentally, the ghost is *the* figure of cinema. I thought that the ghost is not only about fear but rather this falling out of time and place, not belonging anymore, that is, to be on the margins, to be unemployed, or even to be an unloved child—such people feel themselves to be ghosts. And cinema always tells the stories of people who do not belong anymore but who want to belong once again. John Wayne in *The Searchers* is also a ghost. The ghost wants to materialize itself, it wants feelings, skin, and that, for me, is a key theme. Isolation makes one ghostly, and the cinema goers are also ghosts, because they are there and they are not there. And it all feels like a dream.

JF: Of course, you are interested in this in our particular historical moment, how everything has been accelerated with neoliberalism's rapid turning of people into ghosts.

CP: Yes, absolutely. For example, when we watched *The Deer Hunter* [in preparation for *Jerichow*], one sees how the local industry is dying out there, how the steel industry is vanishing, and therefore the male characters go to Vietnam. Not only because they have to, but also because they no longer know what to do with their masculine bodies anymore. And twenty year later, there are hardly any jobs anymore; they are all in Mexico or in China. They are ghosts in such cities, and I think that one has to make films about such ghosts.

JF: What does the car mean throughout your films? What do you find so fascinating about the automobile and mobility in general? Does the car have a special meaning in Germany that it does not possess elsewhere in Europe or in the U.S.?

CP: When I was assistant director with Hartmut Bitomsky, I discovered his film about Wolfsburg [the *VW Komplex*; see the section on *Wolfsburg* above]. I wondered why the automobile has not found a place in German cinema. Of course there are road movies, but they could just as well be riding on horses; there is not really any difference. I wondered: What is specific to the automobile, especially when every second job in Germany is related to the car industry? Why is Germany an enormous Detroit, only more modern, and why are there no stories about it in Germany? What does the automobile change in our perceptions of the world? That's really my concern. Then I read [Paul] Virilio as well as [Georges] Simenon, and they wrote about the automobile and what it means, in particular what it means to fall into this kind of half-sleep while riding in the car. What is cruise control? What is a car radio? And then there is this entire mode of perception and corporeality when sitting in the car that does not have an adequate presence in cinema. And I thought that one should take the automobile seriously, so *Wolfsburg* was a reaction to this thought, a decision to make a film about cars. Of course, it was already somewhat that way in *State I Am In* and even in *Pilots*, where the car is a space not only for movement but a philosophy of life [*Lebensphilosophie*]. The automobile forms individuality, subjectivity, me and the world, by isolating one, as with the hotel. My father, when he had problems at home, would go for a drive. This is the second aspect of the car: the family as it appears in the car, the stereotype of children in the backseat, woman in the passenger seat, and the man behind the steering wheel. What does it then mean for the child, in the backseat, to look at his or her parents but without being able to see their faces, and then to sense that they are in some sort of crisis? So the car is really a social space, not simply a means of transportation.

JF: And of course this is linked to mobility in Germany now, no?

CP: Germany is an unbelievably networked country. I know that American actors who like to shoot in Germany do not come here because they like German cinema but because they can drive three hundred kilometers per hour on the autobahn. Germany is really a nation of freeways; the idea of the freeway is deep in the country. The freeway, in fact, replaced German romanticism. Caspar David Friedrich [the famous German romantic painter, whose compositions Petzold seems to use in *The Sex Thief,* among others] would today paint the freeways. But then again, it is changing even now. I notice that the car is starting to play a smaller role again—my children are not going to get driver's licenses. I think that Tarantino's *Death Proof* did not do very well because the myth of the car is dying out. When you see *Two-Lane Blacktop*, the car is fantastic, but one could not make that anymore. Today there are fifty magazines in Germany about computers, but only three about cars.

JF: You have criticized excessive exposition in films before. More often, you seem to try to convey things through the body of the actors, which is something one sees very clearly with Nina Hoss and Benno

Fürmann. How do you realize this kind of physical reality? How does what you have called "bodily memory" function in your films?

CP: I think in many ways Nazism took our bodies away from us. Nineteen sixty-eight saved us, but if you see cinema of the 1950s, it is clear how dominant dialogue is. People articulate everything, explain everything. On the one hand, one really has to work a lot with the actors so that they do not have a specific task but rather a serenity [*Gelassenheit*]. On the other hand, I think that film production in Germany has so little money, and so few days to shoot, that one simply has to get through it, so the directors just tell the actors how they should cross the street or get in a car.

JF: Yes, that reminds me how often hotels come up in your films. I do not know if you wanted to say something about the hotels in your films, but it reminded me of the difference between place and space that often unfolds in hotels.

CP: Yes, that has many connections. Hotels and cars, they are simply transit spaces in which people have an incredible desire to leave something behind. Two things come to mind: first, Andy Warhol, who found tape recorders fantastic not because you could record something but rather because you could erase something. There's a longing to go to the hotel because you can just push everything away from yourself. But, in this escape to the hotel, there is also an unbelievable loneliness and sadness. And therefore this sort of space of absolute nothingness is filled also with these extremely lonely individuals. And that is what I like about hotels. The hotel is a space of longing but also, at the same time, a place that scares you. One sits there, the television is on, but one can also take out a pistol. How many suicides occur in hotel rooms?

JF: On the other side, there are very often houses, homes, in your films, and there is frequently a shot of the protagonist outside the house looking in, for example in *Jerichow* or *Yella*. And I find that this creates a strong tension between such transit spaces and these homes.

CP: Yes, that is correct. With houses, one thing always interested me. In Germany at least, I do not know if it is true in the U.S.[!], people build their houses like spaceships, like outposts on the moon, as if there is no social context at all. This is where we are building, and this is where we are living, that is our security and safety. But, of course, there is always a window there, and one looks out, and, outside, someone is going by, and they look in, and suddenly one is no longer alone in the world. People always fantasize about their vacations with romantic images of one house, a lake, five trees, and two children, and no one else in the world. Cinema becomes interesting when the second house is built— one wakes up one morning and, right across the way, someone else is building a house. Or in *The Great Gatsby*, people are living there, and then Gatsby builds a house across from them. And immediately there's pressure there. One has to come to terms with it, one has to become social, and that is where I put the camera.

JF: Many of your films concern work, which is a major theme in literature obviously, but not so much in cinema. And in almost every film of yours, work and/or workers play a central role, but a role that is in some way refunctioned—both the worker and the work.

CP: I think that, generally speaking, work does not really take place in cinema. People go to the cinema, after all, to avoid and seek some refuge from work. And yet cinema has not totally forgotten work; there is factory work and alienated work—especially on this latter count, there are bank robbers, craftspeople, people with real "skills" [said in English], for example, people who can break into cars. And I like that. I like to see in Walter Hill's *Driver* how Ryan O'Neal drives—that is really his work, his labor. And in general, it is important that a film unfolds and plays out something that people can comprehend—of working, of kissing, of car-driving. And that the characters have really mastered or learned techniques and skills, I like that in films.

JF: You once said that the spaces in your films should have a kind of soul. What did you mean? What role do places and spaces have in your films?

CP: There is a book by Joel Sternfeld called *On This Site* [he gave German title, *Tatort*] that has beautiful images of houses, and underneath each image there is a caption that says something like, "This is where John Downey was shot," and "Here so and so was run over."[3] And suddenly these spaces have a real aura.

When one goes through a German pedestrian zone or a German mall, one should have the feeling that there is somehow an idea, a ghost, a phantom in these places—maybe just the ghost of the architect or the developer. But something has to be at work behind the space. Tarantino manages to do that in the most unlikely places. In his *Jackie Brown,* there is this really disgusting shopping mall—as I find all these malls disgusting—but nonetheless, in the escalators and in the people who eat there, there is an idea, an idea of a way of life. So spaces have to have soul—not just as background. And if they do not have something like [a soul], if the spaces are completely ugly and broken, then the kiss that the lovers have there has to transform that space, has to enchant it. Yes, with magic. There's a poem by Eichendorf that I always find fantastic and that I liked even as a child: "A song is sleeping in all things" ("Schläft ein Lied in allen Dingen"). That means that in all things, something is sleeping; one just has to be able to see it. I always say that to myself before I shoot. One really cannot forget that.

Notes

1. Petzold had in fact recently directed a theater production, Schnitzler's *Der einsame Weg* (The lonely way) in Deutsches Theater in Berlin, with Nina Hoss and Ulrich Matthes.

2. Ali is the name of the main character in Fassbinder's *Ali: Fear Eats the Soul* (*Angst essen Seele auf;* 1974), a nonethnic German (Moroccan) guest worker in Munich who has an affair with an older ethnic German woman, much to the concern and consternation of both of their social circles.

3. Joel Sternfeld's *On This Site* (1996) is an important work of photography that influenced, among others, Andreas Gursky.

Das Warme Geld (*The Warm Money*; 1992)
Germany
Production Company: Deutsche Film- und Fernsehakademie Berlin GmbH
  (DFFB)
Director: Christian Petzold
Screenplay: Christian Petzold
Dramaturgy: Harun Farocki
Photography: Bernd Löhr
Sound Engineer: Jan Ralske
Editor: Aysun Bademsoy
Production Design: Michael Stehr
Cast: Manuela Brandenstein (Vera), Martina Maurer (Heike), Ulrich Ströhle
  (boss), Mark Schlichter (cook's assistance), Sabahat Bademsoy (server), Halit
  M. Bademsoy (Trensenmann), Andreas Hosang (medical doctor), Kim Kübler
  (girl at pool)
Running Time: 31 min.

Pilotinnen (*Pilots*; 1995)
Germany
Production Company: Schramm Film Koerner and Weber, coproduced by
  Deutsche Film- und Fernsehakademie Berlin GmbH (DFFB), under con-
  tract by Zweites Deutsches Fernsehen (ZDF)
Director: Christian Petzold
Producers: Michael Weber and Florian Koerner von Gustorf
Screenplay: Christian Petzold
Dramaturgy: Harun Farocki
Photography: Hans Fromm
Sound Engineer: Heino Herrenbrück
Music: Georges Delerue
Editor: Monika Kappel-Smith
Costume Designer: Anette Guther
Make-up Artist: Monika Münnich

Production Design: Kade Gruber
Cast: Eleonore Weisgerber (Karin), Nadeshda Brennicke (Sophie), Udo Schenk (Juniorchef), Barbara Frey (Christine), Michael Tietz (Dieter), Ronny Tanner (short police officer), Wolfgang Hahn (tall police officer), Inge-Carolin Gremm (salesperson at supermarket), Kim Kübler (young pharmacist), Imke Barnstedt (older pharmacist), Hans Klima (first attacked policeman), Rüdiger Tuchel (second attacked policeman), Michael Brennicke (saleman for "Dynamic"), Jörg Friedrich (salesman for "Selbstverteidigung"), Klaus Rätsch (station agent), Marie Bondeele (perfumist), Gilles Papelian (Michel), Peter Zarth (man at airport)
Running Time: 72 min.

Cuba Libre (1996)
Germany
Production Company: Cine Images Horst Knechtl, Schramm Film Koerner and Weber, under contract by Zweites Deutsches Fernsehen (ZDF)
Director: Christian Petzold
Producers: Florian Koerner von Gustorf and Horst Knechtl
Screenplay: Christian Petzold
Dramaturgy: Harun Farocki
Photography: Hans Fromm
Sound Engineer: Heino Herrenbrück
Music: Stefan Will
Editor: Bettina Böhler
Production Design: Kade Gruber
Costume Designer: Anette Guther
Make-up Artist: Monika Münnich
Cast: Richy Müller (Tom), Catherine Flemming (Tina), Wolfram Berger (Jimmy), Raoul Schneider (Caddy), Anette Guther (saleswoman), Gilles Papelian (barkeeper), Eleonore Weisgerber (saleswoman), Christoph Krix (guard), Mark Schlichter (commuter), Matthias Viehoff (medical doctor), Marquard Bohm (man from beauty institute), Andrea Brose (girl at bistro), Wilfried Gronau (bum), Jörg Friedrich (bum)
Running Time: 92 min.

Die Beschlafdieben (*The Sex Thief*; 1998)
Germany
Production Company: Schramm Film Koerner and Weber, under contract by Zweites Deutsches Fernsehen ZDF and Arte GEIE
Director: Christian Petzold
Producers: Florian Koerner von Gustorf and Omar Jawal
Screenplay: Christian Petzold
Screenplay Collaboration: Harun Farocki
Photography: Hans Fromm

Sound Engineers: Martin Ehlers and Heino Herrenbrück
Music: Stefan Will
Editor: Katja Dringenberg
Production Design: Kade Gruber
Costume Designer: Anette Guther
Make-up Artists: Geli Baumeister and Monika Münnich
Cast: Constanze Engelbrecht (Petra), Nele Mueller-Stöfen (Franziska), Wolfram Berger (the thief), Richy Müller (police officer), Nadeshda Brennicke (waitress), Andrea Brose (Miriam), Jörg Friedrich (first interviewer), Tilo Nest (second interviewer), Karl-Heinz Knaup (third interviewer), Christoph Krix (man in bar), Bernd Tauber (courier)
Running Time: 86 min.

Die innere Sicherheit (*The State I Am In;* 2000)
Germany
Production Company: Schramm Film Koerner and Weber, coproduced by Hessischer Rundfunk HR, Arte GEIE
Director: Christian Petzold
Producers: Florian Koerner von Gustorf and Michael Weber
Screenplay: Christian Petzold and Harun Farocki
Photography: Hans Fromm
Sound Engineer: Heino Herrenbrück
Music: Stefan Will
Editor: Bettina Böhler
Production Design: Kade Gruber
Costume Designer: Anette Guther
Make-up Artists: Monika Münnich and Kerstin Gaecklein
Cast: Julia Hummer (Jeanne), Barbara Auer (Clara), Richy Müller (Hans), Bilge Bingül (Heinrich), Rogério Jaques (man in the beach bar), Maria João (concierge), Vasco Machado (police officer), Noberto Paula (man at train station), Bernd Tauber (Achim), Katharina Schüttler (Paulina), Günther Maria Halmer (Klaus), Inka Löwendorf (girl in school), Manfred Möck (teacher), Marc Sönnichsen (Heinrich's friend), Ingrid Dohse (restaurant manager), Henriette Heinze (hitchhiker)
Running Time: 106 min.

Toter Mann (*Something to Remind Me*; 2001)
Germany
Production Company: teamWorX Produktion, in collaboration with Arte GEIE, under contract by Zweites Deutsches Fernsehen ZDF
Director: Christian Petzold
Producer: Bettina Reiz
Screenplay: Christian Petzold and Jean-Baptiste Filleau
Dramaturgy: Harun Farocki (consultation)

Photography: Hans Fromm
Sound Engineer: Andreas Mücke-Niesytka
Music: Stefan Will
Editor: Bettina Böhler
Costume Designers: Lisy Christl and Anke Wahnbaeck
Make-up Artist: Monika Münnich
Production Designer: Kade Gruber
Cast: Nina Hoss (Leyla), André M. Hennicke (Thomas), Sven Pippig (Blum), Heinrich Schmieder (Richard), Kathrin Angerer (Sophie), Henning Peker (Ott), Michael Gerber (Agent), Franziska Troegner (Peggy), Johannes Hitzblech (Seifert), Hilmar Baumann (caretaker), Rainer Laupichler (police officer), Ingeborg Schilling (mother), Larissa Rimkus (child), Kai Schuhmann (waiter)
Running Time: 88 min.

Wolfsburg (2003)
Germany
Production Company: teamWorX Produktion GmbH, coproduction with Arte Deutschland TV GmbH, under contract by Zweites Deutsches Fernsehen ZDF
Director: Christian Petzold
Producer: Bettina Reitz
Screenplay: Christian Petzold
Dramaturgy: Harun Farocki (consultation)
Photography: Hans Fromm
Sound Engineer: Andreas Mücke-Niesytka
Music: Stefan Will
Editor: Bettina Böhler
Production Design: Kade Gruber
Costume Designers: Lisy Christl and Anke Wahnbaeck
Make-up Artist: Monika Münnich
Cast: Benno Fürmann (Phillip Wagner), Nina Hoss (Laura Reiser), Astrid Meyerfeldt (Vera), Antje Westermann (Katja), Stephan Kampwirth (Klaus), Matthias Matschke (Scholz), Soraya Gomaa (Françoise), Martin Müseler (Paul Reiser), Anna Priese (Antonia), Florian Panzner (police officer), André Szymanski (new salesman), Peter Kurth (Oliver), Simone von Zglinicki (nurse), Sven Pippig (scrap-metal dealer), Margarita Broich (psychologist), Claudia Geisler (young mother), Andreas Petri (young father), Fritz Roth (mechanic at junkyard), Thorsten Mischweis (security guard), Michael Poth (mechanic at dealership)
Running Time: 90 min.

Gespenster (*Ghosts*; 2005)
Germany and France
Production Company: Schramm Film Koerner and Weber, coproduced by

Les Films des Tournelles, Bayerischer Rundfunk (BR)/Arte, Arte France Cinéma
Director: Christian Petzold
Producers: Florian Koerner von Gustorf and Michael Weber, with Anne-Dominique Toussaint
Screenplay: Christian Petzold and Harun Farocki
Dramaturgy: Harun Farocki (consultation)
Photography: Hans Fromm
Sound Engineer: Andreas Mücke-Niesytka
Music: Stefan Will, Marco Dreckkötter
Editor: Bettina Böhler
Production Design: Kade Gruber and Katrin Schier (assistant)
Costume Designers: Anette Guther and Charlotte Sawatzki (assistant)
Make-up Artists: Monika Münnich and Sabine Schuhmann
Cast: Julia Hummer (Nina), Sabine Timoteo (Toni), Marianne Basler (Françoise), Aurélien Recoing (Pierre), Benno Fürmann (Oliver), Anna Schudt (Kai), Claudia Geisler (shelter director), Philipp Hauß (Mathias), Victoria Trauttmansdorff (Mathias's mother), Peter Kurth (foreman), Annika Blendl (agent), Rosa Enskat (nurse)
Running Time: 85 min.

Yella (2007)
Germany
Production Company: Schramm Film Koerner and Weber (coproduction with Zweites Deutsches Fernsehen ZDF and Arte Deutschland TV GmbH)
Director: Christian Petzold
Producers: Florian Koerner von Gustorf and Michael Weber
Screenplay: Christian Petzold
Dramaturgy: Harun Farocki (consultation)
Photography: Hans Fromm
Sound Engineer: Andreas Mücke-Niesytka
Musik: Stefan Will
Sound effects: Carsten Richter
Editor: Bettina Böhler
Production Design: Kade Gruber
Costume Designers: Anette Guther and Charlotte Sawatzki
Make-up Artist: Monika Münnich
Cast: Nina Hoss (Yella), Devid Striesow (Philip), Hinnerk Schönemann (Ben), Burghart Klaußner (Dr. Gunthen), Barbara Auer (Barbara Gunthen), Christian Redl (Yella's father), Selin Barbara Petzold (Dr. Gunthen's daughter), Wanja Mues (Sprenger), Michael Wittenborn (Schmitt-Ott), Martin Brambach (Dr. Fritz), Joachim Nimtz (Prietzel), Peter Benedict (Friedrich's laywer), Ian Norval (receptionist), Peter Knaack (bankruptcy administrator), Thomas Giese (teller)
Running Time: 88 min.

Jerichow (2008)
Germany
Production Company: Schramm Film Koerner and Weber (coproduction with
   Bayerischer Rundfunk BR and Arte Deutschland TV GmbH)
Director: Christian Petzold
Producers: Florian Koerner von Gustorf and Michael Weber
Screenplay: Christian Petzold
Dramaturgy: Harun Farocki (consultation)
Photography: Hans Fromm
Sound Engineers: Andreas Mücke-Niesytka and Martin Ehlers
Music: Stefan Will
Music Consultant: Aysun Bademsoy
Sound Effects: Carsten Richter, Hanse Warns
Editor: Bettina Böhler
Production Design: Kade Gruber
Costume Designer: Anette Guther
Make-up Artists: Monika Münnich and Parul Banerjee (supplemental)
Cast: Benno Fürmann (Thomas), Nina Hoss (Laura), Hilmi Sözer (Ali), André
   M. Hennicke (Leon), Claudia Geisler (office worker), Marie Gruber (cashier),
   Knut Berger (police officer)
Running Time: 92 min.

Etwas Besseres als den Tod (*Beats Being Dead,* part 1 of *Dreileben,* 2011)
Production Company: Schramm Film Koerner and Weber (under contract with
   Bayerischer Rundfunk BR)
Director: Christian Petzold
Producers: Florian Koerner von Gustorf and Michael Weber
Screenplay: Christian Petzold
Dramaturgy: Harun Farocki (consultation)
Photography: Hans Fromm
Sound Engineer: Andreas Mücke-Niesytka
Musik: Stefan Will
Editor: Bettina Böhler
Production Design: Kade Gruber
Costume Designer: Anette Guther
Make-up Artist: Monika Münnich
Cast: Jacob Matschenz (Johannes) Luna Mijovic (Ana), Vijessna Ferkic (Sarah
   Dreier), Rainer Bock (Dr. Dreier), Konstantin Frolov (Maik), Florian Bar-
   tholomäi (Philip), Stefan Kurt (escapee Frank Molesch), Kirsten Block
   (medical doctor), Deniz Petzold (Edin), Evelyn Gundlach (woman), Kristof
   Gerega (person doing civil service), Thomas Fränzel (male nurse), Eberhard
   Kirchberg (Kreil)
Running Time: 88 min.

Barbara (2012)

Germany

Production Company: Schramm Film Koerner and Weber (in association with Zweites Deutsches Fernsehen ZDF and Arte Deutschland TV GmbH)

Director: Christian Petzold

Producers: Florian Koerner von Gustorf and Michael Weber

Screenplay: Christian Petzold

Screenplay collaboration: Harun Farocki

Photography: Hans Fromm and Pascal Schmit (supplemental)

Sound Engineer: Andreas Mücke-Niesytka and Dominik Schleier

Music: Stefan Will

Sound Effects: Carsten Richter

Editor: Bettina Böhler

Production Design: Kade Gruber and Nina Strathmann

Costume: Anette Guther

Make-up Artist: Barbara Kreuzer and Alexandra Lebedynski

Cast: Nina Hoss (Barbara), Ronald Zehrfeld (Andre), Rainer Bock (Klaus Schütz), Christina Hecke (assistant physician Schulze), Claudia Geisler (nurse), Peter Weiss (medical student), Carlin Haupt (medical student), Deniz Petzold (Angelo), Rosa Enskat (caretaker Bungert), Jasna Fritzi Bauer (Stella), Peer-Uwe Teska (waiter), Mark Waschke (Jörg), Peter Benedict (Gerhard), Thomas Neumann (pensioner in car), Thomas Bading (piano tuner), Susanne Bormann (Steffi), Jannik Schümann (Mario), Alicia von Rittberg (Angie), Selin Barbara Petzold (Maria)

Running Time: 108 min.

Abel, Marco. *The Counter-Cinema of the Berlin School*. Rochester, N.Y.: Camden House, forthcoming.

———. "Imaging Germany: The Political Cinema of Chrisitan Petzold." In *The Collapse of the Conventional: German Film and Its Politics at the Turn of the Twenty-First Century*. Ed. Jaimey Fisher and Brad Prager. Detroit: Wayne State University Press, 2010. 258–84.

———. *Violent Affect: Literature, Cinema, and Critique after Representation*. Lincoln: University of Nebraska Press, 2007.

Abel, Marco, and Christian Petzold. "The Cinema of Identification Gets on My Nerves: An Interview with Christian Petzold." *Cineaste* 33.3 (2008); accessed February 22, 2013. http://www.cineaste.com/articles/an-interview-with-christian-petzold.htm.

Adorno, Theodor and Max Horkheimer. "On the Theory of Ghosts." In *Dialectic of Enlightenment*. New York: Continuum. 215–16.

Albig, Jörg-Uwe, Christoph Gurk, and Christian Petzold. "Der fliegende Holländer: ein Interview." *Texte zur Kunst* 43 (2001), accessed March 22, 2013, http://www.textezurkunst.de/43/der-fliegende-hollander/.

Alter, Nora. *Projecting History: German Nonfiction Cinema, 1967–2000*. Ann Arbor: University of Michigan Press, 2002.

Althen, Michael. "Die Gespenster der Freiheit." *Süddeutsche Zeitung*, January 31, 2001.

Altman, Rick. *Film/Genre*. London: British Film Institute, 1999.

Augé, Marc. *Non-Places: Introduction to an Anthropology of Supermodernity*. London: Verso, 1995.

Aust, Stefan. *Baader-Meinhof: The Inside Story of the R.A.F.* Trans. Anthea Bell. Oxford: Oxford University Press, 1985.

Baer, Hester. "Producing Adaptations: Bernd Eichinger, Christiane F., and German Film History." In *Generic Histories: Film Genre and Its Deviations in German Cinema*. Ed. Jaimey Fisher. Rochester, N.Y.: Camden House, 2013.

Baron, Cynthia, and Sharon Marie Carnicke. *Reframing Screen Performance*. Ann Arbor: University of Michigan Press, 2008.

Bauman, Zygmunt. *Liquid Times: Living in an Age of Uncertainty.* Cambridge: Polity, 2007.

Baute, Michael, Ekkehard Knrer, Volker Pantenburg, Stefan Pethke, and Simon Rothler. "The Berlin School—a Collage." *Senses of Cinema* 55 (2006); accessed September 22, 2011. http://www.sensesofcinema.com/2010/feature-articles/the-berlin-school---a-collage-2/.

Benjamin, Walter. *The Arcades Project.* Harvard University Press, 1999

———. "Excavation and Memory." In *Selected Writings, Volume 2: 1927–1934.* Ed. Michael Jennings with Marcus Bullock, Howard Eiland, and Gary Smith. Cambridge: Harvard University Press, 1999. 576.

Bettelheim, Bruno. *The Uses of Enchantment: The Meaning and Importance of Fairy Tales.* 1975; reprint, New York: Vintage, 1989.

Biehl, Joao. *Vita: Life in a Zone of Social Abandonment.* Berkeley: Univeristy of California Press, 2005.

Biendarra, Anke S. "Ghostly Business: Place, Space, and Gender in Christian Petzold's *Yella.*" *Seminar* 47.4 (2011): 465–78.

Blumenberg, Hans. *Shipwreck with Spectator: Paradigm of a Metaphor for Existence.* Trans. Steven Rendall. 1979; reprint, Cambridge: Massachusetts Institute of Technology Press, 1997.

Blümlinger, Christa. "Slowly Forming a Thought While Working on Images." In *Harun Farocki: Working on the Sightlines.* Ed. Thomas Elsaesser. Film Culture in Transition. Amsterdam: Amsterdam Univeristy Press, 2004. 163–76.

Bourdieu, Pierre, and Loïc Wacquant. "Newliberal Speak: Notes on the New Planetary Vulgate." *Radical Philosophy* 105 (2001): 4–5.

Braudy, Leo. "*Near Dark*: An Appreciation." *Film Quarterly* 64.2 (Winter 2010): 29–32.

Broch, Hermann. "Barbara." *Novellen: Prosa, Fragmente.* 1936; reprint, Frankfurt am Main: Suhrkamp, 1980. 222–47.

Brooks, Peter. *The Melodramatic Imagination: Balzac, Henry James, Melodrama, and the Mode of Excess.* New Haven, Conn.: Yale University Press, 1995.

Buck Caroline M., and Christian Petzold. "Fragen Statt Antworten: Interview mit Chrisitan Petzold." *Neues Deutschland*, February 1, 2001.

Burns, Rob. "Towards a Cinema of Cultural Hybridity: Turkish-German Filmmakers and the Representation of Alterity." *Debatte* 15.1 (2007): 3–24.

Buß, Christian, and Christian Petzold. "Die Musik muss anschaffen gehen." *Die Tageszeitung (taz)*, May 28, 2002.

Carroll, Noel. *The Philosophy of Horror; or, Paradoxes of the Heart.* New York: Routledge, 1990.

Casey, Edward. *Rememerbing: A Phenomenological Study.* Bloomington: Indiana University Press, 1987.

Cawelti, John G. "*Chinatown* and Generic Transformation in Recent American Film." In *Film Genre Reader III.* Ed. Barry Keith Grant. Austin: University of Texas Press, 1979. 243–61.

Clarke, David. *German Cinema since Unification.* London: Continuum, 2006.

Clover, Carol. *Man, Women, and Chain Saws: Gender in the Modern Horror Film.* Princeton, N.J.: Princeton University Press, 1991.

Cohen, Roger. "German Foreign Minister Gives Testimony in Murder Trial." *New York Times,* January 17, 2001.

Corsten, Volker. "Die Blonde Witwe." *Die Welt,* May 26, 2002.

Deleuze, Gilles. "Postscript on the Societies of Control." *October* 49 (1992): 3–7.

Demmerle, Denis, and Christian Petzold. "Nichts ist mehr unschuldig." *Planet-Interview* (2009); accessed July 13, 2011. http://planet-interview.de/interview-christian-petzold-09012009.html.

Derrida, Jacques. *Spectres of Marx: The State of the Debt, the Work of Mourning, and the New International.* Trans. Peggy Kamuf. New York: Routledge, 1993.

Doane, Mary Ann. *The Desire to Desire: The Woman's Film of the 1940s.* Bloomington: Indiana University Press, 1987.

Donald, James. "The Mise-en-Scène of Desire: Introduction." In *Fantasy and the Cinema.* Ed. James Donald. London: British Film Institute, 1989. 136–47.

Elsaesser, Thomas. "Harun Farocki: Filmmaker, Artist, Media Theorist." In *Harun Farocki: Working on the Sightlines.* Ed. Thomas Elsaesser. Film Culture in Transition. Amsterdam: Amsterdam University Press, 2004. 11–40.

———. *New German Cinema.* New Brunswick, N.J.: Rutgers University Press, 1989.

———. "Social Mobility and the Fantastic: German Silent Cinema." In *Fantasy and the Cinema.* Ed. James Donald. London: British Film Institute, 1989. 23–38.

———. *Terror und Trauma: zur Gewalt des Vergangenen in der BRD.* Berlin: Kulturverlag Kadmos, 2007.

———. *Weimar Cinema and After: Germany's Historical Imaginary.* London: Routledge, 2000.

Ertl, Stefan, and Rainer Knepperges. "Drei zu zwei hitverdächtig: Ein Gespräch Mit Christian Petzold." *Filmwärts* 34/35 (1995): 73–76.

Farocki, Harun. "Controlling Observation." In *Harun Farocki: Working on the Sight-Lines.* Ed. Thomas Elsaesser. Film Culture in Transition. Amsterdam: Amsterdam University Press, 2004. 289–96.

Feldvoss, Marli. "Wenn Gespenster Menschen werden: *Die innere Sicherheit* von Christian Petzold." *Neue Zürcher Zeitung,* August 3, 2001.

Fisher, Jaimey. "German Historical Film as Production Trend: European Heritage Cinema and Melodrama in *The Lives of Others.*" In *The Collapse of the Conventional: German Film and Its Politics at the Turn of the Twenty-First Century.* Ed. Jaimey Fisher and Brad Prager. Detroit: Wayne State University Press, 2010. 186–215.

———. "Globalization as Uneven Geographical Development: The 'Creative' Destruction of Place in the Recent Films of Christian Petzold." *Seminar* 47.4 (2011): 447–78.

———. "Hotels." In *Berlin School Glossary: An ABC of the New Wave in German Cinema*. Ed. Roger Cook, Lutz Koepnick, Kristin Kopp, and Brad Prager. Bristol: Intellect, forthcoming.

———. "The Syntax of Terrorism? Terrorists' Border Crossing in Post-2000 German Cinema." In *What Is German? The Toronto German Studies Workshop*. Toronto: Univeristy of Toronto Press, forthcoming.

———. "Times of Transition and Transformation: Christian Petzold's Collaborations with Harun Farocki." Unpublished manuscript.

Fisher, Jaimey, and Brad Prager. Introduction to *The Collapse of the Conventional: German Film and Its Politics at the Turn of the Twenty-First Century*. Ed. Jaimey Fisher and Brad Prager. Detroit: Wayne State University Press, 2010. 1–38.

Fisher, Jaimey, and Nora Alter. "Swimming Pools." In *Berlin School Glossary: An ABC of the New Wave in German Cinema*. Ed. Roger Cook, Lutz Koepnick, Kristin Kopp, and Brad Prager. Bristol: Intellect, forthcoming.

Ganeva, Mila. "No History, Just Stories: Revisiting Tradition in Berlin Films of the 1990s." In *Berlin: The Symphony Continues*. Ed. Carol Anne Costabile-Heming, Rachel J. Halverson, and Kristie A. Foell. Berlin: De Gruyter, 2004. 261–78.

Gansera, Rainer, and Christian Petzold. "Toter Mann, was nun?" *Süddeutsche Zeitung*, October 2, 2002.

———. "Über die Brücke und in den Wald." *Süddeutsche Zeitung*, February 15, 2005.

Göktürk, Deniz. "Turkish Women on German Streets: Closure and Exposure in 'Transnational Cinema.'" In *Spaces in European Cinema*. Ed. Myrto Konstantarakos. Portland, Ore.: Intellect Books, 2000. 64–76.

Gordon, Avery. *Ghostly Matters: Haunting and the Sociological Imagination*. Minneapolis: University of Minnesota, 2008.

Göttler, Fritz. "Fühlen in Einer Kalten Traumwelt." *Süddeutsche Zeitung*, September 12, 2007.

Graf, Dominik, Christoph Hochhäusler, and Christian Petzold. "Die Welt zur Kenntlichkeit entstellen." September 17, 2011; accessed November 12, 2011. http://www.daserste.de/dreileben/allround_dyn~uid,6rdwspg7jn7hiqgl~cm.asp.

———. "Mailwechsel 'Berliner Schule.'" *Revolver* 16 (2007): 7–40.

Hake, Sabine. *German National Cinema*. London: Routledge, 2002.

Halbwachs, Maurice. *The Collective Memory*. Trans. Francis Ditter and Vida Yazdi. 1950; reprint, New York: Harper and Row, 1980.

Hall, Stuart. "The Post-Colonial Question." In *The Post-Colonial Question*. Ed. Iain Chambers and Lidia Curti. London: Routledge, 1996. 242–60.

Harvey, David. *A Brief History of Neoliberalism*. Oxford: Oxford University Press, 2005.

———. *Spaces of Hope*. Berkeley: University of California Press, 2000.

Haupt, Friedericke. "Drei Regisseure retten das deutsche Fernsehen." *Frankfurter Allgemeine Zeitung*, August 28, 2011.

Hauser, Dorothea, and Andreas Schroth. "380 Volt under Oberfläche: Ein Gespäch mit den Regisseuren Romuald Karmakar, Christian Petzold und Andres Veiel." Interview. *Die Tageszeitung (taz)*, June 27, 2002.

Higson, Andrew. *English Heritage, English Cinema: Costume Drama since 1980.* Oxford: Oxford University Press, 2003.

Hirsch, Marianne. "The Generation of Postmemory." *Poetics Today* 29.1 (2008): 103–28.

Hitzemann, Christiane, and Christian Petzold. "Liebe ist das Produkt eines Tausches." *Freitag* September 16, 2005.

Hoch, Jenny, and Chrisitan Petzold. "Beziehungsdrama 'Jerichow': Frosten Im Osten." *Spiegel Online,* November 22, 2009; accessed February 22, 2013. http://www.spiegel.de/kultur/kino/beziehungsdrama-jerichow-frosten-im-osten-a-599513.html.

Homewood, Christopher. "The Return of 'Undead' History: The West German Terrorist as Vampire and the Problem of 'Normalizing' the Past in Margarethe Von Trotta's *Die Bleierne Zeit* (1981) and Christian Petzold's *Die Innere Sicherheit* (2001)." In *German Culture, Politics, and Literature into the Twenty-First Century: Beyond Normalization.* Ed. Stuart Taberner and Paul Cooke. Rochester, N.Y.: Camden House, 2006. 121–36.

Husman, Wenke, and Christian Petzold. "Unsere Idenität bestimmt sich über Arbeit." *Die Zeit,* April 26, 2012.

Huyssen, Andreas. *Present Pasts: Urban Palimpsests and the Politics of Memory.* Stanford, Calif.: Stanford University Press, 2003.

Isenberg, Noah. *Detour.* London: British Film Institute, 2008.

Jameson, Fredric. *Valences of the Dialectic.* New York: Verso, 2009.

Jancovich, Mark. *Horror: The Film Reader.* London: Routledge, 2002.

Jones, Stan. "Turkish-German Cinema Today: A Case Study of Fatih Akın's *Kurz und Schmerzlos* (1998) and *Im Juli* (2000)." In *European Cinema, Inside Out: Images of the Self and Other in Postcolonial European Film.* Ed. Guido Rings and Rikki Morgan-Tamosunas. Heidelberg: Winter, 2003. 75–91.

Kamalzadeh, Dominik, and Christian Petzold. "Was sich im Misstrauensräumen Liebe Entwickelt." *Der Standard,* March 8, 2012.

Khouloki, Rayd, and Christian Petzold. "Schwebezustände: Gespräch Mit Regisseur Chirstian Petzold." *Film-Dienst* 56.20 (2003): 43–45.

Kilb, Andreas. "Zwischen Himmel und Hölle: *Yella.*" *Frankfurter Allgemeine Zeitung,* September 13, 2007.

King, Alisdair. "The Province Always Rings Twice: Christian Petzold's Heimatfilm Noir *Jerichow.*" *Transit* 6.1 (2010): 1–22.

Koepnick, Lutz. "Cars. . . ." In *Berlin School Glossary: An ABC of the New Wave in German Cinema.* Ed. Roger Cook, Lutz Koepnick, Kristin Kopp, and Brad Prager. Bristol: Intellect, forthcoming.

Kopp, Kristin. "Christoph Hochhäusler's *This Very Moment*: The Berlin School and the Politics of Spatial Aesthetics in the German-Polish Borderlands." In

The Collapse of the Conventional: German Film and Its Politics at the Turn of the Twenty-First Century. Ed. Jaimey Fisher and Brad Prager. Detroit: Wayne State University Press, 2010. 285–308.

Körte, Peter. "Implosion der Dritten Generation." *Frankfurter Rundschau,* January 31, 2001.

Kothenschulte, Daniel, and Christian Petzold. "Handapparat für den Film." *Frankfurter Rundschau,* January 8, 2009.

Kracauer, Siegfried. *The Mass Ornament: Weimar Essays.* Trans. Thomas Y. Levin. 1963; reprint, Cambridge, Mass.: Harvard University Press, 1995.

Krakenberg, Jasmin. "Portraiture in Films by Christian Petzold and Andy Warhol." Paper delivered at the National Conference of the Society for Cinema and Media Studies, Boston, March 24, 2012.

Kreist, Ulrich, and Christian Petzold. "Irgendetwas ist nicht in Ordnung: Christian Petzold über seinen neuen Film." *Stuttgarter Zeitung,* September 20, 2005.

———. "Wracks mit Geschichte: Christian Petzold über seinen neuen Film *Yella.*" *Stuttgarter Zeitung,* September 5, 2007.

Ladd, Brian. *Ghosts of Berlin: Confronting German History in the Urban Landscape.* Chicago: University of Chicago Press, 1997.

Lefebvre, Henri. *The Production of Space.* Trans. Donald Nicholson-Smith. 1974; reprint, Malden, Mass.: Blackwell, 2009.

Lenssen, Claudia. "Mit der Kälte des Vermittlers." *Die Tageszeitung (taz),* September 25, 2003.

Lenssen, Claudia, and Christian Petzold. "Diese typische BRD-Generation." *Die Tageszeitung (taz),* February 13, 2003.

Lim, Dennis. "A German Wave, Focused on Today." *New York Times,* May 6, 2009.

Lueken, Verena, Andreas Kilb, Peter Körte, Matthias Glasner, Hans-Christian Schmidt, and Christian Petzold. "Kinoregie will Autonmie." *Frankfurter Allgemeine Zeitung,* February 10, 2012.

Lyons, James K. "Brecht's *Mann ist Mann* and the Death of Tragedy." *German Quarterly* 67.4 (Fall 1994): 513–20.

MacCannell, Dean. *The Tourist: A New Theory of the Leisure Class.* New York: Schocken, 1989.

Maland, Charles. "'Film Gris': Crime, Critique, and Cold War Culture 1951." *Film Criticism* 26.3 (2002): 1–30.

Malik, Sarita. "Beyond 'the Cinema of Duty'? The Pleasures of Hybridity: Black British Film of the 1980s and 1990s." In *Dissolving Views: Key Writings on British Cinema.* Ed. Andrew Higson. London: Cassell, 1996. 200–15.

Margalit, Avishai. *The Ethics of Memory.* Cambridge, Mass.: Harvard University Press, 2002.

Marston, Sallie. "The Social Construction of Scale." *Progress in Human Geography* 24.2 (2000): 219–42.

Martens, René. "Neu im Kino: Die innere Sicherheit." *Die Woche,* February 2, 2001.

Matthias, Bettina. *The Hotel as Setting in Early Twentieth-Century German and Austrian Literature.* Rochester, N.Y.: Camden House, 2006.

Mennel, Barbara. "Bruce Lee in Kreuzberg and *Scarface* in Altona: Transnational Auteurism and Ghettocentrism in Thomas Arslan's *Brothers and Sisters* and Fatih Akın's *Short Sharp Shock.*" *New German Critique* 87 (2002): 133–56.

———. *Cities and Cinema.* London: Routledge, 2008.

Miller, Matthew. "Facts of Migration, Demands on Identity: Christian Petzold's *Yella* and *Jerichow* in Comparison." *German Quarterly* 85.1 (2012): 56–77.

Moeller, Robert G. *War Stories: The Search for a Usable Past in the Federal Republic of Germany.* Berkeley: University of California Press, 2001.

Mitchell, Kalani. "Petzold's Comic Storyboard Constructions." Paper delivered at the National Conference of the German Studies Association, Milwaukee, October 6, 2012.

Mustroph, Tom. "Fremde Gefährten: Die *innere Sicherheit,* ein Film von Christian Petzold." *Neues Deutschland,* January 28, 2001.

Naremore, James. *Acting in the Cinema.* Berkeley: University of California Press, 1988.

———. *More Than Night: Film Noir and Its Contexts.* Berkeley: University of California Press, 1995.

Naughton, Leonie. *That Was the Wild East: Film Culture, Unification, and the "New" Germany.* Social History, Popular Culture, and Politics in Germany. Ed. Geoff Eley. Ann Arbor: University of Michigan Press, 2002.

Neale, Steve. *Genre.* London: British Film Institute, 1980.

———. *Genre and Hollywood.* New York: Routledge, 2000.

Nicodemus, Katja. "Das Phantom der Linken." *Die Tageszeitung (taz),* February 1, 2001.

———. "Kino Als Auto-Analyse." *Die Zeit,* September 25, 2003.

Nord, Cristina, and Christian Petzold. "Ich wollte, dass die DDR Farben Hat." *Die Tageszeitung (taz),* February 11, 2012.

———. "Das Auto ist ein reicher Ort." *Die Tageszeitung (taz),* January 7, 2009.

———. "Mit geschlossenen Augen Hören." *Die Tageszeitung (taz),* February 15, 2005.

Patterson, Orlando. *Slavery and Social Death: A Comparative Study.* Cambridge, Mass.: Harvard University Press, 1982.

Patton, Phil. *Bug: The Strange Mutations of the World's Most Famous Automobile.* Cambridge, Mass.: Da Capo, 2002.

Peck, Jamie, and Adam Tickell. "Neoliberalizing Space." *Antipode* 34.3 (2002): 380–404.

Peitz, Christiane. "Die Angst im Walde." *Der Tagesspiegel,* February 15, 2011.

Peitz, Christiane, and Christian Petzold. "Nach dem Schiffbruch." *Der Tagesspiegel,* January 25, 2001.

———. "Wir haben Sterne ohne Himmel." *Der Tagesspiegel,* September 11, 2007.

Petzold, Christian. "Commentary [Audiokommentar]." *Jerichow.* DVD. Piffl, 2009.

———. "Commentary [Audiokommentar]." *Die innere Sicherheit* Special Edition. DVD. Indigo, 2001.

———. "Commentary [Audiokommentar]." *Wolfsburg*. DVD. ZDF/teamWorx/arte, 2008.

———. "Das Gesicht hinter der Maske: Ein Film mit Peter Lorre, den das Wiener Filmmuseum mit einer Retro ehrt." *Frankfurter Allegemeine Zeitung*, May 13, 2004.

———. "*Gespenster*: Ein ausführliches Booklet." *Gespenster* DVD. Indigo, 2005.

———. "A Gift (91)." In *Minutentexte: The Night of the Hunter*. Ed. Michael Baute and Volker Pantenburg. Berlin: Brinkmann und Bose, 2006. 275.

———. "Hawaiian Getaway." Cartoon. *Cargo: Film/Medien/Kultur* 1 (2009): 50–51.

———. "Lucky to Have Her." Cartoon. *Cargo: Film/Medien/Kultur* 2 (2009): 90–91.

———. "Luzifers Tochter: Demi Moore und *Drei Engele für Charlie*." *Frankfurter Allgemeine Zeitung*, July 6, 2003.

———. "*Barbara*: Pressekonferenz." Berlinale, February 11, 2012.

———. "Vorwort: Am Wegessaum." In *Kinowahrheit*, by Hartmut Bitomsky. Ed. Ilka Schaarschmidt. Berlin: Vorwerk 8, 2003. 7–10.

Petzold, Christian, and Nina Hoss. "Filme, Die Sicherheiten beschwören, sind langweilig." *Filmportal.de* (2007); accessed March 23, 2013. http://www.filmportal.de/node/97377/material/540421.

Polan, Dana. "*Detour*." *Senses of Cinema*, July 17, 2002; accessed November 8, 2011. http://www.sensesofcinema.com/2002/cteq/detour/.

Prager, Brad. "Glimpses of Freedom: The Reemergence of Utopian Longing in German Cinema." In *Collapse of the Conventional: German Film and Its Politics at the Turn of the Twenty-First Century*. Ed. Jaimey Fisher and Brad Prager. Detroit: Wayne State University Press, 2010. 360–85.

Prot, Bénédicte. "Collapsing Regimes and How You Can Survive in Them." *CineaEurope*, February 3, 2012.

Rampetzreiter, Heide. "DDR-Film: Der Wald war abhörfreier Raum." *Die Presse*, March 14, 2012.

Reinecke, Stefan, and Christian Petzold. "Ein Werkstattgespräch mit Regisseur Christian Petzold." *epd film*, October 2, 2003.

Rentschler, Eric. "From New German Cinema to the Post-Wall Cinema of Consensus." In *Cinema and Nation*. Ed. Scott MacKenzie and Mette Hjort. New York: Routledge, 2000. 260–77.

Richter, Gerhard. *Afterness: Figures of Following in Modern Thought and Aesthetics*. New York: Columbia University Press, 2012.

———. "Introduction: Benjamin's Ghosts." In *Benjamin's Ghosts: Interventions in Contemporary Literary and Cultural Theory*. Stanford, Calif.: Stanford Univeristy Press, 2002. 1–19.

Rodek, Hanns-Georg. "*Barbara* Hat Keine Oscar-Chance: Zum Glück." *Die Welt*, August 31, 2012.

———. "Das Auto als Ort der Wahrheit." *Die Welt*, September 24, 2003.

———. "Wer zu lange an seinem Traum festhält." *Die Welt*, January 31, 2001.

Rodek, Hanns-Georg, and Christian Petzold. "Der politische Beobachter." *Berliner Morgenpost*, September 24, 2003.

———. "Totenhemdchen beginnt zu leben." *Die Welt*, September 15, 2005.

Ross, Kristin. *Fast Cars, Clean Bodies: Decolonization and the Reordering of French Culture.* Cambridge: Massachusetts Institute of Technology University Press, 1995.

Rother, Rainer. *Nina Hoss: Ein Porträt, Ich Muss Mir Jeden Satz Glauben.* Leipzig: Henschel, 2009.

Schenk, Ralf, and Christian Petzold. "Christian Petzolds Gespenster." *Berliner Zeitung*, February 15, 2005.

———. "Zwischen Gestern und Morgen." *Berliner Zeitung* March 7, 2012

Scheufler, Eric. "The Ghosts of Autumn Past: History, Memory, and Identity in Petzold's *Die innere Sicherheit.*" *Seminar* 47.1 (February 2011): 103–20.

Schick, Thomas, and Tobias Ebbrecht, eds. *Kino in Bewegung: Perspektiven des deutchen Gegenwartsfilms.* Wiesbaden: VS Verlag fuer Sozialwissenschaften, 2010.

Schwenk, Johanna. *Leerstellen-Resonanzräume: Zur Ästhetik der Auslassung im Werk des Filmregisseurs Christian Petzold.* Baden-Baden: Nomos, 2012.

Schwenk, Johanna, and Christian Petzold. "'Jeder Traum Hat Eine Ordnung': Interview mit Christian Petzold." In *Leerstellen-Resonanzräume: Zur Ästhetik der Auslassung im Werk des Filmregisseurs Christian Petzold.* Ed. Johanna Schwenk. Baden-Baden: Nomos, 2012. 87–93.

Sennett, Richard. *The Culture of the New Capitalism.* New Haven, Conn.: Yale University Press, 2006.

Siebert, Marcus, ed. *Revolver: Kino muss gefaehrlich sein.* Frankfurt am Main: Verlag der Autoren, 2006.

Siemes, Christof, Katja Nicodemus, and Christian Petzold. "'Arm filmt gut? Das gefällt mir nicht': Ein Gespräch mit Christian Petzold." Interview. *Die Zeit,* Jaunary 9, 2009.

Silverman, Kaja. *The Subject of Semiotics.* Oxford: Oxford University Press, 1983.

Simmel, Georg. *The Philosophy of Money.* Trans. David Frisby and Tom Bottomore. Ed. David Frisby. 1978; reprint, London: Routledge, 1991.

Smith, Neil. "Contours of a Spatialized Politics: Homeless Vehicles and the Production of Geographical Space." *Social Text* 33 (1992): 54–81.

———. *Uneven Development: Nature, Capital, and the Production of Space.* Third edition. Athens: University of George Press, 2008.

Soja, Edward. *Thirdspace: Journeys to Los Angeles and Other Real-and-Imagined Places.* Cambridge: Blackwell, 1996.

Sternfeld, Joel. *On This Site: Landscape in Memoriam.* Boston: Chronicle, 1996.

"Stille vor dem Schuß." *Die Frankfurter Allgemeine Zeitung,* January 9, 2001.

Suchsland, Rüdiger. "Geister im Thüringischen Wald." *Berliner Zeitung,* February 16, 2011.

Suchsland, Rüdiger, and Christian Petzold. "Der Schneidetisch eines Films ist wie eine Pathologie." *Artechock,* March 8, 2012; accessed February 22, 2013. http://www.artechock.de/film/text/interview/p/petzold_2012.html.

———. "Ein Roman hält uns nicht zusammen." *Frankfurter Rundschau,* February 17, 2005.

Tom, Mustroph. "Fremde Gefährten: *Die innere Sicherheit,* ein Film von Christian Petzold." *Neues Deutschland,* January 28, 2001.

Trnka, Jamie. "'The Struggle Is Over, the Wounds Are Open': Cinematic Tropes, History, and the RAF in Recent German Film." *New German Critique* 34:2.101 (2007): 1–26.

Truffaut, François, with Helen G. Scott. *Hitchcock.* Rev. ed. New York: Simon and Schuster, 1983.

Uehling, Peter, and Christian Petzold. "Wiederaufstehung in der Prignitz." *Berliner Zeitung,* January 8, 2009.

Urry, John. *Mobilities.* Cambridge, Mass.: Polity, 2007.

———. *The Tourist Gaze: Leisure and Travel in Contemporary Societies.* London: Sage, 1990.

Vahabzadeh, Susan, Fritz Göttler, and Christian Petzold. "Karneval der Seelen, Plot Oder Welt—Ein Gespräch mit Christian Petzold." *Süddeutsche Zeitung,* September 15, 2005.

———. "Kino ist wie ein Bankraub." *Süddeutsche Zeitung,* September 12, 2007.

Von Moltke, Johannes. "Terrains Vagues: Landscapes of Unification in Oskar Roehler's *No Place to Go.*" In *Collapse of the Conventional: German Film and Its Politics at the Turn of the Twenty-First Century.* Ed. Jaimey Fisher and Brad Prager. Detroit: Wayne State University Press, 2010. 157–85.

Wahl, Chris, Marco Abel, and Jesko Jockenhövel. *Im Angesicht des Fernsehens: Der Filmemacher Dominik Graf.* Berlin: Edition Text + Kritik, 2012.

Webber, Andrew J. "Topographical Turns: Recasting Berlin in Christian Petzold's *Gespenster.*" In *Debating German Cultural Identity since 1989.* Ed. Anne Fuchs, Kathleen James-Chakraborty, and Linda Shortt. Rochester, N.Y.: Camden House, 2011. 67–81.

Westphal, Anke, and Christian Petzold. "Unsere lebenden Toten." *Berliner Zeitung,* September 15, 2005.

Williams, Linda. "Film Bodies: Gender, Genre, and Excess." In *Film Genre 3.* Ed. Barry Keith Grant. Austin: University of Texas Press, 2003. 141–59.

———. "Melodrama Revisited." In *Refiguring American Film Genres.* Ed. Nicke Browne. Berkeley: University of California Press, 1998. 42–88.

Wood, Jason, and Christian Petzold. "Many Rivers to Cross: Interview with Christian Petzold." *Sight and Sound* 17.10 (2007): 42.

Wood, Robin. *Hitchcock's Films Revisited.* Rev. ed. New York: Columbia University Press, 2002.

Worthmann, Merten. "Leben nach dem Terror: Christian Petzolds Film *Die innere Sicherheit." Die Zeit,* February 1, 2001.

Wydra, Thilo. "Die innere Unsicherheit." *Frankfurter Allgemeine Zeitung,* May 31, 2002.

Young, Neil. "*Dreileben*: Film Review." *Hollywood Reporter,* March 14, 2011.

Zander, Peter. "Eine Perle: Christian Petzold 'Gespenster.'" *Die Welt,* February 16, 2005.

Zeller, Thomas. *Driving Germany: The Landscape of the German Autobahn, 1930–1970.* Trans. Thomas Dunlap. New York: Berghahn Books, 2006.

Zizek, Slavoj. "Alfred Hitchcock; or, The Form and Its Historical Mediation." In *Everything You Always Wanted to Know about Lacan (but Were Afraid to Ask Hitchcock).* Ed. Slavoj Zizek. 1992; reprint, London: Verso, 2010. 1–12.

Index

39 Steps, The (Hitchcock): as model for *Pilots*, 11, 20, 23–24, 26, 27, 29; as production of desire, 23–24, 27; and wrong-man plot, 26

40m² Germany (Baser), 125

Abel, Marco, 11–14, 23, 26, 42, 51–52, 54, 94, 101, 105, 107, 119

abeyance (*Schwebezustand*): as "balance situation," 17, 19, 77, 141, 154; in *Barbara*, 142; and crisis, 12, 135; and youth/adolescence, 55, 161

acting and actors: and abeyance, 19; awards for, 61; and body, 2, 157–58; collaboration with Nina Hoss, 64–67; direction of, 15, 17; German actors, 165; and method acting, 66–67; and plot, 87; preparing actors, 154, 160; psychology in, 67; recurring actors, 79, 131; turning away and leaving, 66

adolescence. *See* youth

Afghanistan, 119, 126

A Fine Day (*Ein schöner Tag*, Arslan), 92

afterness: in *Ghosts*, 83–84, 86–87, 92, 94–95; in *Jerichow*, 118, 123; in *State I Am In*, 53; in *Yella*, 99, 103

aftershocks (*Nachbeben*), 42, 45–46, 50, 51, 83, 87

airplanes, 20, 25, 40. *See also* mobility; car; train

Akın, Fatih, 21, 125, 144; *Edge of Heaven*, 38, 127, 130, 145; *Head On*, 125; and immigration, 125, 144

Altman, Robert, 155, 156, 162

America, 29, 54, 75, 151, 154, 164; and genre cinema, 75, 120, 155, 156; impact on Germany (Americanization), 8, 122; representation in German culture, 4, 5, 8, 122, 126

American genre films, 155

"amphibian film," 20–21

Antonioni, Michelangelo, 66

archeology (of genre in Petzold's cinema), 11, 16–17, 45, 52, 61, 69, 98, 101, 131, 154

Architect Hans Scharoun, The (Bitomsky), 74–75

Arslan, Thomas, 20–21, 99, 152; *A Fine Day*, 92; *Siblings* 125, 144

art-house cinema and directors, 1, 2, 8, 11–14, 20, 35, 41, 98, 121, 132, 143

Auer, Barbara, 171, 173, 175

Aust, Stefan, 41

automobile. *See* car

Autorenkino/auteurist cinema: and Berlin School 10, 13–14; and Fassbinder, 14; and New German Cinema, 13, 14; in Petzold's cinema (themes, etc.) 13–14, 24, 62, 69, 118, 122, 124, 132, 155; problematization of, 9, 13, 24, 132

Baader (Roth), 38

Baader, Andreas, 39–41

Baader-Meinhof group, 39

Baader-Meinhof Komplex (Edel), 38, 42, 60

Barbara (Petzold), 138–43; and abeyance, 19, 141; awards and recognition 1–2, 145n20; and Broch's "Barbara," 139, 141; and color, 161–62; credits, 175; and (faux) distinction art-house vs. popular, 13; and economy, 93, 135; and ekphrasis, 138–39; and fantasy, 93, 135; and Farocki collaboration, 151; and the German Democratic Republic (East Germany), 99; and ghosts, 4; as heritage (historical) cinema, 139–40; and hotel, 141–42; and labor/work, importance of, 27, 142–43; and makeover theme, 22, 37; and *My Darling Clementine*, 19; and politics, 43, 139–43, 161–62; and preparation of actors/crew, 65, 154, 157; and Rembrandt, 138–39; and scale, 26; and space, 157; and television financing, 21; as westward journey by woman, 32; women protagonist 23, 135

Bauman, Zygmunt, 5, 23–24, 32, 74, 80

Bayerischer Rundfunk (BR), 172, 174

beach, 43, 77, 126–28, 130–31, 171

Beats Being Dead (Petzold). See *Dreileben: Beats Being Dead* (Petzold)

Benjamin, Walter, 16; and "angel of history," 42, 89; and archeology, 17; and ghosts/spectral, 16; and history, 17, 18, 89

Berlin: in *Barbara*, 139; in *Cuba Libre*, 28; in *Ghosts*, 78, 84, 87, 89–92, 105; history of, 6–10; leftist politics in 46; in Petzold's biography, 149, 150, 152, 156, 167; in *Under the Bridges*, 63

"Berlin film," 90–91, 140

Berlin Film Festival, 2, 97

Berlin Republic (post-1990 Germany), 81, 124

Berlin School, 2, 18, 92, 99, 108, 132, 154; and aesthetics, 10–13, 39, 98; and *Autorenkino*, 13; as counter-cinema, 13; definition of, 10–13; and DFFB (German Film and Television Academy, Berlin), 10–11; and historical or heritage film, 140–41

Berlin Wall (including fall of), 6, 9, 85, 88, 152

Bettelheim, Bruno, 135

Biehl, João, 4–5

Bierce, Ambrose, 98

Bigelow, Kathryn, 11, 39, 52, 54, 60, 83; *Near Dark*, 11, 39, 52–54, 58–60, 83, 158

Bitomsky, Hartmut, 9, 22, 150, 163; *The Architect Hans Scharoun*, 74–75; *The VW Komplex*, 75, 76, 163

Blue Gardenia, The (Lang), 101

Bock, Rainer, 174–75

body, 26, 43; and acting, 46, 65–67; "body genre," 104; and genre, 156–57; and labor, 80–81; and masculinity, 156; and neoliberalism, 18–19, 54–56, 58, 60, 102–4, 111, 114, 136, 156–57; as strategy of accumulation, 102–4, 111, 114, 157; transitional bodies, 18–19, 54–56, 60, 80–81, 102–4, 111, 114, 136

border: border crossing in *State I am in*, 47–52, 55, 58, 59, 144n12; changes in, 7; in *Yella*, 97, 100, 157

Böhler, Bettina, 64, 131, 170–75

Boyz n the Hood (Singleton), 120

Brecht, Bertolt, 143; *Mann ist Mann*, 143

Brennicke, Nadeshda, 25, 170–71

Bresson, Robert, 66

bridge (as key space): in *Ghosts*, 81–83, 93; in *Nosferatu*, 81–82; in *Something to Remind Me*, 63–64; in *State I Am In*, 56; in *Yella*, 98, 105, 112, 117

Broch, Hermann, 139, 141

Brose, Andrea, 170–71

bubble space, 55, 63, 73, 81, 94, 108

capitalism, 34, 109, 143n1; and coldness, 24; and domesticity, 123; and migration, 126–29; and mobility, 23; refunctioning people, 23, 106; and space, 72, 107; and transformation, 72; and transit spaces, 25. *See also* creative destruction; economy; labor; mobility; neoliberalism

car, 47, 163, 164; car crash, 59, 77; in *Ghosts*, 92, 96; industry, 68, 163 (see also *Wolfsburg*); in *Jerichow*, 2, 130; as movement space, 23, 25–26, 30, 106; as narratively central 74; in *Near Dark*,

52; as ontology, 71, 73, 74, 164; as private space, 70–71; rejection of, 96; and *Wolfsburg* (Petzold), 67–77; in *Yella*, 106, 107, 113. *See also* airplanes; *Driver*; mobility; movement space; train

Carnival of Souls (Harvey), 11, 98, 100–101, 105, 108, 118, 153, 159, 160

Charlie's Angels: Full Throttle (McG), 18

Chinatown (Polanski), 155–56

Christl, Lisy, 172

cinema audience, 14, 66, 125, 132, 156

cinema of consensus, 91, 153; Rentschler's concept of, 10, 18, 38

cinema of duty, 120

cinematic realism, 81, 108

city, 6–8, 55, 78, 83, 88, 89, 91, 97, 101, 113, 118, 126, 128, 149, 156, 160; and catastrophe, 84–85; and class, 79; and consumerism, 56, 58; and fantasy, 26, 58 and history, 85; and industry, 68, 70, 72, 74, 75; and memories of the past, 70–71; and migration 121–22, 148; and renovation/make-over, 90–91; and unemployment/economics, 98–99. *See also* Berlin; *Wolfsburg*

clothing, 30–31, 55–56, 89–90, 92, 102, 113–14, 134, 145n21. *See also* body; consumerism; cosmetics

coldness, 12, 67, 111; and capitalism 5, 24, 62, 116; interpersonal coldness, 31, 136; and melodrama, 70

cold war, 6, 8, 11, 88

collaboration, 17, 22, 64, 66, 131–32, 151. *See also* Böhler; Farocki; Fromm; Graf; Hochhäusler; Hoss

collective, 19, 73, 103, 108, 132, 137, 139, 144. *See also* collective memory

collective memory, 44, 45, 47, 54, 89. *See also* common memory

color, 140, 141, 161–62; and aesthetics, 140

common memory (Margalit), 44–46, 49–50, 56. *See also* collective memory

consumerism, 54–56, 142

Corsten, Volker, 64

cosmetics, 21–23, 26, 31, 37, 107, 140. *See also* body; transformation

counter-cinema, 11, 13, 51

country, the, 121–22, 126, 158

creative destruction, 35, 105, 106, 107, 116, 123

crime: in *Cuba Libre*, 32; and economic fantasies, 27; in film noir/gris, 152; in *Ghosts*, 90, 95; and immigrants, 121; in *Jerichow*, 121, 126; and "normal" life, 20, 27, 28, 38, 90; by Petzold's characters, 4, 59, 69–70; in *Pilots*, 20, 24, 27; in *Sex Thief*, 34, 38; in *State I Am In*, 59; and Sternfeld's photos of, 87; in *Wolfsburg*, 69–70, 75, 77. *See also Yella*

crime-thriller genre, 12, 61, 101, 133

crisis, 135, 141, 150, 155; and abeyance, 12, 15, 135, 154; and transitions, 15, 19, 53, 54, 78, 161, 164

Cuba Libre (Petzold), 28–32; budget of, 143; credits, 170; and criminality, 38; and desire, 44; and *Detour*, 11, 28–30, 153; and economy, 31–32, 80; and fantasies of space, 32; and genre, 11, 28–30, 153; and labor/work, 119; and make-over theme, 37, 119; and (cash) money, 31; and movement space, 28–30; and outsiders, 80; and the past, 32, 85; plot of, 28–29; and politics, 157; strangers meeting in, 107; and television financing, 21; and transit space, 27, 29, 30–32, 33; and westward journey of women, 32

Dardenne, Jean-Pierre and Luc, 11, 28, 65, 81, 192

Das kleine Fernsehspiel, 21, 28. *See also* television; ZDF

Death Proof (Tarantino), 164

debt, 5, 28, 31, 35, 160. *See also* economy; labor

Deer Hunter, The (Cimino), 122, 163

Deleuze, Gilles, 50, 76; and societies of control, 50, 76

Derrida, Jacques, 16

desire, interwoven with economics, 67, 68, 98, 136, 137, 141

Detour (Ulmer), 11, 15, 29–31, 153

Detroit, 163

Deutsche Film- und Fernsehakademie Berlin. *See* DFFB

DFFB (German Film and Television Academy Berlin), 9, 10, 12, 20, 22, 27, 35, 74, 150, 152, 156, 169
Die Innere Sicherheit. See State I am In
difference (class and ethnic) 69, 121, 126, 153
diversity, ethnic, 121–22, 126
Divine Comedy, The (Dante), 135
documentary filmmaking, 57, 74. *See also* Farocki; Bitomsky
documentary realism (Dardenne brothers), 17
domesticity, 27, 44, 55, 123, 128
Donald, James, 44
Donnersmarck, Florian Henckel von, 140; *Lives of Others*, 140, 141
drama, historical. *See* heritage/historical-drama cinema
dreams (vs. reality), 5, 20, 25–27, 30, 33, 44, 54, 81, 93, 98, 101, 104, 110, 112, 162; of home, 33. *See also* fantasies
Dreileben: Beats Being Dead (Petzold), 131–38; and abeyance, 134; and the body, 135; and the bridge/dam, 56, 82; and car, 135–37; and class, 136; as collaboration, 131–32; credits, 174; and desire, 109; and economy, 135–36; and fairy tale, 135; and fantasies of economy, 135; and forest, 134, 137; and genre, 12, 132; and the German Democratic Republic (East Germany), 99; and ghost, ghost-zone, 134, 137; and isolation, 109; and *Last Picture Show*, 15, 154; and love/antiromance, 135–36; and "Mail Exchange" (Mailwechsel) among Petzold, Graf, and Hochhäusler, 12, 132; and movement space, 26, 48, 134, 136–38; and mythology, 101, 133–34; and Ondine myth, 133–34; and the past, 48; plot of, 132–33; and river, 48, 101; and Rübezahl, 134; and scale, 26; and romance (*see* love); and sex, 134, 136–37; and space (location of), 133–34; surveillance, 36, 134; as television project, 1, 131–32; and transformation, 154; and transit space, 27, 134;

and walking, 136–37; and westward journey of women, 32, 135; and young people/adolescence, 161
Driver (Hill), 70–71, 153, 166. *See also* car; labor

East Germany. *See* German Democratic Republic
Eastwards (*Ostwärts*, Petzold), 87, 99, 152
"Economic Miracle" (1950s), 6, 75
economy: adaptability (transformations), 5, 22, 37, 117, 126, 136; and afterness, 83; American practices of, 8, 24; "becoming economic," 1–2, 4, 18; and body/corporeality, 18, 81, 97–100, 102, 103; and criminality, 28, 38, 105; and debt, 5; and desire, 44, 67, 68, 98, 112, 120, 136, 137, 141; and fantasy (impact upon), 23, 26, 44, 58, 92–97, 114, 135; and the GDR, 124; German economy, 68, 71; and ghosts, 4, 5, 6, 16, 19, 26, 106, 113, 135, 137; and lack of opportunity, 86, 118, 142; and love/sexuality, 4, 20, 32, 86, 90, 94, 136, 137; and migration, 32, 97–100, 101, 120, 128, 141; and refunctioning of people, 5, 27, 109–13, 126; and social transformation, 5, 6, 9, 48, 74, 86, 100, 107, 117–18, 139; themes of in Petzold's work, 14, 18; and women, 32, 76, 80, 97–100, 102, 103, 109–13; in *Yella*, 109–13, 117–18. *See also* capitalism; neoliberalism; transformation
Edge of Heaven, The (Akın), 38, 127, 130, 145n18
Edukators (*Die fetten Jahre sind vorbei*, Weingartner), 38
Eichinger, Bernd, 64, 65
Eighteenth Brumaire of Louis Napoleon (Marx), 59
ekphrasis, 139
Elsaesser, Thomas, 20, 22, 40, 54, 62, 156
employment. *See* labor
Ensslin, Gudrun, 40, 57
ethnic Turks. *See* Turkish ethnicity in Germany

ethnicity, 118, 120, 122, 124, 126, 160
European Cinema, 11, 64, 65, 143, 155
European Union, 6
exiles, 46, 47, 158

Face behind the Mask, The (Florey/Mac-
 Donald), 109
factory, 72–75, 144, 166
fairy tales, 79, 81, 82, 83, 95, 97, 133,
 134, 135
family: and domesticity, 122; as economic
 structure, 71, 76, 110, 116, 137; and
 ethnic diversity, 125; exile of in *State I
 am in*, 39, 47, 44, 48, 144n12; obsolescence of, 53, 55, 83–86; and paranoia,
 34, 39, 49–50; ridding self of, 23; and
 shared memories, 60; and terrorism,
 41, 42, 50–51
fantasies: and body, 53–56, 65, 136; of
 car, 74; criminal fantasies, 26–28; of
 domesticity, 124, 166; and economics/
 capitalism, 5, 20, 23, 26, 44, 92–97,
 110–14, 114, 135, 137; erotic fantasy,
 92, 101, 109, 136; and generation,
 46; in *Ghosts*, 79–82, 87; and politics,
 42–44, 58, 60, 141; vs. reality, 98, 104,
 133; spatial, 34, 43–44, 135, 166; of
 travel, 33, 118, 131; and utopia, 44; and
 Weimar cinema (fantastical), 65, 82; in
 Yella, 98, 104
Farocki, Harun: collaboration work with
 Petzold, 19, 22, 83, 118, 169–75; and
 Deleuze's, 76; *Georg K. Glaser, Author
 and Smith*, 46, 51–53, 54, 151; *How to
 live in the German Federal Republic*,
 64; *The Interview*, 35–36, 110, 159;
 manual theme and labor, 54; *Nothing
 Ventured*, 110, 116, 160; as teacher at
 the DFFB, 9, 150–51; *Workers Leave
 the Factory*, 144
Fassbinder, Rainer Werner, 9, 12, 28,
 118, 128, 150, 160; and emotional
 exploitation, 94; *Fear Eats the Soul*,
 128, 167; and genre, 14, 153; and immigration, 167; *Marriage of Maria
 Braun*, 136; *Merchant of Four Seasons*,
 118, 126

Fear Eats the Soul (Fassbinder), 128, 167
film noir: ethnicity in, 122; as genre,
 155; and homosociality, 31; influence
 on Petzold, 29, 30, 31, 101; and lack
 of solidarity, 131; metteur-en-scene
 in, 130; money in, 107; neo-noir, 121;
 spaces of, 30, 127; urban settings of,
 30. See also *Detour, Postman Always
 Rings Twice, Vertigo*
Fisher, Jaimey, 40–41, 147
Fonda, Henry, 19, 154
Ford, John, 19, 101; *My Darling Clementine*, 19, 111, 154; *The Searchers*,
 163
freeway, 27, 130, 122, 164. *See also* car;
 road
Freie Universität Berlin, 8–9
Freud, Sigmund, 104, 112; and the
 dreamwork, 112
Friedrich, Jörg 170–71
Fromm, Hans, 17, 19, 64, 131, 169,
 170–75
Fürmann, Benno, vi, 3, 125, 157, 165,
 172–74

Ganeva, Mila, 91
Garnett, Tay, 12; *Postman Always Rings
 Twice*, 4, 11, 15, 120, 122, 123, 126,
 127
gaze, 12, 94, 103, 105, 138
GDR. *See* German Democratic Republic
Geisler, Claudia, 172–75
gender: and ethnicity, 126; female protagonists in Petzold's films 23, 135; in
 the GDR, 141; generational relations
 among women, 20–21, 142; and horror, 104–5, 113–18; masculinity, 156,
 160, 163; and melodrama, 76–77; and
 (esp. westward) migration, 99, 100–
 101, 161; and mobility, 97–98, 101–2,
 161; and westward journey of women,
 32, 101; and women under economic
 duress, 20; and work, 100–101, 107,
 109
generations, 10, 14–15, 20, 39, 40–47, 51,
 54–58, 60, 142. *See also* family
generic model, 4, 52–53, 98, 118

genre: archeology of, 14–15, 19, 62, 68, 69, 70, 98, 101, 127, 136, 139, 153–54; vs. art-house cinema 12–14, 132; and the body, 156–57; body genres, 104; fragmenting and recasting of genre works, 54, 58, 61, 64, 82, 88, 96, 105, 115, 118; genre cinema, 12, 14, 18, 132, 139, 153 24; genre films, 8, 13, 16, 19, 28–29, 30, 39, 52, 61–62, 81, 98, 118, 136, 153, 155–56; late genre, 16–17, 35, 52, 58; and non-fiction film, 36; transitional/transformational types, 23, 53, 67, 133. *See also* film noir; guest-worker films; Heimat film; heritage/historical-drama cinema; horror films/genre; hotel film; Western

Georg K. Glaser, Author and Smith (Farocki), 46, 51–53, 54, 151

Gere, Richard, 18, 156

"German Autumn," 39–41

German Democratic Republic (East Germany): Americanization, 122; anti-Fascism, its failure, 153; in *Barbara*, 138–42; ethnic diversity in, 120, 160–62; in Petzold's biography, 7–8, 99; as setting for *Postman Always Rings Twice*, 118; transition to unified German and capitalism, 2, 97, 99, 100–103, 105, 133

German film industry, 14, 20–21, 33, 60, 64, 65, 132, 154, 158, 159

German legends and myths, 46, 95, 100–101, 133–34

German New Wave, 2

gestures, 15, 17, 46, 65, 66, 96, 112

ghost and the ghostly, 42, 51, 117, 124; actors playing, 17; and economics/labor, 4, 5, 16, 19, 26, 106, 113, 135, 137; in fairy tales, 79; as the film audience, 162–63; and the former German Democratic Republic 106, 135, 137, 139; and history, 5, 16, 42, 51, 83, 135, 137, 139; and space, 166

Ghosts (*Gespenster*, Petzold), 72–97; and abeyance, 161; and afterness, 83–86, 94–95; and Berlin film, 91–92, 140; and bridge, 56, 63, 81–82; budget of, 143n6; and bubble spaces, 108; and

"Burial Shirt" (Totenhemdchen) of Grimm brothers, 79–80; credits of, 172–73; and crisis, 161; and desire, 44; and dreamlike tone, 81; and "Earth-quake in Chile" of Kleist, 84–85; and economy, 80–84; and emotional exploitation, 93–94; ending, 117; and fairy tale, 79–80, 81, 82, 95–96; and family, 85–86; and fantasy (also blurred line to reality), 44, 54, 92–93, 96; and forests, 82–83, 94–95, 107, 134–35; and French aspects, 84; and genre (citation and critique of), 17, 98, 140; and ghost/ghostly, 80–84; and Ghost Trilogy, 16; and history (vs. memory), 72, 88–89, 90–91; and horror, 17, 109; and hotel, 86, 109, 141; and labor reform 80–81, 83–84; and labor/work, 80–81; and landmarks, avoidance of, 28; and love (entwinement with economy), 86; and nature, 105; and *Nosferatu*, 81–82; and past as present, 85–86; plot of, 78–79; and Potsdamer Platz, 86–90, 99; public vs. private, 89–90; and space (urban), 28, 86–90, 99, 102; and strangers' encounter in, 107; and transit space; and trauma, 85; and Weimar cinema, 81–82; and the *Wende* (1989/1990), 9; and youth/adolescence, 55, 161

Ghost trilogy: endings of films in, 117; and genre, 98; ghost aspect, 51; and horror, 98; and remnants/remains, 16; and the past's return in the present, 42; and space, 124; and *State I Am In*, 97; and *Yella*, 97. *See also* economy; *Ghosts*; ghosts and the ghostly; *State I Am In*

Glaser, Georg, 46, 51–53, 54, 151

globalization, 101, 106, 107, 122. *See also* uneven geographical development

Godard, Jean-Luc, 14, 148, 153–54

Go, Trabi, Go (Timm), 10

Göttler, Fritz, 66, 67, 84, 87, 100, 144

Graf, Dominik, 12–14, 61, 132–33, 143, 150

Grand Hotel (Goulding), 109

Great Gatsby, The (Fitzgerald), 166

Grube, Kade, 170–75

guest-workers, 118–21, 124, 125, 126, 167
guest-worker films, 120–23, 125–26, 140
guilt, 23–24, 69–70, 130, 157. *See also* debt
Gustorf, Florian Koerner von, xi, 143, 169–71, 173–75
Guther, Anette 169–71, 173–75

Hake, Sabine, 20–21
Hall, Stuart, 119–21
Halloween (Carpenter), 54, 104, 137
Haneke, Michael, 11, 158
Hartz IV Reforms, 72, 123
Harvey, David: and body as strategy of accumulation, 102, 157; *Brief History of Neoliberalism*, 143; and creative destruction, 35, 105–7, 116, 123; *Spaces of Hope*, 102–3, 105; and uneven geographical development, 101–2, 107
Head-On (*Gegen die Wand*, Akın), 125
Heaven (Tykwer), 135
Heimat, 122–23, 126, 148. *See also* home
Heimat film, 122
heritage/historical-drama cinema, 10, 140–41, 145
Hennicke, André, 61, 63, 172, 174
Herrenbrück, Heino, 169–71
Herzog, Werner, 9, 10
Higson, Andrew, 145
Hirsch, Marianne, 45
history: afterness, 83, 84; aftershocks of, 42, 45–46, 50–51, 83, 87; archeological history, 16; and the "Berlin film," 88–91; falling out of (by characters), 51, 150–51, 158; of Germany 5–6, 8, 50, 68, 71–72, 75–76, 78, 84–85, 89–90, 100, 157; and ghosts, 5, 16, 42, 51, 83, 135, 137, 139; historical disjuncture, 49, 51; politics over the course of, 38, 59; posthistoire, 84; "progress" of, 5, 18, 43; public history, 79, 88, 90–91; repetition as farce, 59; transformation, 17
Hitchcock, Alfred, 11, 20, 23–24, 32, 38, 60–64, 90, 102, 105, 109; *The 39 Steps*, 11, 20, 23–24, 26, 27, 29; and acting, 66; criminality theme, 62, 117; and the long shot, 114; MacGuffin, 24, 26; *Marnie*, 102; *Psycho*, 32, 109, 113;

reframing in his cinema, 62, 90, 105; *Vertigo*, 11, 60–64; wrong-man theme, 23, 26, 29–31
Hitler, Adolf, 68, 88, 158
Hochhäusler,Christoph, 11–13, 132–33; *Dreileben: Eine Minute Dunkel*, 132–33
Hollywood, 8, 29, 101, 150, 155, 162
Hollywood genre films, 8, 29, 101. *See also* New Hollywood
Holocaust, the, 39, 57. *See also* history; Nazism
home: childhood home, 33–35, 37, 44, 103–4, 108–9, 119, 123–29; and the collective past, 70; dreams of, 33–34, 44, 73, 112, 114, 116, 165; homeland, 39, 47, 126; homelessness, 27, 28, 44, 78, 108–9, 123–29, 131, 135, 148, 161; homesickness, 128; hometown, 97, 103–4, 118–19, 122–29, 124, 126, 129; ruins of, 108–9, 123
horror films/genre: gender in, 104–5, 113–18; generic syntax/grammar of, 98, 104–5; influence on Petzold's cinema, 45, 54, 81, 104–6, 113–18, 155, 161; spaces of (forest, hotels, house, etc.), 83, 87–88, 109; subjective vs. objective POV in, 54, 104–5, 115. See also *Carnival of Souls*; *Nosferatu*; *Psycho*; *The Shining*
Hoss, Nina, 19, 61, 63–67, 97, 111, 112, 115, 160, 164, 167, 172–75
Hot Summer (*Heißer Sommer*, Hasler), 162
hotels: in *Barbara*, 141–42; and class, 28; in *Dreileben*, 161; and economy, 108–9, 141–42, 161; fantasies of, 112, 113, 164–65; in *Ghosts*, 78, 86, 89, 95; and homelessness: 22–23, 30, 33, 108–9; social isolation in, 165–65; as symbol of mobility, 28, 33, 37, 107–13, 118; as transit space 7, 20, 53; in *Yella*, 107–13, 116–18
hotel film, 109
house. *See* home
How to Live in the German Federal Republic (*Leben: BRD*, Farocki), 64
Huyssen, Andreas, 89

iconography (of genre), 23, 53, 124, 127
identity, 29–31, 84, 86; nonidentity, 16;
  and work, 84; wrong-man theme, 23,
  26, 29–31
immigration: in *Barbara*, 142; and border,
  49, 52; in *Face behind the Mask*, 109;
  guest-worker, 118–21, 124, 125, 126,
  167; guest-worker films, 120–23, 125–
  26, 140; in *Jerichow*, 118, 131, 160. *See
  also* home, homelessness
Indian Grave, The (*Das indische Grabmal*, May), 82
Interview, The (*Die Bewerbug*, Farocki),
  35–36, 110, 159

Jackie Brown (Tarantino), 167
Jameson, Fredric, 44
Jancovich, Mark, 104
Jerichow (Petzold), 118–31; and abeyance; and Akın, Fatih, 126; and Americanization, 122; and beach, 77, 126–29;
  and car, 2–4, 74, 124, 130–31; and
  cinema of duty, 120, 125; and creative
  destruction, 123; and credits, 174; and
  criminality, 28; and *Deer Hunter*, 122,
  163; and domestic, 55, 122–23, 124,
  165; and economy, 2–4, 105, 118–19,
  122, 123–26; and *Edge of Heaven*, 126;
  and ethnicity, 160; and Fassbinder,
  118, 127, 128; and fantasies, 93; and
  Fear Eats the Soul, 128; and film noir,
  131; and forest, 135; and GDR (East
  Germany), 99, 152; and genre, 4, 11–
  12, 118, 130–31, 140, 153; and ghost/
  ghostly, 3–4, 118; and ghetto film, 120,
  124; and guest-workers, 120–22; and
  guest-worker films, 120–22; and Stuart
  Hall, 120–21; and *Head-On*, 126; and
  Heimat ("Heimat-Building"), 122, 123;
  and home/house, 55, 122–23, 124, 165;
  and labor/work, 143; and landscape,
  122; and love, 118, 129–30; and memory, 123; and *Merchant of Four Seasons*, 118, 126, 127–28; and migration,
  120–26, 130–31; and movement space,
  2–4, 122, 129–31; and *Ossessione*,
  144n17, 120, 123; and the past vs. present, 123; and place vs. space, 103; plot

of, 119–20; and *Postman Always Rings
  Twice*, 3, 118, 119, 123, 127, 128; and
  Bob Rafelson, 128; and refunctioning people, 4–5; and remnants/ruins
  (social), 85; and scale, 26; setting of,
  119, 133; and sex, 136; and solidarity,
  lack of, 130–31; and space, 77, 123–27,
  133; and strangers, encounter with,
  107, 124; and television financing, 21;
  and "third space," 126–29; and transit
  space, 2–4, 122, 124–26; and Turkish
  people, 118–22, 124–25, 129–30; and
  walking, 134; and *The Wire*, 122
jet, 25, 40. *See also* airplanes; car; mobility; movement spaces

Kings of the Road (*Im Laufe der Zeit*,
  Wenders), 8
Kleist, Heinrich von: "The Earthquake in
  Chile," 85 "On the Gradual Formation
  of Thought in Speaking," 151
Kluge, Alexander, 23, 89
Koepnick, Lutz, xi
Kopp, Kristin, 11, 119
Körte, Peter, 49–50
Kothenschulte, Daniel, 119–20
Kracauer, Sigfried, 108
Kreist, Ulrich, 66, 67, 80, 83, 84, 91, 101,
  102, 103, 104, 139
Krix, Christoph, 170, 171
Kübler, Kim, 169–70
Kurth, Peter, 172–73

labor and work: and body, 80, 102, 162;
  control function of, 35; creative destruction of, 35, 107; demateralization
  of, 23, 34, 54, 74–75, 84; flexibility"
  of, 5; and paranoia, 34; in *Pilots*, 27;
  surveillance of, 21, 37, 76, 34; as (usually absent) topic in cinema, 22, 27, 65;
  transformation of, 20, 22, 26, 37, 54,
  68, 75, 80–82, 84; and women, 23. *See
  also* body; economy; gender; Hartz IV
  reforms; solidarity
Ladd, Brian, 88–89
landscape: and business people, 122; vs.
  economy, 122; and history, 72; industrial landscapes, 6, 68; and memory,

103; with movement spaces, 2, 102; and myth, 133; Western landscape, 154. *See also* Sternfeld, Joel

Last Picture Show, The (Bogdanovich), 15–16, 53–54, 83, 154

Lenssen, Claudia, 71, 72, 144

Liane, the Girl from the Jungle (*Liane, das Mädchen aus dem Urwald*, von Borsody), 148

Little Big Man (Penn), 54

Lives of Others, The (Donnersmarck), 140, 141

Lonely Way, The (*Der einsame Weg*, Arthur Schnitzler), 167

Long Goodbye, The (Altman), 155, 156, 162

love: in *The 39 Steps*, 24; absence of, 23; in *Barbara* 141–43; contextually determined love, 24, 62, 69, 97–118, 136; in *Detour*, 29–30; in *Dreileben* 133–34, 136; and economy/work, 4, 20, 32, 86, 90, 94, 136, 137; and ghosts, 163; in *Jerichow*, 120; in *The Last Picture Show*, 154; and melodrama, 77; and public/private space, 63; in *Something to Remind Me*, 62; in *Vertigo*, 62; in *Wolfsburg*, 69; in *Yella*, 97–118. *See also* coldness; economy; romance

Mädchen Rosemarie (Eichinger), 64

"Mail Exchange" (Mailwechsel) among Petzold, Graf, and Hochhäusler, 12, 132

make-up. *See* cosmetics

Maltese Falcon (Huston), 30

Margalit, Avishai, 44–45

Marianne and Juliane (von Trotta), 57

Marnie (Hitchcock), 102

Marriage of Maria Braun, The (Fassbinder), 136

masculinity, 156, 160, 163

Marx, Karl, 16, 59, 153

melodrama: and domesticity, 70, 71; and family, 86, 90, 96; generic fragments of, 61, 71; and heritage cinema, 141, 144; and (romantic) love, 77; maternal melodrama, 69; as mode, 70; moral legibility of, 69, 144n14; of Douglas Sirk, 162; and *Wolfsburg*, 68–77

memory: bodily memory, 165; collective memory, 44, 46, 47, 89; common memory, 44–47, 49, 50, 55, 60; political memory, 43–45, 58; private memory, 90, 123; shared memory, 44–47, 49, 55, 56, 60; in *State I am in*, 42–47. *See also* history; Margalit, Avishai

Menace II Society (Hughes)

Merchant of Four Seasons (Fassbinder), 118, 126

metteur-en-scène, 60, 130

Middle High German, 149

migrants, 98, 109, 121, 129, 131; domestic migrants, 126; and longing for home, 128; in Petzold's biography, 147, 160

migration, 102; domestic, 99; gendered, 100–101. *See also* immigration

mobility, 14, 17, 19, 38–40, 42, 65, 130, 152, 175. *See also* movement space

Moby Dick (Melville), 41

modernism, 88

modernity, 14

monster, 104, 105, 113, 114, 116

Moore, Demi, 18

movement space: and bubble space, 73; definition of, 2; in *Dreileben*, 138; in *Jerichow*, 130–31; and private space, 70; in *Wolfsburg*, 67–77; and *Yella*, 113. *See also* airplanes; cars; jet; train; walking

Mücke-Niesytka, Andreas, 172–75

Müller, Richy, 170–71

multiculturalism, 120

Münnich, Monika, 169–74

Murnau, Friedrich Wilhelm, 10, 53, 81

music: and Berlin School, 11; diegetic music, 55–56, 78, 137–38; and flashback in *Cuba Libre*, 29; of home in *Jerichow*, 126; musicals and *Barbara*, 162; music credit in films, 169–75; nondiegetic in *State I Am In*, 144n12; and rights to, 144n13; and young people, 55–56, 137–38. *See also* Schlager; sound

My Darling Clementine (Ford), 19, 111, 154

Naked City (Dassin), 30

National Socialism. *See* Nazism

Nazism, Nazi Germany: and bodies, 65, 165; and car industry, 68–75; and GRD, 99, 141, 147, 153; quote from *Night and Fog* (Resnais), 57; traces of in present, 72; and *Wolfsburg* (Petzold), 68–75. *See also* history, Holocaust

Near Dark (Bigelow), 11, 39, 52–54, 58–60, 83, 158

neoliberalism: and body, 18–19, 54–56, 58, 60, 102–4, 111, 114, 136, 156–57; and capitalism, 32, 88; definition of, 143n1; and gender in *Yella*, 95, 98, 160; and ghosts, 163; and surveillance, 37; and transformation of Germany 2, 5, 14. *See also* economy, labor

neorealism, 120. *See also* documentary realism

New German Cinema: as auteurist cinema, 13, 14; and Eichinger, 64; and gender, 144n7; and film schools, 9; influence on Petzold, 91, 153, 156; and television, 20. *See also* Fassbinder, Rainer Werner; Sander, Helke; *Shirin's Wedding*; Wenders, Wim

New Hollywood: and balance situation/crisis, 155; and coldness, 70; and genre, 162; influence on Petzold, 150. *See also* Altman, Robert; Polanski, Roman; Rafelson, Bob; Vietnam War

Nicodemus, Katja, 1, 46, 59, 71–72, 74

Night and Fog (Resnais), 57

nonplace. *See* space, abstract

Nord, Cristina, 2, 22, 71, 79, 80, 88, 99, 140, 142

Nosferatu (Murnau), 81–82. *See also* horror films/genre

Oberhausen Manifesto, 9–10

Odyssey, The (Homer), 90

On this Site (Sternfeld), 87, 95, 166, 167n3

Oscar: Petzold's nomination for, 2, 138, 145n20

Ossessione (Visconti), 120, 123, 126, 144

Ozu, Yasujiro, 66

Papelian, Gilles, 170

paranoia: in contemporary economy, 6; in *Cuba Libre*, 30–32; in family relationships, 34, 51; in love relationships, 30–32; in *Sex Thief*, 34; in *State I am in*, 40, 45, 50, 51; and terrorism, 40, 45, 50, 51

Peck, Jamie, 5, 21, 34, 37

Peitz, Christiane, 40–42, 46–47, 51, 66, 100, 102, 106, 133

People on Sunday (*Menschen am Sonntag*, Siodmak, Gliese, Ulmer), 29

performance. *See* acting and actors

Petzold, Christian; biography, 6–9; physicality, 18–19, 65, 67, 94, 156. *See also* individual film titles

Pilots (*Pilotinnen*), 20–28; and *The 39 Steps*, 11, 23–24, 26; actors/performance in, 66; and *Barbara*, similarities to, 37; and car, 74, 164; and coldness between people, 24; and control societies, 35; and creative destruction, 107; credits of, 169–70; and criminality, 38; and desire, 98; economy, 20–28, 32; ending of, 32; and fantasies, 26, 32, 44, 134; and fantasized geography, 26; and fantasized plot, 134; and Harun Farocki, 21; and genre, 11, 20–24, 29, 30; and ghost/ghostly, 26; and Alfred Hitchcock, 11, 23–24, 26, 61; and homelessness, 27; and hotels, 108; labor/work, 23–25, 27–28, 31, 141, 143; and landscape with business people, 122; and make-over theme, 37; and make-up theme, 22–23, 37; and movement space, 2, 22–27, 74; plot of, 21; and the past vs. present; and politics, 157; and refunctioning people, 31; and remnants/remains, 107; and scale, 26; and space, 6, 26, 30; and strangers, 142; and television financing, 20–21; and transformation, 23; and transit space, 22–23, 25–27, 33; travel, 33; and women characters/protagonists, 43, 142; and women's mobility, 97; and women under economic duress, 20

Pippig, Sven, 67, 172

Polan, Dana, 29, 30

Poland, 86

Polanski, Roman, 155–56

police: in *Barbara*, 140, 142; in *Dreileben*, 132; and immigrants, 121, 124; in *Pilots*, 24, 28; in *Sex Thief*, 33, 35, 37; in *Something to Remind Me*, 67, in *State I am in*, 47, 49–52, 59; and terrorism, 40, 41.

politics: in *Barbara*, 141–42; of Berlin, 91; vs. consumerism, 59, 142; and immigration, 49; intergenerational politics, 51, 54, 59; leftist politics, 42, 43; radical politics, 38, 40, 58; and passing of time, 42, 43, 46, 49, 56, 59.

posthistoire, 84

Postman Always Rings Twice, The: Cain novel, 11, 15, 118–22, 126, 131; Garnett film, 4, 15; Rafelson film, 12, 15, 128

Potsdamer Platz, 84, 86–90, 94, 99

Prager, Brad, 10, 44

Pretty Woman (Marshall), 18, 156–57

production trends, 140

Psycho (Hitchcock), 32, 109, 113

RAF (Red Army Faction): films about, 60; and German history, 39–42, 144n8; and passing of time, 46, 85; radicalization of, 57; and *State I Am In*, 39–42, 157.

Rafelson, Bob, 12, 128. See also *Postman Always Rings Twice, The*

Ray, Nicholas, 162

realism. *See* documentary realism, neorealism

Red Army Faction. See RAF

refugees, 7, 98, 147–49, 153

Reinecke, Stefan, 69, 70, 73

Rembrandt, 138–39, 145

remnants/remains: archeological/generic remains in Petzold's cinema, 16–19, 70, 82, 139; in *Barbara*, 139; in *Ghosts*, 78, 79, 83–87, 91; in *Jerichow*, 118, 123; in *Last Picture Show*, 15; of melodrama, 70; of public history, 79; social remains, 5; in *State I Am In*, 42, 45, 46, 52, 57; in *Yella*, 99, 103, 105, 111, 118. *See also* afterness, aftershocks, ghosts and the ghostly, posthistoire

Rentschler, Eric, 9, 38

Resnais, Alain, 58

Revolver (journal), 11, 12, 143n3

Richter, Carsten, 173–75

Richter, Gerhard (painter), 17, 139

Richter, Gerhard (theorist/scholar), 16, 83

river, 48, 97–98, 101, 110, 112–13, 138

road, 30, 33, 59, 72, 74, 101, 107. *See also* car; freeway; movement space; transit space

road movies, 163

Rodek, Hans-Georg, 40, 41, 49, 59, 72, 82, 142, 145

romance, 59–63, 133–5, 162; anti-romance, 135–36. *See also* love

Rote Armee Fraktion. See RAF

Rother, Rainer, 65–67

rubble. *See* ruins

Ruhr region, 6–7, 21, 142, 147

ruins: from creative destruction, 34–35, 105–6, 123; of genre, 62, 139; of home, 108; and ghosts, 99, 102, 103. *See also* creative destruction, economy, remnants

Running on Empty (Lumet), 42, 52

Sander, Helke, 9

scale, 26, 108

Schanelec, Angela, 10

Schlager, 69

Schleyer, Hanns-Martin, 40

Schlichter, Mark, 169–70

Schlöndorff, Volker, 13

Schneider, Helge, 69

Schramm Film Koerner and Weber, 143n6, 169–75

Schwebezustand. See abeyance

Schwenk, Johanna, 66, 80, 83, 119, 142

Searchers, The (Ford), 163

Sebald, W. G., 136; *Rings of Saturn*, 145n20

Sennett, Richard, 32, 73, 74, 143

Sex Thief (*Die Beischlafdiebin*), 32–38; and adrift characters, 101, 123; and archeological approach, 110; and control societies, 35; and creative destruction, 34–35, 107; credits of, 170–71; and criminality, 37–38; and desire, 44; and domestic, 33, 103, 123;

Sex Thief (*Die Beischlafdiebin*) (continued), and economy, 33–34, 35–37, 110; and family, 34; and fantasies, 32–34; 44; and Harun Farocki, 35–37, 110; and Caspar David Friedrich, 164; and ghost/ghostly; and home/house, 33, 103, 123; and *The Interview*, 35–37, 110; and make-over theme, 37; movement space, 97; and neoliberalism, 36–37; and paranoia, 34; and the past vs. present; and place vs. space, 33, 103, 123, 125; plot of, 33; and politics, 157; and refunctioning people 35–37, 102; and remnants/remains, 107; and Gerhard Richter (painter), 17; and sex, 136; and space, 6; and surveillance, 36–37, 80, 145n19; and tourism, 32; and transformation, 102; and travel, 33; and transit space, 33; and women protagonists, 20; and women's mobility, 97; and *Yella*, similarities to, 34

shared memories, 44–47, 49–51, 55–58, 60

Shining, The (Kubrick), 109

Shirin's Wedding (Sanders-Brahms), 120

Siblings (*Geschwister*, Arslan), 125, 144

Sleeper (*Schläfer*, Heisenberg), 38

socialism, 153

solidarity, 24, 30, 31, 76–77, 127, 129, 131

Something to Remind Me (*Toter Mann*, Petzold), 60–67; and abeyance; and acting/performance, 61, 64–67; and actor preparation, 65; and biography/career of Petzold, 60–61; and the body, 65; and bridge, 63; and car, 2–4; credits, 171–72; and economy, 2–4; and Harun Farocki, 60; and femme fatale, 62; Benno Fürmann, 65; and the GDR (East Germany), 99; and genre, 4, 11, 61; and ghost/ghostly, 3–4; and Alfred Hitchcock, 61–62, 66; and Nina Hoss, 64–67, 160; and *How to live in the German Federal Republic*, 64; Helmut Käutner, 63; love, 62; and method acting, 66–67; and metteur-en-scene, 62; and movement space, 2–4; and the past vs. present, 85; and plot, 61–62; and prizes for, 60–61; and public spaces,

62–63; and refunctioning people, 4–5; and setting, 62, 65–66, 97; and space, 62; and Steadicam, 82; and swimming pool, 61–62; and television financing, 60, 144n13, 159; and transit space; and trauma, 85; and *Under the Bridges*, 63–64; and *Vertigo*, 61–62, 63–64; and walking, 66 103; and Wittenberge, 65–66, 97

sound: of different socioeconomic scales, 26; in *Dreileben*, 136; lack of sound, 59; sound point-of-view, 112, 117; and the uncanny, 110, 111; of wind, 80. *See also* music

space: abstract, 108–10, 112; of *afterness*, 86; and creative destruction, 107; in *Detour*, 30; domestic space 33, 35, 71, 134–35, 137; and genre/generic recasting, 62; and history, 72, 88–89, 102; liminal space, 16, 108; importance in Petzold's work, 87, 147–48, 165–66; in mise-en-scene, 66; and mobility, 4; and nation, 49; vs. plot, 95; private space, 70; public space, 63; rivers, 48; rural space, 125; spatial fantasies, 5, 45–46, 105, 134–35; third (utopian) space, 127–28, 129; urban space, 78–79. *See also* beach, Berlin, border, bubble space, car, home, hotels, mobility, movement space, Potsdamer Platz, transit space

Specters of Marx (Derrida), 16

Stasi, 151–52

State I am In (*Die innere Sicherheit*), 38–60; and adrift characters, 101; and aftershocks, 42–43; and archeology of Petzold's films, 16; and the Berlin School, 10, 38; in the biography/career of Petzold, 10, 61, 65, 78, 152–53, 157–58, 159; and the body, 54–56, 60, 94, 102; and borders, 47–52, 97; and bridge, 56, 63, 82; and bubble space, 73, 74, 108; and car, 2–4, 71, 73, 74, 164; and collective memory, 44, 47, 54; and common memory, 44–46; and consumerism (vs. politics), 54–56, 142; and context for, 39–42; credits of, 171; and criminality, 58–59, 90; and economy, 2–4; and ending of, 117; and family (incl. obsolescence of), 38–47, 51, 85; and fantasy (incl. dream-like tone), 43–44, 54, 58, 60, 81, 93, 141; and Harun Farocki, 46, 151; and forest, 134; and gas station, 27; and generations, 44–45; and genre, 4, 11, 16–17, 52–54, 98; and *Georg K. Glaser, Author and Smith*, 46, 53–54, 151–52; and German Autumn, 40–41; and *The German Sisters*, 57; ghost/ghostly, 3–4, 46, 52–54, 78; and *Ghosts*, 78–79; and Ghost trilogy, 16; and George Glaser, 46, 51, 53–54, 151–52; and history, 48–49, 72, 84; and the Holocaust, 57; and home/house, 43, 103; and homelessness; and horror, 17, 53–55; and idyllic openings, 105; and love, 44, 143; and Sidney Lumet, 42; and make-over theme, 102; and memory, 42–47, 57, 60; and migration, 49; and *Moby Dick*, 41–42; and movement space, 2–4; and music, 43; and *Near Dark*, 39, 52–54, 58, 59; and neoliberalism, 42–43; and *Night and Fog*, 57; and the past vs. present, 72; and place vs. space, 103; plot, 39; and politics (incl. over time), 38–39, 42–43, 53–54, 142, 143, 157–58; and postmemory, 45; prizes awarded to, 1, 38; and refunctioning people, 4–5; and remnants/remains, 42–43; and *Running on Empty*, 42; and sex, 136; and shared memory, 44–46; and strangers' meeting, 111; success of, 67, 78, 39; and surveillance, 36, 51, 59–60; and terrorism 38–42, 57–60, 157–59; title, original, 78; and tourism, 38–40; and transformation, 47–48, 53, 54–56, 85; and transit space, 27, 47–50; and travel, 38–40, 47–48; and Margarethe von Trotta, 57; and utopia, 44, 60, 93; and vampires, 53–55; and Westerns, 53–54, 58; and youth/adolescence, 161

Sternfeld, Joel, 87, 95, 166, 167
strangers: and economy, 109; fantasies of, 96–97, 112; partnership with, 32, 107, 111; promise of meeting stranger, 32, 107, 135, 142; refunctioning self through, 32, 95–97, 135

student movement, 8, 39
subsidy system, 20. *See also* television
Suchsland, Rüdiger, 1, 21, 66, 82–85, 91, 96, 143
Süden (*South*, Petzold), 87, 150
surveillance: in *Barbara*, 140–41; and contemporary economy, 37, 59; and fantasy, 145n19; in interviews, 36; in personal relationships, 86, 134; in *State I am in*, 59; in workplace, 21, 76

Tarantino, Quentin: *Death Proof*, 164; *Jackie Brown*, 167
Tauber, Bernd, 171
television: American television series, 122; and *Cuba Libre*, 28; and *Dreileben*, 1, 131–32; financing through television, 20–21, 131–32, 158, 159; in the GDR, 100; and genre, 12, 14, 154; in *Ghosts*, 92; and *Pilots*, 20–21; and *Sex Thief*, 32; and *Something to Remind Me*, 60–61, 78, 159; and *Wolfsburg*, 67, 78.
Teorama (Pasolini), 161
terrorism and terrorists: fading relevance, 51, 58, 60, 157–58; and family, 46–47, 157–58; historical context for *State I Am In*, 38–41; and memory, 45, 47–48, 55; and paranoia, 45. See also *Baader-Meinhof Komplex*; border; *Marianne and Juliane*; politics; *State I Am In*
theater, 64, 138, 148, 155, 157, 159, 167
Third Reich. *See* Nazism
third (utopian) space, 127–28, 129
This Man Must Die (Chabrol), 77
tourism, 33, 39, 148
train, 24, 28–31, 33, 97, 98, 102, 105. *See also* airplanes; car; movement spaces
transformation: of bodies, 54, 60, 102–3, 111, 114, 136; of borders, 49, 97; of economy, 22, 31, 67, 91, 95, 97, 99; of film genre, 52; historical transformation in films, 15, 17, 52–53, 67, 71, 124; of individuals, 19, 20, 24, 31, 97, 102–3, 111, 114, 117, 139; of labor, 5, 74, 152; of space, 2, 56, 91, 138, 167; of state, 9, 22, 49, 91, 99, 139, 153. *See also* bridge; history; politics; space

transit space: in *Barbara*, 141; in biography of Petzold, 7, 147–48; in *Cuba Libre*, 28, 33 definition of, 26; in *Detour*, 30; in *Dreileben*, 134–35; in Farocki's work, 151; gas station, 27, 29, 30, 134; in *Ghosts*, 89; in *Jerichow*, 118, 122; in *Near Dark*, 158; and non-space, 89; in *Pilots*, 20, 23, 26, 27, 33; of rest area, 20, 27, 29, 49; in *Sex Thief*, 33; in *Wolfsburg*, 67; in *Yella*, 103, 107–8. *See also* home, hotels, Volkswagen

travel. *See* mobility, movement space, tourism

Truffaut, Francois, 13, 114, 118, 162

Turkish ethnicity in Germany, 118–21, 124–31, 144, 153, 160

Two-Lane Blacktop (Hellman), 164

Uehling, Peter, 8, 68, 118, 122, 123

Ulmer, Edgar G., 11, 29–31

Under the Bridges (*Unter den Brücken*, Käutner), 63, 64

uneven geographical development, 101–2, 107, 127, 130. *See also* Harvey, David

Unification, German, 4, 6, 38, 99, 102, 152

Urry, John, 2, 4, 23, 93

utopia, 44, 58, 60, 77, 93, 94, 99, 125

Vahabzadeh, Susan, 66, 67, 84, 87, 144

vampires, 52–53, 58–60, 81, 158

Vertigo (Hitchcock), 11, 60–64

victim and victimization: in *Barbara*, 138–39; and gender, 113; in horror films, 104; and immigrants 120–21; and Petzold's characters, 23, 33; in melodrama, 69; in *Yella*, 160

violence, 41–42, 58–59, 138, 140, 142. *See also* crime

Vietnam War, 40, 155, 163

Visconti, Luchino: *Ossessione*, 11, 120, 123

Volkswagen, 68, 72, 75–76

von Donnersmarck, Florian Henckel 140

von Moltke, Johannes, 144n7

von Trotta, Margarethe, 57

VW Komplex, The (Bitomsky), 75, 76, 163

walking: characters walking away, 66, 103; in *Ghosts*, 93, 96; in *Jerichow*, 119, 124; in preparation for shooting, 157; sleepwalking, 101

Warm Money, The (*Das warme Geld*, Petzold) 20, 66, 169

Warsaw Pact, 6, 7, 100, 139

Weimar Cinema: and bodies, 65; and fantasy, 82; as legitimate cinema, 10; reframing in, 62; subjective vs. objective POV in, 54; and Ulmer's career, 29

Weimar Germany, 41

Weisgerber, Eleonore 25, 170

Wende, 91, 152. *See also Ghosts* (Petzold)

Wenders, Wim, 8, 9, 14; *Kings of the Road*, 8

Western (genre): as ancient drama, 155; coldness of, 70; in *Ghosts*, 96; landscape in, 154; in *Last Picture Show*, 15; *My Darling Clementine*, 19, 111, 154; in *Near Dark* and *State I Am In*, 52–54, 58, 60

West Germany: in Petzold's biography, 6–8; in *Pilots*, 26; in *State I Am In*, 50; in *Wolfsburg*, 68; in *Yella* 97–98

Will, Stefan, 170–75

Williams, Linda, 69, 104

Wire, The, 122

Wittenberge, 97, 100, 102, 109, 113, 139

Wolfsburg (Petzold), 68–77; and actors/performance, 65; and *Architect Hans Scharoun*, 74; in biography/career of Petzold, 61; and Hartmut Bitomsky, 74–75, 163; and bubble space, 73, 108; and car, 68–77, 106, 130, 163–64; and class, 136; and control societies, 76; credits of, 172; and criminality, 28; and Gilles Deleuze, 76; and distribution/theatrical release, 66–67, 144n13; and domestic, 68–69, 125; and *Driver*, 153; and economy, 71–72; and fantasies, 135; and genre, 69–70, 153; and guilt for Nazi past, 70–71, 74–75; and history, 68, 70–72; and home/house, 68–69, 125; and labor/work (incl. reform), 65, 71–72, 75; and landscape with business people, 72, 122; and love, 85, 136; and melodrama, 69–70, 86;

and movement space, 2, 85; and place vs. space, 125; plot, 68–69; setting of, 68–69; and stranger, 135; and suicide, 137; and surveillance, 36, 76, 145n19; and television financing, 60, 159; transit space; and *VW Komplex*, 75, 163; and women protagonists, 67

women. *See* gender

Women (*Weiber*, Petzold), 150

work. *See* labor

Workers Leave the Factory (*Arbeiter verlassen die Fabrik*, Farocki), 144n15

World War II, 6, 7, 88, 91, 147

Worthmann, Merten, 40, 42, 49

Yasemin (Bohm) 120

Yella (Petzold), 97–118; and abeyance, 99, 111; and adrift characters, 101; and archeology of genre, 98; and Marc Augé, 107–8; and Ambrose Bierce, 97; in biography/career of Petzold, 99; and the body (incl. as strategy of accumulation), 102–3, 104, 114, 157; and border, 98, 157; and bridge, 82; and bubble space, 108; and car, 74, 105–7; and *Carnival of Souls*, 98–100, 159–60; and creative destruction, 104–6, 125; credits of, 173; and criminality, 28; and desire, 44, 98; and domestic, 55, 103, 112, 115–17, 165; and economy, 98–101, 105–7, 110–18; and ending, 117–18; and *Face Behind the Mask*, 109; and family, 85; and fantasized plot, 134; and fantasy (incl. blurry line to reality), 44, 54, 93, 98, 108; and Harun Farocki, 34, 36, 110–13; and forest, 135; and Freud, 104, 112; and genre, 11, 12, 98, 100–101, 153, 159; and the GDR, 97–100, 141, 152; and ghost/ghostly, 99, 106, 113; and Ghost trilogy, 16, 98; and *Halloween*, 104; and David Harvey, 101, 105; and Herk Harvey,

98; and Alfred Hitchcock, 99, 105, 114; and home/house, 55, 103, 112, 115–17, 165; and homelessness, 101, 107–10; and horror, 17, 81, 88, 104–6, 109–10, 111, 113–17; 137; and Nina Hoss, 67, 97; and hotels, 27, 107–10; and hotel film, 109–10; and labor/work, 99–100, 143; and landscapes with business people, 122; and Henri Lefebvre, 108; and love, 107, 112–17; and Peter Lorre, 109; make-over theme, 102–3, 114; and *Marnie*, 102; migration, 100–101, 109–10; movement space, 106; and neoliberalism, 99–100, 110–14; and nonplaces, 107–8; and *Nothing Ventured*, 110–13; "Occurrence at Owl Creek Bridge," 98; and place vs. space, 112, 123, 125; and politics, 93; and *Psycho*, 113; and refunctioning people, 102–3, 114–16; and remains/remnants, 85, 99; and scale, 26; and setting, 66, 139; and space, 107–12; and strangers' encounter, 107; and *Tagesreste*, 104, 112–13; and television financing, 21; and transit space, 27, 103–4, 107–8, 165; and transformation of people, 67, 102–3, 117–18; and the *Treuhand Anstalt*, 100; and uneven geographical development (globalization), 101–2, 130; and unemployment, 99–100; and *Wende* (1989/1990), 99; and Westerns, 32; and westward journey of women, 32, 97, 100–101; and Wittenberge, 66, 97, 139; and woman protagonist, 102–3

youth and adolescence in Petzold's cinema (as time of crisis and abeyance), 55, 161. *See also Dreileben; State I Am In*

ZDF (Zweites Deutsches Fernsehen), 21, 28, 169–75

Zizek, Slavoj, 24, 139

Jaimey Fisher is an associate professor of German and Director of Cinema and Technocultural Studies at the University of California, Davis. He is the author of *Disciplining Germany: Youth, Reeducation, and Reconstruction after the Second World War* and the coeditor of *Collapse of the Conventional: German Film and Its Politics at the Turn of the Twenty-First Century*.

Books in the series Contemporary Film Directors

Nelson Pereira dos Santos
  Darlene J. Sadlier

Abbas Kiarostami
  Mehrnaz Saeed-Vafa and Jonathan Rosenbaum

Joel and Ethan Coen
  R. Barton Palmer

Claire Denis
  Judith Mayne

Wong Kar-wai
  Peter Brunette

Edward Yang
  John Anderson

Pedro Almodóvar
  Marvin D'Lugo

Chris Marker
  Nora Alter

Abel Ferrara
  Nicole Brenez, translated by Adrian Martin

Jane Campion
  Kathleen McHugh

Jim Jarmusch
  Juan Suárez

Roman Polanski
  James Morrison

Manoel de Oliveira
  John Randal Johnson

Neil Jordan
  Maria Pramaggiore

Paul Schrader
  George Kouvaros

Jean-Pierre Jeunet
  Elizabeth Ezra

Terrence Malick
  Lloyd Michaels

Sally Potter
  Catherine Fowler

Atom Egoyan
  Emma Wilson

Albert Maysles
  Joe McElhaney

Jerry Lewis
  Chris Fujiwara

Jean-Pierre and Luc Dardenne
  Joseph Mai

Michael Haneke
  Peter Brunette

Alejandro González Iñárritu
  Celestino Deleyto
  and Maria del Mar Azcona

Lars von Trier
  Linda Badley

Hal Hartley
  Mark L. Berrettini

François Ozon
  Thibaut Schilt

Steven Soderbergh
  Aaron Baker

Mike Leigh
  Sean O'Sullivan

D.A. Pennebaker
  Keith Beattie

Jacques Rivette
  Mary M. Wiles

Kim Ki-duk
  Hye Seung Chung

Philip Kaufman
  Annette Insdorf

Richard Linklater
  David T. Johnson

David Lynch
  Justus Nieland

John Sayles
  David R. Shumway

Dario Argento
  L. Andrew Cooper

Todd Haynes
  Rob White

Christian Petzold
  Jaimey Fisher

The University of Illinois Press
is a founding member of the
Association of American University Presses.

Composed in 10/13 New Caledonia
with Helvetica Neue display
by Lisa Connery
at the University of Illinois Press
Manufactured by Sheridan Books, Inc.

University of Illinois Press
1325 South Oak Street
Champaign, IL 61820-6903
www.press.uillinois.edu